A dictionary of Chinese charac

'The whole thrust of the work is that it is more helpful to learners of Chinese characters to see them in terms of sound, than in visual terms. It is a radical, provocative and constructive idea.' Dr Valerie Pellatt, University of Newcastle.

By arranging frequently used characters under the phonetic element they have in common, rather than only under their radical, the Dictionary encourages the student to link characters according to their phonetic. The system of cross referencing then allows the student to find easily all the characters in the Dictionary which have the same phonetic element, thus helping to fix in the memory the link between a character and its sound and meaning.

More controversially, the book aims to alleviate the confusion that similar looking characters can cause by printing them alongside each other. All characters are given in both their traditional and simplified forms.

Appendix A clarifies the choice of characters listed while Appendix B provides a list of the radicals with detailed comments on usage. The Dictionary has a full pinyin and radical index.

This innovative resource will be an excellent study-aid for students with a basic grasp of Chinese, whether they are studying with a teacher or learning on their own.

Dr Stewart Paton was Head of the Department of Languages at Heriot-Watt University, Edinburgh, from 1976 to 1981.

A dictionary of
Chinese characters
Accessed by phonetics

Stewart Paton

Routledge
Taylor & Francis Group

LONDON AND NEW YORK

First published 2008 by Routledge
2 Park Square, Milton Park, Abingdon, OX14 4RN

Simultaneously published in the USA and Canada by Routledge
270 Madison Ave, New York, NY 10016

Routledge is an imprint of the Taylor & Francis Group, an informa business

Typeset in 10/12pt GraphSwift Light by Graphicraft Limited, Hong Kong
Printed and bound in Great Britain by TJ International Ltd, Padstow, Cornwall

British Library Cataloguing in Publication Data
A catalogue record for this book is available from the British Library

Library of Congress Cataloging in Publication Data
Paton, Stewart.
A dictionary of Chinese characters : accessed by phonetics / Stewart Paton.
   p. cm.
   Includes bibliographical references and index.
   1. Chinese characters–Dictionaries.   I. Title.
   PL1171.P285 2008
   495.1'321–dc22

                                                      2007042986

ISBN10: 0-415-46046-8 (hbk)
ISBN10: 0-415-46047-6 (pbk)
ISBN10: 0-203-92820-2 (ebk)

ISBN13: 978-0-415-46046-0 (hbk)
ISBN13: 978-0-415-46047-7 (pbk)
ISBN13: 978-0-203-92820-2 (ebk)

Contents

Foreword

This Dictionary of selected Chinese characters, together with its cross-references, has been prepared with the aim of helping non-Chinese-speaking students of the characters who are just emerging from the initial stage of study. It is in the form of a supplement to the standard Chinese–English dictionary, adding two features not present in such a dictionary, in the hope of offering these two further aids to the memory in the difficult task of fixing the link between the character, the sound and the meaning.

The first, and more significant, of these features aims to stress the importance of the phonetic element in the Chinese characters by grouping together the most frequently used characters which have the same 'phonetic' under one 'key' character and linking them by cross-references.

The second feature attempts to deal with a simple but persistent difficulty for the foreigner: the tendency to confuse similar looking characters which need to be distinguished one from another. These difficult cases are confronted by printing the characters next to one another and again linking them with cross-references.

As a student of the Chinese characters I have found, and continue to find, the use of these two aids in memorising characters increasingly useful. In presenting this list, primarily for the use of students, may I invite comments from all those interested in the process of acquiring a reading knowledge of Chinese.

Acknowledgements

I would like to express my gratitude in the first place to two specialists in Chinese, Dr Valerie Pellatt of the University of Newcastle-on-Tyne and Dr Nigel Wiseman of Chang Gung University, Taiwan, who, over a number of years, encouraged me to persist in my efforts to acquire a reading knowledge of Chinese. They, together with a number of other friends, were kind enough to read through and make comments on the various drafts of the material which was being compiled during this rather lengthy process and which then formed the basis of this Dictionary. I remain conscious of the debt of gratitude I owe to them and to Jackie Addison, Moira Bambrough, Professor Greg Benton of Cardiff University, Jim Doyle of Napier University, Edinburgh, and to two former colleagues in the Department of Languages of Heriot-Watt University, Edinburgh: Professor Ian Mason and Dr Jerry Payne.

Even though I did not always accept the comments and criticism offered, I was always glad of the opportunity to discuss the points raised and, while incorporating some of the suggestions made, I must stress that I bear the sole responsibility for the arguments put forward in the Preface and Introduction to the Dictionary and for any errors which occur in the entries in the Dictionary.

Stewart Paton
Edinburgh April 2008

Introduction

For the foreigner studying the Chinese characters there is bound to be much 'brute' memory work, to quote John DeFrancis.[1] However, the situation is not as bad as it sounds, since this kind of memory work is required principally for a limited number of frequently used characters which we could categorise as 'simple', in the sense that they consist of one shape without additions of any kind. Such simple characters would be for example 刀 *dāo* (knife), or 人 *rén* (man).

However, the overwhelming majority of Chinese characters are 'compound' characters, and with a compound character help is being offered by each of the two elements which compose it. These are a 'radical', which gives a general indication of the meaning, and another element which gives an indication of the sound and is therefore referred to as the phonetic. Such a compound character would be for instance 吸 *xī* (breathe in), where the radical is 口 *kǒu* (mouth) and the phonetic is 及 *jí* (reach).

The radicals, 214 in number in the traditional count (see Appendix B), are the modern conventionalised forms of the original pictograph characters, under which the Chinese characters are ordered in the dictionaries. Radical No. 30 is 口 *kǒu* (mouth), as in the example above. All the compound characters in which it appears are listed in the dictionary under radical 30, giving therefore a general indication of the meaning, so that one finds here the characters for 'to breathe', 'to smoke', 'to spit', 'to kiss', etc. This of course is a useful aid for the student: but the main aim of this Dictionary is to direct the attention to the other element in the character, the phonetic, since the radical generally gives no help at all with the sound of a particular character.

As a student I have found that the most useful 'hook' for the memory is to fix in the mind the link between one shape and one sound. Thus 分 is pronounced *fēn* (divide), and this continues to be the case, except for a change in tone,[2] in such compound characters as 粉 *fěn* (powder) and 份 *fèn* (portion). The entry in the Dictionary for this character (No. 199) also includes two compounds which, while using the same phonetic, have two variant pronunciations: 盆 *pén* (basin) and 贫 *pín* (poor). As a general rule each phonetic appears only once as a key character in the Dictionary, linked to the one sound, and I do continue to find this approach useful.

I have also tried to include in the Dictionary another 'hook' to help the memory. This is an attempt to confront the tendency to confuse similar looking characters by printing them alongside one another, following but considerably expanding the practice in the Mathews dictionary.[3] Clearly this is a more controversial issue, since

---

[1] John DeFrancis: *The Chinese Language: Fact and Fantasy*, University of Hawaii Press, 1984, p.128.
[2] For a note on the Chinese tones see p.x.
[3] R.H. Mathews: *Chinese–English Dictionary*, Harvard University Press, 1943.

by its nature it has to be partially subjective, and since what I confuse may not worry others. But objectively, when faced with 各 and 名, 哀 and 衷, or 末 and 未 the difference can be said to be slight, perhaps one stroke only. In other cases another student may very well dismiss my suggestion of possible confusion as misplaced. (These items in the Dictionary are marked D.f. = distinguish from).

In choosing which characters to include in the Dictionary, either as one of the key characters or as one to be referred to in the cross-references, the overriding factor has been that of usefulness. By this is meant frequency of use and I have relied heavily for these decisions on the recently published character frequency count by Liu Yuan and his colleagues (for details see Appendix A). For each character he gives what might be called a 'usage number' and, for reasons given in Appendix A, I have included in the Dictionary, either as a key character or in the cross-references, only those characters having a usage number of 200 or more.

The method advocated in this list can best be illustrated by taking a typical Chinese character such as 场 pronounced *chǎng*,[4] meaning 'a place where people gather', and consisting of a radical 土 often, as here, placed on the left, plus a phonetic, i.e. a shape which gives an indication of the sound.

The helpful feature for the student, and indeed the principal justification for producing this Dictionary for the study of the Chinese characters, is that the phonetic, once learned is a kind of constant, which occurs in combination with many other radicals, meaning many different things, but generally all pronounced in a similar and sometimes in an identical way. A conscious attempt to memorise the more frequently occurring phonetics has certainly, for me, accelerated the learning process.

Having memorised the shape for *chǎng*, and given a cross-reference list, one has also effectively learned to recognise very easily many other characters with the same phonetic, such as the following five:

+ radical 130:	肠 *cháng* intestines	(radical 130 = flesh);
+ radical 85:	汤 *tāng* soup	(radical 85 = water);
+ radicals 85&86:	烫 *tàng* to scald	(radical 86 = fire);
+ radical 64:	扬 *yáng* to raise	(radical 64 = the hand);
+ radical 75:	杨 *yáng* the poplar tree	(radical 75 = tree).

The pinyin for the last four characters above is underlined, as it is in the Dictionary, to indicate a variant pronunciation.[5]

The system of cross-references used in the list ensures that all the frequently used compound characters with a particular phonetic are readily available, listed under the entry for the key character, which in this instance is entry No. 77 for 场, *chǎng*.

One important further feature of the Dictionary is that it presents both the traditional (unsimplified) and simplified forms of the characters listed. Simplified

---

[4] The sound of the Chinese character is given in 'pinyin'. This is the term used for the officially accepted system for the representation of the sounds of Chinese in a Western alphabet. Where pinyin is used it is printed in italics, thus: *pīnyīn*. The diacritic indicates the tone to be used (see note on the tones on p.x).

[5] See p.xi of this Introduction for further examples of variant pronunciation.

forms of the Chinese characters were introduced in the 1950s for a large number of the traditional forms and, where both simplified (S) and traditional (T) forms exist for any particular character mentioned, the T form is given in brackets immediately after the S form.

Thus the layout for entry No. 77 begins as follows:

77 *chǎng*   场(場) a place where people gather.

D. phonetic in T form f: 易 *yì* easy, No. 826 in list.

The second line of this entry is an example of the second 'hook' for the memory: to help to distinguish between very similar characters. In this case the 'helpful hint' would only apply when reading a text printed in traditional (unsimplified) characters. As here, the characters to be distinguished one from another are printed in close proximity to each other. (D.f. = distinguish from).

These first two lines of entry No. 77 are then followed by those compound characters, chosen for their frequency, which are formed with this phonetic, beginning in this instance with:

+ 130: 肠(腸) *cháng* intestines.

The radicals used in the entries in the list are designated by their number in the traditional list, see pp. xiv–xv and Appendix B.[6]

The layout of the entries in the list follows the pattern indicated above for entry No. 77: 1. Key character with basic phonetic, followed by 2. either items in the 'distinguish from' (D.f.) category and/or 3. compound characters using the basic phonetic.

As has been indicated, it is intended that this list should be used together with a Chinese–English dictionary. For all the characters in the list, the *pīnyīn*, the appropriate tone mark,[7] and the meaning are also given, making the list usable with any Chinese–English dictionary. However, students are strongly advised to make use of a full Chinese–English dictionary particularly to verify the range of meanings for any particular character. A recommended dictionary is: *A Chinese-English Dictionary*, ed. Wu Jingrong, Beijing 1987.

The Dictionary is provided with a full pinyin and radical index. These include all the characters mentioned in it, either as key characters or in the cross-references.

Two further examples will illustrate in greater detail the benefits of the phonetic approach to the study of the Chinese characters.

---

[6] In the reign of Emperor Kang Xi the system of classifying the Chinese characters under 214 'significs' (radicals) was used in the dictionary of 1716. Since then it has remained the traditional way of classifying the characters.

[7] The tones. Chinese is a tonal language, each character is a syllable and each syllable must be pronounced with one of four tones. They are indicated by diacritics placed above the appropriate vowel. Tone 1 is high level, as in both syllables of *pīnyīn*; tone 2 is 'high rising', as in *mén* (gate); tone 3 is 'low dipping' as in *chǎng* (a place where people gather); tone 4 is 'high falling', as in the first syllable of *tàitai* (lady). Exceptionally, some syllables are toneless, as is the second syllable of *tàitai*, and are then left unmarked.

The character 中 *zhōng* (centre) is one of the simple characters which beginners must learn at an early stage. But it is also one of the very useful phonetics, since every compound character in which it appears is also pronounced *zhong* or *chong*, sometimes with a change of tone. The great advantage with this phonetic is that one can turn immediately to the appropriate pages in the alphabetical-pinyin dictionary without having to resort to the cumbersome and time-consuming traditional method: determining under which radical the character is likely to be listed (not always an easy task), and then finding it in the tables according to the number of strokes it is made up of.

This phonetic is key character No. 910 in the Dictionary and the entry includes five other commonly used compound characters, all having this pronunciation, which otherwise one would have had to find under five different radicals. It is notable also that this phonetic is even more useful in reading the simplified forms of the characters, since in the simplification process it has been used to replace three different forms of the corresponding phonetics in the traditional characters.

However, not all phonetics are as helpful and reliable as 中. With some phonetics the pronunciation of particular characters can vary and this list differs from the usual dictionary, and aims to be particularly useful to the student, by grouping these variations in the entry for the key character which uses the phonetic common to them all. Thus entry No. 540 has the key character: 钱(錢) *qián* (money), and lists three further compound characters with this phonetic, of which one is pronounced *qián*, whereas the other two have the pronunciations <u>*cán*</u> and <u>*xiàn*</u>. The *pīnyīn* for these two characters is underlined here, as it is in the Dictionary, to show an unexpected variation from the pronunciation of the phonetic in the key character (the difference between tones, and between the aspirated and unaspirated versions of the same sound, are not considered variations in this sense).

In using this Dictionary, which lists the most useful Chinese phonetics and the relevant cross-references, it is suggested that the student, on meeting an unfamiliar character, should pay particular attention to the phonetic element and note those phonetics which occur most frequently. I have found that this not only makes it easier to track down a character in the Dictionary but also helps to fix the character in the memory.

Terms and abbreviations used in the Dictionary

alt.form	alternative form.
basic	that element in a character to which a radical (or radicals) is added to form a compound character. It frequently gives an indication of the way the character is pronounced.
Beijing dictionary	*A Chinese–English Dictionary*, ed. Wu Jingrong, Beijing 1987.
combination	'used in combination' indicates that the character conveys a given sense only when used in combination with other characters.
compound character	any character consisting of a basic element to which a radical (or radicals) has been added.

the Dictionary	this Dictionary of 943 key characters plus cross-references.
D.f.:	distinguish from.
key character	those characters numbered 1 to 943 making up the Dictionary.
Mathews	Mathews' *Chinese–English Dictionary*. Revised American Edition, Harvard University Press, 1943.
No. xxx	refers to the key character with this number in the Dictionary.
phonetic	that element of a character which gives an indication of the way it is pronounced.
pinyin	the conventional system for the representation of the sounds of Chinese characters in the Roman alphabet.
a plus (+) sign preceding a number	indicates the radical to be added to form a particular compound character, the number used being that assigned to it in the traditional list (see pp. xiv–xv and Appendix B). If the plus sign is preceded by (T), this indicates that the radical is to be added to the phonetic of the T form of the key character.
a radical	one of the 214 modern conventionalised versions of the original Chinese pictographs, under which characters are ordered in the dictionaries (see pp. xiv–xv and Appendix B).
a simple character	consists of one basic shape without any additional elements.
S form:	indicates the simplified form of the character.
T form:	indicates the traditional (unsimplified) form of the character.
tones	see footnote (7) of the Introduction.
usage number	a figure indicating the frequency of use of a particular Chinese character, given to it in the frequency count by Liu Yuan (see p. 190).
a useful character	a character which fits into the frequency of use criteria given in Appendix A.
variant pronunciation	an unexpected variation from the basic phonetic shown in the key character. In the Dictionary the pinyin for these pronunciations is underlined.
×2, ×3	indicates the number of times of the repeated use of the same character.

List of the traditional 214 radicals

The 214 radicals, in the traditional count used in the Kang Xi dictionary, are given below. For the 24 radicals which have both S and T forms, both forms are given.

1	一	30	口	59	彡	88	父	117	立
2	丨	31	囗	60	彳	89	爻	118	竹
3	丶	32	土	61	心忄	90	爿	119	米
4	丿	33	士	62	戈	91	片	120	丝(絲)
5	乙	34	夂	63	戶	92	牙	121	缶
6	亅	35	夊	64	手扌	93	牛	122	网(網)
7	二	36	夕	65	支	94	犬犭	123	羊
8	亠	37	大	66	攴攵	95	玄	124	羽
9	人亻	38	女	67	文	96	王	125	老
10	儿	39	子	68	斗	97	瓜	126	而
11	入	40	宀	69	斤	98	瓦	127	耒
12	八	41	寸	70	方	99	甘	128	耳
13	冂	42	小	71	无	100	生	129	聿
14	冖	43	尢尣	72	日	101	用	130	肉月
15	冫冰	44	尸	73	曰	102	田	131	臣
16	几	45	屮	74	月	103	疋	132	自
17	凵	46	山	75	木	104	疒	133	至
18	刀刂	47	川	76	欠	105	癶	134	臼
19	力	48	工	77	止	106	白	135	舌
20	勹	49	己	78	歹	107	皮	136	舛
21	匕	50	巾	79	殳	108	皿	137	舟
22	匚	51	干	80	毋	109	目	138	艮
23	匸	52	幺	81	比	110	矛	139	色
24	十	53	广	82	毛	111	矢	140	艹
25	卜	54	廴	83	氏	112	石	141	虍
26	卩巳	55	廾	84	气	113	示礻	142	虫
27	厂	56	弋	85	水氵	114	禸	143	血
28	厶	57	弓	86	火灬	115	禾	144	行
29	又	58	彐彑	87	爪	116	穴	145	衣衤

146	西	160	辛	174	青	188	骨	202	黍
147	见(見)	161	辰	175	非	189	高	203	黑
148	角	162	辶	176	面	190	髟	204	黹
149	讠(言)	163	阝	177	革	191	鬥	205	黾(黽)
150	谷	164	酉	178	韦(韋)	192	鬯	206	鼎
151	豆	165	釆	179	韭	193	鬲	207	鼓
152	豕	166	里	180	音	194	鬼	208	鼠
153	豸	167	钅(金)	181	页(頁)	195	鱼(魚)	209	鼻
154	贝(貝)	168	长(長)	182	风(風)	196	鸟(鳥)	210	齐(齊)
155	赤	169	门(門)	183	飞(飛)	197	卤(鹵)	211	齿(齒)
156	走	170	阝	184	饣(食)	198	鹿	212	龙(龍)
157	足	171	隶	185	首	199	麦(麥)	213	龟(龜)
158	身	172	隹	186	香	200	麻	214	龠
159	车(車)	173	雨	187	马(馬)	201	黄		

A Dictionary of Chinese characters
Accessed by phonetics

The 943 characters (with cross-references and comments).

To be used in conjunction with a Chinese–English dictionary.

Recommended dictionary: *A Chinese–English Dictionary*, ed. Wu Jingrong, Beijing.

A

1	*āi*	哎	Oh! Look out!

| 2 | *āi* | 挨 | to get close to; |
| | *ái* | | to suffer; endure. |

Basic: 矣 *yǐ* (particle) indicating (a) completion (b) distress.

+ 32:* 埃 *āi* dust;

+ 30: 唉 *āi* & *ài* (exclamation) OK!; What?; alas!

3   *ǎi*   矮 short; low.

Basic: 委 *wěi* to entrust; appoint, No. 716.

4   *ài*   爱(愛) love.

D.f. phonetic in: 暖 *nuǎn* warm, No. 514;

D.f.: 受 *shòu* to receive, No. 630.

5   *ān*   安 peaceful.

+ 84: 氨 *ān* ammonia, see No. 535 for 气 *qì* gas;

+ 64: 按 *àn* press down;

D. this f.: 接 *jiē* to receive, No. 340;

+ 130: 胺 *àn* amine.

6   *àn*   案 table; case.

D.f.: 牵(牽) *qiān* to lead along.

---

* The plus sign followed by a number indicates the radical to be added to the basic element to form the compound character referred to. The number used is that assigned to the radical in the traditional list (see pp. xiv–xv and Appendix B).

7 *àn* 暗 dark.

Basic: 音 *yīn* sound, No. 831.

D.f. phonetic in: 倍 *bèi* times; -fold, No. 34.

8 *āo* 凹 concave.

D.f.: 凸 *tū* protruding; convex.

9 *āo* 熬 to boil.
  áo

D. left-hand element f. that in: 殷 *yīn* abundant, see also No. 597.

10 *ào* 奧 profound.
  + 30: 噢 *ō* (exclamation) Oh!

B

11	bā	八 **eight** Radical 12.

+ 40:   穴 <u>*xué*</u> cave; den, radical 116.

12	bā	巴 **to hope earnestly.**

+ 30:   吧 *bā* (sound) crack! and *ba* (imperative) Let us!;

+ 64:   把 *bǎ* hold, and *bà* a handle;

+ 88:   爸 *bà* pa; dad, for 父 *fù* father, see No. 214;

+ 87:   爬 *pá* to crawl; creep, see also entry No. 920 for
抓 *zhuā* to seize;

+ 127:   耙 *pá* rake;

+ 130:   肥 <u>*féi*</u> fat; fertile.

13	bá	拔 **to pull out.**

14	bà	罢(罷) **to stop; dismiss.**

+ 64:   摆(擺) <u>*bǎi*</u> to put; place.

15	bái	白 **white** Radical 106.

+ 64:   拍 <u>*pāi*</u> to clap; beat;

+ 9:   伯 <u>*bó*</u> uncle;

+ 85:   泊 <u>*bó*</u> to moor; berth;

+ 162:	迫 <u>pò</u> to compel;	
+ 61:	怕 <u>pà</u> fear; perhaps;	
+ 115, 42 and 59:	穆 <u>mù</u> solemn, see also No. 763.	

16   *bǎi*   百 **hundred.**

+ 9, 40 and 120:   缩 <u>suō</u> to shrink, No. 663.

17   *bài*   败(敗) **to be defeated.**

This character is 贝(貝) *bèi* shellfish, radical 154, plus radical 66.

+ 32:   坝(壩) <u>bà</u> dam; dyke.

18   *bài*   拜 **to do obeisance.**

D.f.:   邦 *bāng* nation, No. 23.

19   *bān*   班 **class; team.**

D.f.:   斑 *bān* spot; speck.

20   *bān*   般 **sort; kind.**

D.f.:   船 *chuán* boat, No. 113;

D.f.:   股 *gǔ* thigh, see also entry No. 597 for 设 *shè* to set up, for other compounds with radical 79: 殳.

+ 64:   搬 *bān* to remove;

+ 108:   盤 T form for *pán* tray; dish, S form: 盘.

21   *bàn*   办(辦) **to do.**

D. S form f.:   为 S form for *wéi* to act as, No. 713, T form: 為;

D. T form f.:   辨 *biàn* to differentiate, No. 47.

+ 140:   苏(蘇) <u>sū</u> to revive (also used in proper names);

+ 24:   协(協) <u>xié</u> joint; common.

22 *bàn* 半 **half.**

  + 64: 拌 *bàn* to mix;

  + 18: 判 *pàn* to distinguish; discriminate.

23 *bāng* 邦 **nation; state.**

  + 50: 帮(幫) *bāng* to help.

24 *bāo* 包 **wrap.**

D.f.: 句 *jù* sentence, No. 371;

D.f. phonetic in: 约 *yuē* to arrange, No. 863.

  + 130: 胞 *bāo* afterbirth; of the same parents;

  + 184: 饱 *bǎo* be full; eat one's fill;

  + 18: 刨 *bào* to plane;

  + 64: 抱 *bào* to hold in the arms; to embrace;

  + 85: 泡 *pāo* and *pào* spongy; bubble; to soak;

  + 86: 炮 *páo* to roast, and *pào* a gun;

  + 157: 跑 *pǎo* to run.

25 *bǎo* 宝(寶) **treasure; precious.**

For 玉 *yù* jade, see entry No. 706 for 王 *wáng* king.

26 *bǎo* 保 **to protect; defend.**

  Basic: 呆 *dāi* slow-witted; blank.

D.f.: 吊 *diào* to hang; suspend, No. 159;

D. also f.: 杏 *xìng* apricot;

  + 32: 堡 *bǎo* fort; fortress.

| 27 | *bào* | 报(報) report; newspaper. |

Left-hand part of the T form: 幸 is *xìng* good fortune, see also No. 899;

| | + 130: | 服 *fú* clothes, No. 211. |

| 28 | *bào* | 暴 sudden and violent. |
| | + 86: | 爆 *bào* to explode. |

| 29 | *bēi* | 卑 low; inferior. |
| | + 91: | 牌 *pái* tablet; signpost. |

| 30 | *bēi* | 背 to carry on the back. |
| | *bèi* | the back of the body. |

| 31 | *běi* | 北 the north. |

| 32 | *bèi* | 备(備) to be equipped with. |

| 33 | *bèi* | 被 a quilt; by (agent of the passive). |
| | Basic: | 皮 *pí* skin, No. 521. |

| 34 | *bèi* | 倍 times; -fold. |

D.f. phonetic in: 暗 *àn* dark, No. 7;

	+ 170:	陪 *péi* to accompany;
	+ 32:	培 *péi* to earth up; to foster;
	+ 163:	部 *bù* part; section, No. 59.

| 35 | *bēn* | 奔 to run quickly. |
| | *bèn* | to head for. |

| 36 | *běn* | 本 root of a plant. |

D.f.: 木 *mù* tree; wood, No. 487;

| | + 9: | 体 S form for *tǐ* body, No. 679, T form: 體; |

D. this f.: 休 *xiū* to stop; cease, No. 780;

| | + 140: | 苯 *běn* benzene; benzol. |

37	*bí*	鼻 nose. Radical 209.

38	*bǐ*	比 compare. Radical 81.
	+ 24:	毕(畢) *bì* to finish; accomplish;

> D. both forms f.:   华(華) *huá* magnificent, see No. 287
> for   化 *huà* to change;

| | + 64: | 批 *pī* to slap. |

39	*bǐ*	笔(筆) **pen.**

> The S form is   毛 *máo* hair, plus radical 118, for 毛 see No. 463;
> The T form is   聿 *yù* radical 129, plus radical 118, for 聿 see note to
>   entry No. 350 for 津 *jīn* a ferry.

40	*bì*	币(幣) **money; currency.**
	+ 55:	弊 *bì* fraud; abuse.

41	*bì*	必 **must; have to.**

> D.f.:   心 *xīn* the heart, No. 767;

	+ 115:	秘 *mì* secret;
	+ 40 and 46:	密 *mì* close; dense; secret, No. 473.

42	*bì*	避 **to avoid.**
	Basic:	辟 *pì* to open up (land), and *bì* monarch.
	+ 32:	壁 *bì* a wall;
	+ 130:	臂 *bì* the arm;
	+ 18:	劈 *pī* to split; chop.

43	*biān*	边(邊) **side.**

> D.f.:   迈 S form for *mài* to step; stride, T form: 邁.

44	*biān*	编 **to weave; organise.**
	Basic:	扁 *biǎn* flat;

D. this f.:	扇	*shān* fan; stir up.

+ 162:	遍	*biàn* all over; everywhere;
+ 9:	偏	*piān* slanting; partial;
+ 118:	篇	*piān* a piece of writing; a sheet of paper.

45 *biàn* 变(變) **to change.**

+ 57:	弯(彎)	*wān* curved; tortuous;
+ 57 and 85:	湾(灣)	*wān* a gulf; a bay.

46 *biàn* 便 **convenient.**

Basic: 更 *gēng* to change, and *gèng* more, No. 236;

D.f.:	使	*shǐ* to use; to send; to cause, No. 618.

47 *biàn* 辨 **to differentiate.**

D.f.:	辦	T form for *bàn* to do, No. 21, S form: 办.

+ 149:	辩	*biàn* to argue; dispute.

48 *biāo* 标(標) **a mark; sign.**

S form is basic	示	*shì* to show; notify, No. 620, plus radical 75;
T form is basic	票	*piào* ticket, No. 523, plus radical 75.

49 *biǎo* 表 **surface; a watch.**

50 *bié* 别 **to leave; other; don't!**
　　 biè

Basic: 另 *lìng* other, No. 438;
+ 64: 拐 *guǎi* to turn; to limp.

51 *bīng* 兵 **weapons; a soldier.**

52 *bìng* 并(並) **to combine.**

D.f.:	井	*jǐng* a well, No. 359.

+ 184:	饼	*bǐng* a round flat cake;
+ 98:	瓶	*píng* a bottle; a flask;
+ 44:	屏	*píng* screen;
+ 64:	拼(拚)	*pīn* to put together;
+ 112:	碰	*pèng* to bump; to run into.

This character uses an alternative form of No. 52, 並, which should be distinguished from 业 S form for *yè* business; occupation, No. 811.

53	*bìng*	病 ill; disease.
	Basic:	丙 *bǐng* third.

D. this f.:	内	*nèi* inner; inside, No. 499;
and f.:	两	*liǎng* two; both, No. 431.

+ 75:	柄	*bǐng* a handle;
+ 86:	炳	*bǐng* bright; splendid.

54	*bó*	博 rich.

D. phonetic f.:	專	T form for *zhuān* special, No. 921, S form: 专.

+ 140 and 85:	薄	*bó* slight; meagre, and *báo* thin; flimsy;
+ 9:	傅	*fù* to teach; instruct.

55	*bǔ*	补(補) to mend; make up for.
	Basic for S form:	卜 *bǔ* divination; fortune-telling.
	(T) + 64:	捕 *bǔ* to seize; arrest (this one form only);
	(T) + 167:	铺 *pū* to spread; extend, and *pù* a shop (this one form only);
	+ 64:	扑(撲) *pū* to throw oneself on; to pounce;
	+ 9:	仆(僕) *pú* a servant;

D. this T form phonetic f.:	業	T form for *yè* business, No. 811, S form: 业,
and note similarity to	叢	T form for *cóng* thicket, S form: 丛;

(T) + 159:	辅	*fǔ* to assist; to supplement (this one form only);
+ 156:	赴	*fù* to go to; to attend (this one form only).

56   *bù*   不 **no; not.**

D.f. phonetic in: 坏 *pī* base; earthen brick, see also entry No. 264.

+ 75:   杯 *bēi* cup; glass;

+ 30:   否 *fǒu* to deny; whether . . . , No. 208;

+ 162:   还(還) *hái* still and *huán* return, No. 264;

+ 61:   怀(懷) *huái* bosom; to cherish, see No. 264;

+ 32:   坏(壞) *huài* bad; evil, see also No. 264;

+ 96:   环(環) *huán* a ring; to surround, see No. 264;

+正 *zhèng* (straight), No. 894: 歪 *wāi* crooked.

57   *bù*   布 **cloth; to proclaim.**

D.f.:   市 *shì* market, No. 619.

The lower part of No. 57 is 巾 *jīn* a piece of cloth, radical 50.

58   *bù*   步 **step; pace.**

+ 181:   频 *pín* frequently;

+ 85:   涉 *shè* wade; ford.

59   *bù*   部 **part; department.**

D.f.:   都 *dōu* all, No. 167.

Note that No. 59 is the phonetic in: 倍 (*bèi* times, No. 34) plus radical 163.

C

60	*cái*	才 **ability.**
	+ 75:	材 *cái* timber; material;
	+ 154:	财 *cái* wealth; money;
	+ 169:	闭 *bì* to close, for 门 *mén* door, see No. 468;
	+ 31:	团(團) *tuán* round; a group;

The phonetic in the T form 專 is the T form for *zhuān* special, No. 921 (S form: 专), d. this T form f. the phonetic in: 博 *bó* rich, No. 54.

61	*cái*	裁 **to cut into parts.**
	D.f.:	栽 *zāi* to plant; to grow;
	D.f.:	载 *zǎi* year, and *zài* to transport;
	D.f.:	截 *jié* to cut; a section;
	Note:	戴 *dài* to wear, No. 134.

62	*cǎi*	采(採) **to pick; to select.**

D.f. phonetic in: 探 *tàn* to seek, and see No. 601 for 深 *shēn* deep.

	+ 59:	彩 *cǎi* colour;
	+ 140:	菜 *cài* vegetables; a dish; a course.

63	*cān*	参(參) **to join; take part in.**

D.f. phonetic in: 趁 *chèn* to take advantage of, No. 90, see also No. 781.

	+ 64:	掺 = 攙 *chān* to mix.

64	*cāng*	仓(倉) **storehouse.**
	+ 18:	创(創) *chuāng* wound, and *chuàng* start;
	+ 75:	枪(槍) *qiāng* a rifle;
	+ 64:	抢(搶) *qiǎng* to rob; loot.

65	*cáng*	藏 to hide; to store.
	zàng	a storing place; Tibet.
	+ 130:	臟 T form for *zàng* the internal organs, S form: 脏;

The phonetic for this S form: 庄 is S for *zhuāng* village, No. 922, and also occurs in the S form of the following character:

| | + 130: | 脏(髒) *zāng* dirty; filthy. |

| 66 | *cāo* | 操 to grasp; hold. |
| 67 | *cè* | 册(冊) volume; book. |

| | D.f. phonetic in: | 棚 *péng* canopy; shed, No. 520. |

| 68 | *céng* | 曾 once. |

| | D.f.: | 會 T form for *huì* meet; be able, No. 298, S form: 会; |
| | D.f.: | 普 *pǔ* general; universal, No. 527; |

	+ 44:	層 T form for *céng* layer; storey, S form: 层, note that basic for this S form is 云 *yún* cloud, No. 866;
	+ 9:	僧 *sēng* Buddhist monk;
	+ 32:	增 *zēng* to add; increase.

69	*chā*	差 difference.
	chà	to differ from; to fall short of.
70	*chā*	插 to stick in; insert.
71	*chá*	茶 tea.

| | D. phonetic here f.: | 余 *yú* surplus, No. 851. |

72	*chá*	查 to check; examine.
	+ 85:	渣 *zhā* dregs; sediment.
73	*chá*	察 to examine.
	Basic:	祭 *jì* hold a memorial ceremony for.
	+ 170:	際 T form for *jì* border; inter-, S form: 际;

+ 64:　擦 _cā_ to rub; wipe.

74　*chán*　缠(纏) **to twine; tie up; pester.**

75　*chǎn*　产(產) **to give birth to; to produce.**

The T form includes　生 _shēng_ to bear a child; life, No. 604;

D.f.:　严 S form for _yán_ strict, No. 800, T form: 嚴;

+ 167:　铲(鏟) _chǎn_ shovel;

+ 140 and 170:　萨(薩) _Sà_ a surname; used in foreign names;

+ 59 and 181:　颜 _yán_ face; colour.

76　*cháng*　长(長) **long. The T form is radical 168.**
　　zhǎng　　　**older; senior.**

+ 57:　张 _zhāng_ to open; display;

+ 85 and 57:　涨 _zhǎng_ to rise, and _zhàng_ to swell;

+ 50:　帐 _zhàng_ curtain; an account;

+ 130:　胀 _zhàng_ to expand; swell.

77　*cháng*　场(場) **a level open space.**
　　chǎng　　　**a place where people gather.**

D. phonetic in T form f.:　易 _yì_ easy, No. 826;

+ 130:　肠(腸) _cháng_ intestines;

Note:　傷 T form _shāng_ wound, No. 591, S form: 伤;

+ 85:　汤(湯) _tāng_ hot water; soup;

+ 85 and 86:　烫(燙) _tàng_ scald; burn;

+ 170:　陽 T form for _yáng_ the sun, note S form: 阳
　　　　　(for 日 _rì_ the sun, see No. 574);

+ 64:　扬(揚) _yáng_ to raise;

+ 75:　杨(楊) _yáng_ the poplar tree.

78　*cháng*　尝(嘗) **to taste.**

+ 9:　偿(償) _cháng_ to repay; compensate for.

This T form phonetic　赏 is T form for _shǎng_ to reward, S form: 赏.

79	*cháng*	常 ordinary; often.
80	*chǎng*	厂(廠) factory.

	D.f.:	广 S form for *guǎng* wide, No. 255, T form: 廣; T form has basic phonetic: 尚 *shàng* still; yet, No. 594.

81	*chàng*	唱 to sing.
	Basic:	昌 *chāng* prosperous;

	D.f.:	冒 *mào* to emit, No. 464.

82	*cháo*	朝 court, dynasty; towards.

	D.f.:	胡 *hú* non-Han; recklessly, No. 282;

	+ 85:	潮 *cháo* tide;
	+ 53:	廟 T form for *miào* temple, S form: 庙, see No. 843.
83	*chē*	车(車) a vehicle. Radical 159.

	D.f.:	东(東) *dōng* east, No. 164;
	D.f. phonetic in:	拣(揀) *jiǎn* to choose; to pick up
	The basic in this T form is	柬 *jiǎn* a card,
	see also No. 427 for	练(練) *liàn* white silk; to train;
	D. S form f.:	年 *nián* year, No. 504;

	+ 175:	辈 *bèi* lifetime, for 非 *fēi*, bad, see No. 196;
	+ 九 *jiǔ*:	轨 *guǐ* rail; track, for 九 nine, see No. 362;
	+ 14:	军 *jūn* the armed forces, No. 378;
	+ 53:	库 *kù* warehouse, No. 399;
	+ 162:	连 *lián* link; even, No. 424;
	+ 76:	软 *ruǎn* soft, for 欠 *qiàn*, see No. 541;
	+ 170:	阵 *zhèn* battle array; front,

	D. this character f.:	陈 *chén* to lay out; to state, No. 88.

84	*chè*	撤 to remove.

	D.f.:	撒 *sā* to let go, see No. 585 for 散 *sǎn* to come loose.

85	*chén*	尘(塵) dust; dirt.

	The S form is	小 *xiǎo* small, No. 763, plus radical 32;
	D.f.:	尖 *jiān* point; sharp, No. 324.

86	*chén*	臣 an official; a subject. Radical 131.

	D.f.:	巨 *jù* huge, No. 370;

	+ 人 *rén*, No. 569:	臥 T form for <u>*wò*</u> to lie, No. 727, S form: 卧.

87	*chén*	沉 (alt.form: 沈) to sink; deep. The alternative form is also used for *Shěn* Shenyang.

88	*chén*	陈(陳) to lay out; explain.
	Basic:	东(東) *dōng* east, No. 164;

	D.f.:	阵(陣) *zhèn* battle array; front, see also No. 83.

89	*chèn*	衬(襯) to line a garment.

	The T phonetic	親 T form for *qīn* parent, No. 548, S form: 亲,
	The S phonetic	寸 *cùn* tiny; a unit of length, No. 127.

90	*chèn*	趁 to take advantage of.

	D. phonetic f.:	参 *cān* to join, No. 63;
	and f. phonetic in:	修 *xiū* to repair, No. 781;

	+ 96:	珍 *zhēn* treasure; precious.

91	*chēng*	称(稱) to call; to name.
	Basic for S form:	尔 *ěr* you, see No. 502 for 你 *nǐ* you.

| 92 | *chéng* | 成 to accomplish; to become. |

| | D.f. phonetic in: | 越 *yuè* to get over; to exceed, No. 865. |

	+ 149:	诚 *chéng* sincere; honest;
	+ 32:	城 *chéng* city wall; wall;
	+ 108:	盛 *chéng* to fill; to ladle, and *shèng* flourishing.

| 93 | *chéng* | 呈 to assume; to submit. |

| | D.f.: | 皇 *huáng* emperor, No. 292, |
| | and see also: | 王 *wáng* king, No. 706. |

| | + 115: | 程 *chéng* rule; regulation. |

| 94 | *chéng* | 承 to bear. |

| | D.f.: | 乘 *chéng* to ride, No. 95; |
| | D. phonetic f. that in: | 蒸 *zhēng* to steam food; to evaporate. |

| 95 | *chéng* | 乘 to ride. |

| | D.f.: | 承 *chéng* to bear, No. 94. |

| | + 18: | 剩 *shèng* surplus. |

| 96 | *chī* | 吃 to eat. |
| | Basic: | 乞 *qǐ* to beg, No. 533. |

97	*chí*	持 to hold.
	Basic:	寺 *sì* a temple, see also entry No. 615.
	+ 60:	待 *dāi* to stay and *dài* to deal with;
	+ 72:	時 T form for *shí* time, No. 615, S form: 时.

| 98 | *chǐ* | 尺 a unit of length; a ruler. |
| | + 162: | 迟 S form for *chí* slow, T form: 遲. |

Note: 尽 S form for *jìn* to the greatest extent, No. 352, T: 盡, see entry No. 352 for note on the abbreviated form of radical 15: 冰.

99	*chǐ*	齿(齒) tooth. Radical 211.
100	*chì*	赤 red; bare. Radical 155.

	D.f.:	亦 *yì* also, No. 823;
	× 2:	赫 *hè* conspicuous; grand, see also entry No. 747.

101	*chōng*	冲(衝) to rush; to dash.
	chòng	with vim; facing towards.
	Basic:	中 *zhōng* centre, No. 910;

The T form is 行 *xíng* to go, radical 144, No. 774,

plus: 重 *chóng* repeat, No. 104, placed in the centre.

For other examples of the use of radical 144 see No. 341 for 街 *jiē* street.

102	*chōng*	充 sufficient.
	+ 120:	统 *tǒng* system; to unite.

103	*chóng*	虫(蟲) insect. S form is radical 142.
	+ 天:	蚕(蠶) *cán* silkworm,
	for	天 *tiān* heaven, see No. 681.
	+ 148:	触(觸) *chù* to touch, No. 111;
	+ 94:	独(獨) *dú* only; alone;
	+ 140:	茧(繭) *jiǎn* cocoon;
	+ 184:	蚀 *shí* to lose; corrode.

104	*chóng*	重 repeat; again.
	zhòng	weight; heavy, listed separately as No. 912.
	+ 144:	衝 T form for *chōng* to rush; dash, No. 101, S form: 冲;
	+ 140:	董 *dǒng* to supervise;
	+ 140 and 61:	懂 *dǒng* to understand;
	+ 19:	動 T form for *dòng* to move, No. 166, S form: 动.

105	*chòu*	臭 smelly; foul.

	D.f.:	皇 *huáng* emperor, No. 292.

106 *chū* 出 to go or come out.

+ 44: 屈 *qū* to bend; injustice.

107 *chū* 初 at the beginning.

This character is 刀 *dāo* knife, No. 140, plus radical 145.

108 *chú* 除 to get rid of; except.

Basic: 余 *yú* surplus, No. 851.

109 *chǔ* 处(處) to get along with.
chù place; office.

D.f.: 外 *wài* outside, No. 702.

110 *chǔ* 楚 clear.

This character is 林 *lín* forest, No. 435, plus radical 103, for use of radical 103, see also 定 *dìng* to decide; fix, No. 163.

111 *chù* 触(觸) to touch.

This character is 角 *jiǎo* a horn; an angle, radical 148, No. 336, plus
in the S form 虫 *chóng* insect, radical 142, No. 103,
and in the T form: 蜀 *Shǔ* Sichuan,
note similar forms in 属(屬) *shǔ* to belong to, No. 634.

+ 94: 独(獨) *dú* only; alone.

112 *chuān* 穿 to pierce; penetrate.

This character is 牙 *yá* tooth, No. 795,

+ 116: 穴 *xué* cave, see entry No. 11 for 八 *bā* eight.

113   *chuán*   船 boat; ship.

D.f.:   般 *bān* sort; kind, No. 20;

The left-hand element here 舟 is radical 137, *zhōu* boat;

Note 137 + 147:   舰 S form for *jiàn* warship, T form: 艦, for 见 *jiàn*, to see, radical 147 see No. 328; for 監 *jiān* to supervise see No. 327.

+ 167:   铅 *qiān* lead;

+ 85:   沿 *yán* along and *yàn* water's edge, No. 801.

114   *chuàn*   串 to string together.

D.f.:   呂 T form for *Lü* (third tone) Lu, a surname, S form: 吕.

This phonetic + 167:   鋁 T form for *lü* (third tone) aluminium S form: 铝,

and + 40:   宮 T form for *gōng* (a palace) S form: 宫.

+ 61:   患 *huàn* (trouble; to suffer from).

115   *chuāng*   窗 window.

116   *chuáng*   床 bed.

This character is   木 *mù* tree, radical 75, No. 487, plus radical 53;

D.f.:   庆 S form for *qìng* celebrate, No. 553, T form: 慶;

and D. also f.:   庄 S for *zhuāng* village, T: 莊, see Nos. 65 and 922.

117   *chuī*   吹 to blow.

This character is   欠 *qiàn* to owe, radical 76, No. 541, plus 口,

for   口 *kǒu* mouth, radical 30, see No. 396.

118   *chuí*   垂 to hang down.

+ 167:   锤 *chuí* a hammer;

+ 109:   睡 *shuì* to sleep.

119 *chūn* 　春 spring.

120 *chún* 　纯 pure; simple.

+ 163: 邨 T form for *cūn* village, S form: 村 see No. 127;

+ 30: 吨 *dūn* ton;

+ 181: 顿 *dùn* pause.

121 *cí* 　词 word; poetry.

Basic: 司 *sī* to take charge of;

+ 184: 饲 *sì* to raise; rear.

122 *cǐ* 　此 this.

+ 7: 些 *xiē* these;

+ 172: 雌 *cí* female;

+ 75: 柴 *chái* firewood;

+ 30 and 148: 嘴 *zuǐ* mouth, No. 935;

+ 120: 紫 *zǐ* purple.

123 *cì* 　次 order; time.

+ 98: 瓷 *cí* porcelain;

+ 108: 盗 *dào* to steal; a thief;

+ 154: 资 *zī* expenses; to provide.

124 *cì* 　刺 thorn; splinter.

+ 118: 策 *cè* plan; scheme.

125	*cóng*	从(從) from; ever; to obey.
	cōng	used in the first tone only in the expression

从容(從容) *cōng róng* calm; plentiful. For 容 see No. 577.

+ 120:	纵(縱) *zòng* from north to south; vertical;
Note:	丛 S form for *cóng* a thicket, T form: 叢;

D. part of this T form f.: 業 T form for *yè* business, No. 811, S form: 业,

and also f. phonetic in: 撲 T form for *pū* to pounce on, S form: 扑, and

see also reference in entry No. 55 for *bǔ*: 补.

126	*cún*	存 to exist.
127	*cùn*	寸 unit of length; very small. Radical 41.
	+ 145:	衬 S form for *chèn* to line a garment, No. 89, T: 襯;
	+ 75:	村(邨) *cūn* a village;

Phonetic for this T form is 屯 *tún* to collect, for other uses see No. 120;

+ 29:	对 S form for *duì* answer; opposite, No. 177, T: 對;
+ 37:	夺 S form for *duó* to seize, No. 179, T form: 奪;
+ 9:	付 *fù* to hand over; to pay, No. 215;
+ 162:	过 S form for *guò* to cross; to pass, No. 263, T: 過;
+ 126:	耐 *nài* to be able to bear, No. 493;
+ 72:	时 S form for *shí* time, No. 615, T form: 時;
+ 40:	守 *shǒu* to guard, No. 627;
+ 149:	讨 *tǎo* to suppress; to beg for.

D

128   *dā*   搭 **to build.**

+ 118 and − 140:   答 *dā* and *dá* to answer;

+ 32:   塔 *tǎ* a pagoda; a tower;

see also No. 274 for 合 *hé* to close; to join.

129   *dá*   达(達) **to extend; to reach.**

Basic for S form: 大 *dà* big, No. 131;

D. T form f.:   遠 T for *yuǎn* distant, S form: 远 see No. 860;

D. phonetic in T form f.:   幸 *xìng* good fortune,

and also f.:   辛 *xīn* pungent, No. 768.

130   *dǎ*   打 **to strike.**

Basic: 丁 *dīng* man, No. 162.

131   *dà*   大 **big.   Radical 37.**

+ 162:   达 S form for *dá* to extend, No. 129, T form: 達;

+ 53:   庆 S form for <u>qìng</u> to celebrate, No. 553, T: 慶.

132   *dài*   代 **to replace; dynasty.**

D.f. phonetic in: 伐 *fá* to fell,

and f. that in: 找 *zhǎo* to look for, No. 884;

+ 145:   袋 *dài* bag; sack;

+ 154:   贷 *dài* loan; borrow;

D. this f.:   货 *huò* goods, No. 303.

133   *dài*   带(帶) **belt; to bring.**

134   *dài*   戴 **to put on; to wear.**

D.f.:   裁 *cái* to cut into parts, No. 61.

135	*dān*	单(單)	**one; single.**
	+ 57:	弹(彈)	*dàn* bullet, and *tán* to shoot;
	+ 62:	戰	T form for *zhàn* war, S form: 战.
136	*dān*	担(擔)	**to carry a burden.**
	dàn		**a unit of weight.**
	+ 130:	胆(膽)	*dǎn* courage;
	+ 9:	但	*dàn* but; only (this one form only), see also No. 787.
137	*dàn*	蛋	**egg.**

Note another character with the meaning 'egg': 卵 *luǎn* see also No. 212.

138	*dāng*	当(當)	**ought; must.**
	dàng		**proper; to treat as.**

D. T form f.:   堂 *táng* a hall, No. 672;

	+ 64:	挡(擋)	*dǎng* to ward off; block;
	+ 75:	档(檔)	*dàng* shelves; files.
139	*dǎng*	党(黨)	**political party.**

D.f.:   堂 *táng* a hall, No. 672 in list.

140	*dāo*	刀	**knife. Radical 18.**

D.f.:   刃 *rèn* the edge of a knife etc., see also No. 571;

	+ 145:	初	*chū* at the beginning of, No. 107;
	+ 30:	召	*zhào* to call together, see also entry No. 883.
141	*dǎo*	岛(島)	**island.**

D.f.:	鸟(鳥)	*niǎo* bird, No. 506;
D.f.:	乌(烏)	*wū* crow;
D. T form f.:	焉	*yān* here; how?

142	*dào*	到	to arrive.
	+ 9:	倒	*dǎo* to fall and *dào* upside down; to pour.
143	*dào*	道	road; way.
	Basic:	首	*shǒu* head, No. 628;
	+ 41:	導	T form for *dǎo* to lead; guide, S form: 导;

D. the above S form   导 f. 异 *yì* different, No. 824.

144	*dào*	稻	rice; paddy.
145	*dé*	得	to get; obtain.
	de		(particle: showing possibility).
	děi		need; must.
146	*dé*	德	virtue.

This phonetic is also seen in 聽 T form for *tīng* to listen to, No. 685, S form: 听.

147	*de*	的	(particle of possession).
	dí		in: 的确 *díquè* indeed; really.
	dì		target; bull's eye.
148	*dēng*	登	to ascend; to step on.
	+ 86:	燈	T form for *dēng* lamp; light, S form: 灯,
	for	丁	*dīng* man, see entry No. 162;
	+ 163:	鄧	T form for *Dèng* Deng, a surname, S form: 邓;
	+ 149:	證	T form for *zhèng* to prove, S form: 证,
	for	正	*zhèng* straight, see entry No. 894.
149	*děng*	等	rank; to wait.
	Basic:	寺	*sì* temple,

for other uses of this basic see No. 615 for 時 T form for *shí* time, S form: 时.

| 150 | *dī* | 低 | low. |

D. phonetic f.:   氏 *shì* family name; surname, for other compound characters using this phonetic see entries Nos. 299 and 903.

+ 53:   底 *dǐ* bottom; base;

+ 64:   抵 *dǐ* to support; sustain.

151   *dī*   滴 **to drip.**

D. phonetic f.:   商 *shāng* to discuss; commerce, No. 592;

+ 66:   敵 T form for *dí* enemy, S form: 敌,
see No. 596 for 舌 *shé* tongue;

+ 162:   適 T form for <u>*shì*</u> fit; proper, S form: 适 see No. 596;

+ 64:   摘 <u>*zhāi*</u> to pick; pluck.

152   *dì*   地 **the earth.**
       de   **(adverbial indicator.)**

This character is   也 *yě* also, No. 809, plus radical 32.

153   *dì*   弟 **younger brother.**

D.f.:   夷 *yí* smooth; safe;

+ 162:   递 S form for *dì* to hand over, T form: 遞, for note on
phonetic of T form see No. 283 for 虎 *hǔ* tiger;

+ 118:   第 *dì* (sign of an ordinal number).

154   *dì*   帝 **Supreme Being; emperor.**
      + 140:   蒂 *dì* the base of a fruit.

155   *diǎn*   典 **standard; dictionary.**

D.f.:   曲 *qū* crooked and *qǔ* a tune; melody;

+ 112:   碘 *diǎn* iodine.

156   *diǎn*   点(點) **a drop; spot.**

The T form is   黑 *hēi* black, radical 203, No. 276,
plus: 占 S. form for *zhàn* to occupy, No. 879, T form: 佔.

157   *diàn*   电(電) electricity.
       + 9 and 37:   俺 *ǎn* I; we;
       + 120 and 30:   绳 *shéng* a rope, No. 606.

158   *diàn*   店 shop.

This character is   占 S form for *zhàn* to occupy, No. 879, T form: 佔, plus radical 53.

159   *diào*   吊 to hang; suspend.

D.f.:   呆 *dāi* slow-witted, see No. 26 for 保 *bǎo*, defend.

160   *diào*   调 to transfer; a tune.
       tiáo   to mix; fit in.

This shape has another sound, a series of characters pronounced *zhou* or *chou* of which the most frequently seen is 周 *zhōu* all around; a week, No. 914.

161   *diào*   掉 to fall; to drop.
       Basic: 卓 *zhuō* tall; eminent;

D.f.:   桌 *zhuō* table;

       + 122:   罩 *zhào* to cover.

162   *dīng*   丁 man.
       + 109:   盯 *dīng* to stare at;
       + 167:   钉 *dīng* and *dìng* nail;
       + 181:   顶 *dǐng* the crown of the head;
       + 149:   订 *dìng* to agree on; fix;
       + 27:   厅 S form for *tīng* a hall, T form: 廳;

Note this same phonetic in 亭 *tíng* kiosk, and 停 *tíng* to stop, No. 686;

       + 40:   宁 S form for *níng* peaceful, No. 507, T form: 寧;

+ 64: 打 *dǎ* to strike, No. 130 in list;

+ 86: 灯 S form for *dēng* light, T form: 燈, see No. 148.

163 *dìng* 定 **calm; to fix.**

No. 163 is radical 103 疋 (T form for *pǐ* be equal to, S form: 匹) plus radical 40;

For other uses of this radical see entry No. 110 for *chǔ*: 楚 clear,

and also No. 137 for *dàn*: 蛋 egg.

+ 167: 锭 *dìng* a tablet.

164 *dōng* 东(東) **east.**

D.f.: 车(車) *chē* a vehicle, No. 83;

D. S form f.: 年 *nián* year, No. 504;

D. T form f.: 束 *shù* to tie, see No. 656 for 速 *sù*, speed.

+ 15: 冻(凍) *dòng* to freeze;

+ 170: 陈(陳) *chén* to lay out; explain, No. 88.

165 *dōng* 冬 **winter.**

For note on the form of radical 15 冰 *bīng* ice, used in No. 165, see No. 352.

+ 31: 图(圖) *tú* picture; map, No. 695;

+ 120: 终 *zhōng* the end; entire.

166 *dòng* 动(動) **to move.**

Basic for S form: 云 *yún* cloud, No. 866;

Basic for T form: 重 *chóng* repeat, No. 104 and *zhòng* heavy, also listed separately as No. 912;

D. T form f.: 勒 *lè* to rein in, see No. 231: 革 *gé* change;

and also f.: 勤 *qín* diligent, No. 550;

and also f.: 勸 T form for *quàn* to advise, S form: 劝.

+ 61: 恸(慟) *tòng* deep sorrow.

167	*dōu*	都 all.
	dū	capital city.
	Basic:	者 *zhě* (person performing an action) No. 887.

| | D.f.: | 部 *bù* part; section, No. 59; |
| | D.f.: | 那 *nà* that, No. 491; |

168	*dòu*	斗(鬥) struggle. S form is radical 68.
		T form is radical 191.
	dǒu	a unit of measure for grain.

| | D. T form f.: | 鬥 T form for *mén* door, No. 468, S form: 门; |

	+ 64:	抖 *dǒu* to tremble;
	+ 115:	科 *kē* a branch of study, No. 386;
	+ 119:	料 *liào* to anticipate; material.
169	*dòu*	豆 beans. Radical 151.
	+ 181:	頭 T form for *tóu* head, No. 692 in list, S form: 头;
	+ 111:	短 *duǎn* short, No. 173;
	+ 46:	豈 T form for *qǐ* (question particle), S form: 岂,
		see also entry No. 316 for 己 *jǐ* oneself;
	+ 131 and 29:	豎 T form for *shù* vertical, S form: 竖, see also entry
		No. 325 for 坚 *jiān* firm.

| 170 | *dú* | 毒 poison. |

Note also entry No. 486 for 母 *mǔ* mother.

| 171 | *dù* | 度 degree. |

| | D.f.: | 席 *xí* mat; seat; |

	+ 85:	渡 *dù* to cross a river, the sea etc.
172	*duān*	端 end.
173	*duǎn*	短 short.

| This character is | 豆 *dòu* beans, No. 169 in list, plus radical 111. |

174   *duàn*   段 section.

D.f.:   殷 *yīn* abundant; hospitable;
D.f. phonetic in: 假 *jiǎ* false, and *jià* holiday, No. 323.

+ 167:   锻 *duàn* forge.

175   *duàn*   断(斷) break.
+ 120:   继(繼) *jì* to continue, No. 318.

176   *duì*   队(隊) team; group.
+ 162:   遂 *suì* to satisfy,

see also entry No. 652 for 送 *sòng* to deliver; to accompany.

177   *duì*   对(對) answer; opposite.

The right-hand element of these forms is 寸 *cùn* very small, radical 41, No. 127.

178   *duō*   多 many.
+ 88:   爹 *diē* dad, for 父 *fù* father, see No. 214;
+ 115:   移 *yí* to move; change;
+ 句 (*jù*):   够(夠) *gòu* enough, for *jù* sentence, see No. 371.

179   *duó*   夺(奪) to seize.

Both forms have radicals 37: 大 *dà* big, No. 131, and 41: 寸 *cùn* very small,
No. 127, but the T form has also radical 172: 隹 *zhuī*, see No. 335;
D.f.:   寿 S form for *shòu* longevity, No. 629, T form: 壽.

180   *duǒ*   躲 to hide; avoid.

This character is: 朵 *duǒ* (a measure word), for flowers,
plus: 身 *shēn* the body, radical 158, No. 600.
D.f.:   染 *rǎn* dye.

E

181   è
      ě

   Basic: 恶(惡) **evil.**

              亚(亞) *yà* inferior, No. 796.

182   ēn   恩 **kindness.**

   Basic: 因 *yīn* because of, No. 829.

   + 30:   嗯 *ng* second tone: What?, third tone: What!,
              fourth: H'm.

   Note: 惠 *huì* kindness,
   phonetic + 115:   穗 *suì* the ear of grain; fringe.

183   ér   儿(兒) **child; son.**   Radical 10.

184   ér   而 **and**   Radical 126.

   D.f.:   面 *miàn* face, No. 476;

   + 46 and 117:   端 *duān* end, No. 172;

   + 41:   耐 *nài* to be able to bear, No. 493;

   + 173:   需 *xū* need, No. 785;

   + 67:   斋(齋) *zhāi* to practise abstinence.

185   ěr   耳 **ear.   Radical 128.**

   + 184:   饵 *ěr* cakes; pastry;

   + 30 and 159:   辑 *jí* to collect; edit;

   + 29:   取 *qǔ* to take; get, No. 559;

   + 64 and 3 × 128: 攝 T form for *shè* to absorb; to photograph, S form: 摄;

   + 96 and 30:   聖 T form for *shèng* sage; saint, S form: 圣;

   + 169:   闻 *wén* to hear; to smell, No. 724;

   + 只 *zhǐ*:   职 S form for *zhí* job, T form: 職, for *zhǐ* see No. 902.

186   èr   二 **two.   Radical 7.**

   + 9:   仁 *rén* benevolence, No. 570.

F

187	*fā*	发(發) to send out.
	fà	发(髮) hair.

D. T form f.: 號 the T form of 号, *hào*, name; number, No. 272.

+ 64: 拨(撥) *bō* to move with the hand etc.;

D. this S form f.: 拔 *bá* to pull out, No. 13;

+ 53: 废(廢) *fèi* to give up; abandon.

188	*fǎ*	法 law.

This character is basic *qù* 去 to go away, No. 560, plus radical 85.

189	*fān*	番 time; occasion.
	+ 40:	審 T form for *shěn* careful, S form: 审 see No. 599;
	+ 124:	翻 *fān* turn over;
	+ 64:	播 *bō* sow; broadcast.
190	*fán*	凡 anyone.

D.f.:	丹 *dān* red;
D.f.:	瓦 *wǎ* tile, No. 701;
D.f. phonetic in:	讯 *xùn* interrogate, No. 793.

+ 48 and 61: 恐 *kǒng* fear, No. 395.

191	*fán*	繁 numerous; manifold.

D.f.:	緊 T form for *jǐn* tight, S form: 紧, No. 353;
D.f.:	繫 T form for *xì* system; to tie, S form: 系 No. 745, also pronounced *jì* to tie; to button up.

192   *fǎn*   反 **to turn over; return.**

    + 162:   返 *fǎn* to return;

    + 184:   饭 *fàn* cooked rice; a meal;

    + 64:   扳 *bān* to pull; turn;

    + 91:   版 *bǎn* printing plate; edition;

    + 75:   板 *bǎn* board; plank, note T form: 闆.

193   *fàn*   犯 **to violate.**

    + 140 and 85:   范 S form for *fàn* model, T form: 範 see No. 342.

194   *fāng*   方 **square.   Radical 70.**

    D.f. phonetic in: 伤 S form for *shāng* wound, T form: 傷, No. 591;

    + 140:   芳 *fāng* fragrant;

    + 170:   防 *fáng* defend;

    + 63:   房 *fáng* house; room;

    + 149:   访 *fǎng* to visit;

    + 120:   纺 *fǎng* to spin;

    + 66:   放 *fàng* to let go.

    + 195:   鲂 *fáng* bream;

    + 9:   仿 *fǎng* copy;

195   *fēi*   飞 (飛) **to fly.   Radical 183.**

196   *fēi*   非 **wrong.   Radical 175.**

    + 22:   匪 *fěi* bandit;

    + 64:   排 *pái* to put in order, No. 515;

    + 159:   辈 (輩) *bèi* lifetime, for 车 (車) *chē* vehicle, see No. 83;

    + 告: 靠 *kào* to lean on, for 告 *gào* to tell see No. 229;

    + 122:   罪 *zuì* crime; guilt, No. 937.

197   *fēi*   肺 **lungs.**

    D. this phonetic f.:   市 *shì*, market, No. 619.

198   *fèi*   费(費) fee; to cost.

199   *fēn*   分 to divide.
          fèn   component.
          + 164:   酚 *fēn* phenol;
          + 119:   粉 *fěn* powder;
          + 9:   份 *fèn* share; portion;
          + 108:   盆 *pén* basin;
          + 154:   贫 *pín* poor, see also No. 267 for 含 *hán* contain.

200   *fèn*   奋(奮) to exert oneself.

201   *fèn*   粪(糞) excrement.

202   *fēng*   丰(豐) abundant.

203   *fēng*   风(風) the wind.   Radical 182.

204   *fēng*   封 a seal.

205   *féng*   缝 to stitch; sew.
          fēng
          + 46:   峰 *fēng* a peak, summit;

D. this phonetic f. that in:　降 *jiàng* to fall;
and f. that in:　隆 *lóng* grand.

206　*fèng*　　奉 **to give with respect.**
+ 75:　棒 *bàng* a club; a cudgel;
+ 64:　捧 *pěng* hold or carry in both hands.

Note the following characters in which the upper half has the same shape as *fèng*:

春 *chūn* spring, No. 119;
秦 *Qín* a proper name; the Qin dynasty;
泰 *tài* peaceful; Thai;
奏 *zòu* to play music, No. 932;

D. the upper half of *fèng* from the upper half of 卷 *juǎn* roll up, No. 374; and also from the upper half of the phonetic in 腾 *téng* to gallop.

207　*fó*　　佛 **Buddha.**
fú　　　　(as in 仿佛 *fǎngfú* seem.)

D. basic:　弗 *fú* not,
f.:　兼 *jiān* double, No. 326;
and f.:　弟 *dì* younger brother, No. 153.

+ 84:　氟 *fú* fluorine;
+ 154:　费 *fèi* fee; cost, No. 198.

208　*fǒu*　　否 **to deny; whether.**
for　　　不 *bù* not, see No. 56; for 口 *kǒu* the mouth, see No. 396.

209　*fū*　　夫 **husband.**
+ 64:　扶 *fú* to support with the hand.

210　*fú*　　伏 **to bend over.**

This character is radical 9, plus one form of radical 94: 犬 *quǎn* dog.

+ 94 and 149: 狱 *yù* prison;

D. No. 210 伏 f.: 优 *yōu* excellent,
for   尤 *yóu* outstanding, see No. 842.

| 211 | *fú* | 服 clothes. |
| | *fù* | a dose. |

D.f.: 报 S form for *bào* to report, No. 27, T form: 報.

212	*fú*	浮 to float.
+ 卵 *luǎn* egg:	孵 *fū* to hatch; brood;
+ 5:	乳 *rǔ* the breast; milk.

213	*fú*	福 good fortune.
+ 50:	幅 *fú* width of cloth;
+ 162:	逼 *bī* to force (note alt.form has radical 9 instead of 162);
+ 18:	副 *fù* deputy;
+ 40:	富 *fù* rich.

214	*fù*	父 father. Radical 88.
+ 8:	交 *jiāo* to hand over, No. 334;
+ 多 *duō*:	爹 *diē* dad, for *duō* many, see No. 178;
+ 巴 *bā*:	爸 *bà* pa; dad, for *bā* hope, see No. 12;
+ 26:	爷 S form for *yé* father, T form: 爺.

215   *fù*   付 to hand over.

This character is radical 9 plus radical 41 寸 *cùn* very small, No. 127.

+ 53:	府 *fǔ* government office;
+ 53 and 肉:	腐 *fǔ* rotten, for 肉 *ròu* meat, see No. 578;
+ 170:	附 *fù* to add.

216	*fù*	负(負) to bear; carry.
+ 束:	赖(賴) *lài* to rely on, No. 407,
for	束 *shù* to tie, see entry No. 656 for 速 *sù* speed.

217 *fù* 妇(婦) woman.

+ 64: 扫(掃) *sǎo* to sweep;

D.f.: 归(歸) *guī* to return.

218 *fù* 复(復) duplicate; complex.

D.f.: 夏 *xià* summer, No. 748;

+ 130: 腹 *fù* belly;

Note also: 覆 *fù* to cover; overturn.

G

| 219 | *gāi* | 该(該) **ought to; should.** |

+ 39: 孩 *hái* child;

+ 75: 核 *hé* stone; nucleus;

+ 18: 刻 *kè* to carve.

| 220 | *gǎi* | 改 **to change.** |

| 221 | *gài* | 盖(蓋) **a lid; to cover.** |

The S form is   羊 *yáng* sheep, No. 805, radical 123; plus radical 108.

D.f.:   益 *yì* benefit; profit, No. 827.

| 222 | *gài* | 概 **aproximate.** |

Basic: 既 *jì* already; since, No. 317.

| 223 | *gān* | 干(乾) **to do; dry.**   **S form is radical 51.** |
| | *gàn* | 干(幹) **trunk of a tree.** |

D.f.:   千 *qiān* thousand, No. 538;

D.f.:   于 S form for *yú* in; at, No. 849, T form: 於;

+ 130: 肝 *gān* liver; courage;

+ 75: 杆 *gān* pole, and 杆(桿) *gǎn* shaft; arm;

+ 115: 秆(稈) *gǎn* stalk;

+ 156: 赶(趕) *gǎn* to catch up with;

+ 85: 汗 *hàn* sweat;

+ 18: 刊(刊) *kān* to print; publish;

+ 72: 旱 *hàn* drought;

D.f.:   早 *zǎo*, early, No. 873;

+ 72 and 86: 焊 *hàn* to weld; solder;

+ 27 and 46: 岸 *àn* bank; shore.

224   *gān*   甘 sweet. **Radical 99.**

     + 135:   甜 *tián* sweet.

225   *gǎn*   敢 bold; to dare.

This character forms the phonetic for the T form of *yán* 嚴 strict, S form: 严, No. 800.

226   *gǎn*   感 feel.

     D. phonetic f.:   或 *huò* perhaps, No. 302.

     + 30:   喊 *hǎn* to shout;

     + 15:   减 *jiǎn* to subtract;

     + 112:   碱 *jiǎn* alkali; soda;

     Basic: 咸 S form for *xián* salted; salty, T form: 鹹, for salt see also *yán* 盐（鹽）, No. 802.

227   *gāng*   刚（剛）firm; only just.

     D.f.:   网（網）*wǎng* net, No. 707;

Referring to the T form phonetics above, see also No. 503 for 逆 *nì* contrary.

     D.f.:   风（風）*fēng* the wind, No. 203.

     + 120:   纲（綱）*gāng* guiding principle; programme;

     + 167:   钢（鋼）*gāng* steel, and *gàng* to sharpen;

     + 46:   岗（崗）*gǎng* hillock.

228   *gāo*   高 tall. **Radical 189.**

     + 64:   搞 *gǎo* to do;

     +115:   稿 *gǎo* a stalk; draft document;

     + 66:   敲 *qiāo* to knock.

229   *gào*   告 to tell.

     + 175:   靠 *kào* to lean on, No. 385 (for 非 *fēi* wrong, see No. 196);

     + 162:   造 *zào* to make, create.

| 230 | *gē* | 哥 (elder) brother. |
| | + 76: | 歌 *gē* song, to sing. |

| 231 | *gé* | 革 leather; to change.   Radical 177. |
| | + 19: | 勒 *lè* to rein in; |

| D.f.: | 動 T form of *dòng*, to move, S form: 动, see No. 166, |
| and f.: | 勤 *qín* diligent, No. 550. |

| 232 | *gé* | 隔 separate. |

| D.f. phonetic in: | 锅 S form for *guō* pot, T form: 鍋, No. 260; |

| | + 142: | 融 *róng* to melt. |

| 233 | *gè* | 个(個) a measure word. |

| The T form is | 固 *gù* firm, plus radical 9. See also entry 243. |

| 234 | *gè* | 各 each; every. |

| D.f.: | 名 *míng* name, No. 480. |

	+ 75:	格 *gé* squares; division;
	+ 167:	铬 *gè* chromium;
	+ 102:	略 *lüè* brief; summary;
	+ 157:	路 *lù* road, No. 449;
	+ 40:	客 *kè* guest, No. 390;
	+ 140 and 85:	落 *luò* to fall; drop, No. 455;
	+ 85:	洛 *Luò* Luo, a proper name.

| 235 | *gěi* | 给 to give. |

| This character is | 合 *hé* to close; to join, No. 274, plus radical 120. |

236   *gēng*   更 to change.
          gèng   more; even more.

D.f.:   史 *shǐ* history;
D.f. phonetic in: 使 *shǐ* to send, No. 618.

+ 9:   便 *biàn* convenient, No. 46;
+ 112:   硬 *yìng* hard; tough.

237   *gēng*   耕 to plough.

This character is 耒 *lěi* a plough, radical 127, plus 井 *jǐng* a well, No. 359;
D. radical 127 f. the left-hand element in: 栽 *zāi* to plant, see also No. 61.

238   *gōng*   工 a worker; labour.   Radical 48.
+ 19:   功 *gōng* merit; achievement;
+ 66:   攻 *gōng* to attack;
+ 154:   贡 *gòng* tribute;
+ 121:   缸 *gāng* vat; jar;
+ 64:   扛 *káng* to carry on the shoulder;
+ 120:   红 *hóng* red;
+ 116:   空 *kōng* and *kòng* empty (space); air, No. 393;
+ 凡 and 61:   恐 *kǒng* fear, No. 395 (for 凡 *fán*, anyone, see No. 190);
+ 85:   江 *jiāng* (large) river; the Yangtze;
+ 181:   项 *xiàng*, nape of the neck; an item.
+ 85:   汞 *gǒng* mercury (radical 85 here in full form,
                                   see No. 643).

D. this phonetic f.: 永 *yǒng* forever, No. 840.

239   *gōng*   弓 bow.   Radical 57.
+ 2:   引 *yǐn* to draw; to attract, No. 832.

240   *gōng*   公 public; common.
                               松(鬆) *sōng* pine tree; loose; to relax;
+ 181:   颂 *sòng* to praise.

241   *gòng*   共 **common; general.**

D.f.:   井 *jǐng* a well, No. 359;

D.f.:   其 *qí* his, No. 531.

+ 9:   供 *gōng* to supply and *gòng* to confess;

+ 86:   烘 *hōng* to dry or warm; bake;

+ 85:   洪 *hóng* big; vast;

+ 85 and 26:   港 *gǎng* port; Hong Kong;

+ 26:   巷 *xiàng* lane; alley;

+ 44 and 79:   殿 *diàn* hall; palace;

+ 102:   異 T form for *yì* different, S form: 异, No. 824.

242   *gōu*   勾 **to retain; to cancel.**

D.f.:   句 *jù* a word; a sentence, No. 371.

+ 167:   钩(鉤) *gōu* a hook;

The phonetic of this T form is identical to 句 *jù* sentence, No. 371;

+ 85:   沟(溝) *gōu* a ditch;

+ 75:   构(構) *gòu* to form; compose;

+ 154:   购(購) *gòu* to buy;

The phonetic of the above three T forms is identical to that in the T form of 講 *jiǎng* to speak, tell, S form: 讲, No. 333.

243   *gǔ*   古 **ancient.**

D.f.:   吉 *jí* lucky.

+ 31:   固 *gù* firm; solid, see also entry No. 233;

+ 66:   故 *gù* incident; reason;

D.f.:   姑 *gū* aunt;

+ 75:	枯 *kū* withered; dried up;
+ 140:	苦 *kǔ* bitter, No. 398;
+ 130:	胡 *hú* non-Han, No. 282.

244 *gǔ* 骨 **bone. Radical 188.**

D.f. phonetic in: 過 T form of *guò* to pass, S form: 过, No. 263.

| + 85: | 滑 *huá* slippery; smooth. |

245 *gǔ* 鼓 **drum; to rouse. Radical 207.**

246 *gù* 顾(顧) **turn round and look at.**

Note use of the T form phonetic in 僱 T form for *gù* to hire, S form: 雇.

247 *guā* 瓜 **melon. Radical 97.**

D.f.:   爪 *zhuǎ*, claw, as seen in 抓 *zhuā*, to arrest, No. 920.

| + 57: | 弧 *hú* arc. |

248 *guà* 挂(掛) **to hang.**
Basic:	圭 *guī* ceremonial jade.
+ 112:	硅 *guī* silicon;
+ 75:	桂 *guì* laurel tree;
+ 30:	哇 *wā* noise of crying;
+ 38:	娃 *wá* a baby;
+ 27 and 46:	崖 *yá* a precipice; a cliff;
+ 9:	佳 *jiā* fine

D.f.:   住 *zhù* to live, No. 918;

+ 144:	街 *jiē* street, No. 341;
+ 177:	鞋 *xié* shoes; boots;
+ 41:	封 *fēng* a seal; a letter, No. 204.

249   *guài*   怪 strange; odd.

Note basic: 圣 of this character is the S form of *shèng* saint,
                     S form: 圣, T form: 聖.

250   *guān*   关(關) to close.
       + 128:   联(聯) *lián* to unite, No. 425;
       + 163:   郑(鄭) *Zhèng* a surname;

Note also + 64:   掷(擲) *zhī* or *zhì* to throw.

251   *guān*   观(觀) to look at.
       Basic: 见(見) *jiàn* to see, radical 147, No. 328.
       + 76:   欢(歡) *huān* joyous;
       + 75:   权(權) *quán* right; power;
       + 19:   劝(勸) *quàn* to urge; advise;
       (T) + 121:   罐 *guàn* a pot (this one form only);
       (T) + 85:   灌 *guàn* to irrigate (this one form only);

See No. 846 for 又 *yòu* again for examples of its use as the phonetic in the S form
of numerous compound characters. Note particularly also:
+ 85: 汉 the S form for *Hàn* Chinese, T form: 漢 No. 269.

252   *guān*   官 official.
       + 118:   管 *guǎn* a tube; to be in charge of;
       + 184:   馆 *guǎn* hotel; embassy.

253   *guàn*   贯 to pass through.

D.f.:   贵 *guì* dear; expensive, No. 258;
D.f. phonetic in: 喷 *pēn* to spurt; gush.

+ 61:   惯 *guàn* to be used to.

254   *guāng*   光 light.

     + 军: 辉 *huī* brightness, for 军 *jūn* army, see No. 378.

255   *guǎng*   广(廣) wide; vast.

> Note T form basic: 黄 *huáng* yellow, No. 293;
>
> D. S form   广 f. 厂 S form for *chǎng* factory, T form: 廠 No. 80.

     + 112:   矿(礦) *kuàng* ore deposit;

     + 64:   扩(擴) *kuò* to expand.

256   *guī*   规 regulation; rule.

257   *guǐ*   鬼 ghost; spirit.   Radical 194.

     + 32:   塊 T form for *kuài* piece, S form: 块, see also No. 375;

     + 164:   醜 T form for *chǒu* ugly, S form: 丑 (for other characters using this shape see entry No. 509, 扭 for *niǔ* to turn round).

258   *guì*   贵(貴) expensive; dear.

> D.f.:   贯(貫) *guàn* to pass through, No. 253;
>
> D.f. phonetic in: 喷 *pēn* to spurt; gush.

     + 162:   遗(遺) *yí* to lose; leave behind.

259   *gǔn*   滚(滾) to roll; trundle.

> D.f. phonetic in: 棱(稜) *léng* edge, No. 416;
>
> D.f. phonetic in: 酸 *suān* acid; sour, No. 658.

260   *guō*   锅(鍋) pot.

> D. T form phonetic f.:   骨 *gǔ* bone, No. 244;
>
> D. S form phonetic f.:   隔 *gé* separate, No. 232.
>
> 162 + T form phonetic: 過 T form for *guò*, No. 263, to cross, S form: 过.

     + 113:   祸(禍) *huò* disaster;

+ 85:   涡(渦) *wō* whirlpool;

+ 116:   窝(窩) *wō* nest.

261   *guó*   国(國) **country.**

262   *guǒ*   果 **fruit.**

+ 149:   课 *kè* course, No. 391;

+ 75:   棵 *kē* a measure word, e.g. for trees;

+ 181:   颗 *kē* a measure word, e.g. for beans.

263   *guò*   过(過) **to cross; pass.**

This S character is radical 162 plus radical 41: 寸 *cùn* very small, No. 127;

This T character is radical 162 plus the phonetic of the T form of *guō* 鍋 No. 260.

H

264	*hái*	还(還) still; yet.
	huán	return.
	+61:	怀(懷) *huái* bosom; to cherish;
	+32:	坏(壞) *huài* bad;

D.f.:   坯 *pī* base, see also entry No. 56;

	+96:	环(環) *huán* a ring; to surround;

S forms are   不 *bù* no; not, No. 56, plus radicals 162, 61, 32 and 96.

265	*hǎi*	海 the sea.
	Basic:	每 *měi* each; every, No. 466.
266	*hài*	害 evil.

D.f.:   善 *shàn* good, No. 590.

	+18:	割 *gē* to cut.
267	*hán*	含 to contain.

The following characters need to be noted and distinguished one from another:

No. 267 without radical 30: 今 *jīn* today, No. 347;

No. 267 with radical 154: 贪 *tān* corrupt;

D.f.:   贫 *pín* poor, see No. 199 for 分 *fēn*;

D. also *jīn*, above,   今 from 令 *lìng* order, No. 439;

Note: 函 *hán* with meaning similar to No. 267 (to contain). See also No. 770.

268	*hán*	寒 cold.

D.f.:   塞 *sāi* to squeeze in, No. 583.

Note also entry No. 165 for 冬 *dōng* winter.

269   *Hàn*   汉(漢) Chinese.

D. phonetic in T form f.:   莫 *mò* no; not, No. 484,

and also f.:   黄 *huáng* yellow, No. 293;

The S form phonetic   又 is *yòu* again, No. 846, also used for the S forms

listed in No. 251, e.g.:   观 *guān* look at, T form: 觀,

and in No. 496, e.g.:   难 *nán* hard, T form: 難;

       + 30:   叹(嘆) *tàn* sigh.

270   *háo*   毫 writing brush; (not) at all.

       + 152:   豪 *háo* a hero; unrestrained;

Note also: 毛 *máo* hair, No. 463.

271   *hǎo*   好 good; fine.
         hào   to like.

272   *hào*   号(號) name; number.
         háo   to howl.

D. T form f.:   發 T form for *fā* to send out, No. 187, S form: 发;

The right-hand part of the T form 虎 is *hǔ* the tiger, No. 283.

273   *hē*   喝 to drink.
         hè   to shout.

       + 145:   褐 *hè* coarse cloth; brown;

       + 64:   揭 *jiē* to tear off;

       + 76:   歇 *xiē* to have a rest.

274   *hé*   合 close; join.

       + 108:   盒 *hé* box; case;

D. this f.:   盖 *gài* lid; cover, No. 221;

       + 30:   哈 *hā* to breathe out;

       + 64 and 140:   搭 *dā* to build, No. 128;

+ 120:	给	*gěi* to give, No. 235;
+ 64:	拾	*shí* to pick up;
Note also + 64:	拿	*ná* to hold; take, No. 490.

275	*hé*	和	**gentle; and; with.**
	hè		**to join in the singing; compose a poem in reply.**

276	*hēi*	黑	**black. Radical 203.**
	+ 32:	墨	*mò* ink.

277	*hěn*	很	**very.**

D. phonetic f.:	良	*liáng* good; fine, No. 428;

+ 94:	狠	*hěn* ruthless;
+ 61:	恨	*hèn* hate;
+ 75:	根	*gēn* root; base; origin;
+ 157:	跟	*gēn* heel; to follow;
+ 162:	退	*tuì* to retreat, No. 698;
+ 170:	限	*xiàn* limit; bounds;
+ 109:	眼	*yǎn* the eye, No. 803;
+ 167:	银	*yín* silver.

278	*hòu*	后(後)	**behind.**

279	*hòu*	厚	**thick.**

D. phonetic f.:	享	*xiǎng* to enjoy, No. 758;
and f. the phonetic in	哼	*hēng* to groan; snort.

280	*hòu*	候	**to wait.**

D.f.:	侯	*hóu* a nobleman.

281	*hū*	乎	**at; in; from.**

D.f.:	平	*píng* flat; even, No. 525;

+ 30:	呼	*hū* to breathe out.

282   *hú*   胡 non-Han; recklessly.

This character is   古 *gǔ* ancient, No. 243, plus radical 130.
D. between No. 282 胡 and 朝 *cháo* dynasty, No. 82.

+ 85:   湖 *hú* lake;
+ 119:   糊 *hú* paste.

283   *hǔ*   虎 tiger.

Note the right-hand element in 號 T form for *hào*, name, No. 272, S form: 号;
Note similar shape in 虛 *xū* empty, No. 784.

+ 59:   彪 *biāo* a young tiger; a name;
+ 27 and 162:   遞 T form for *dì* to hand over, S form: 递 see No. 153.

284   *hù*   户 door; household.   Radical 63.

D.f.:   尸 *shī* a corpse, No. 608, radical 44;

+ 64:   护(護) *hù* to protect (the phonetic in this T form

can also be seen in 獲 the T form for 获 *huò* to capture, No. 304);

+ 130:   肩 *jiān* shoulder;
+ 85:   沪(滬) *Hù* Shanghai;
+ 86:   炉 S form for *lú* a stove, No. 446, T form: 爐;
+ 30:   启(啟) *qǐ* to open;
+ 123:   扇 *shān* to fan, or *shàn* a fan.

285   *hù*   互 mutual; each other.

D.f.:   丑 S form for *chǒu* ugly, T form: 醜, note that other
                              characters with this phonetic sound *niǔ* e.g. 扭
                              twist, No. 509.

286   *huá*   划(劃) **to row a boat; to cut; scratch.**
         huà   **to differentiate; to plan.**

The S form is   戈 *gē* a dagger-axe, radical 62, plus radical 18,
see also No. 884   找 *zhǎo* to look for, for another use of radical 62.
The T form phonetic   畫 is the T form for *huà* to draw, No. 289, S form: 画.

287   *huà*   化 **to change.**
         huā   **to spend.**
         + 24:   华(華) *huá* magnificent; China;

D.f.:   毕(畢) *bì* to finish, see entry No. 38 for *bǐ* 比;

         + 140:   花 *huā* flower;
         + 24 and 75: 桦(樺) *huà* a birch tree;
         + 149:   讹 *é* erroneous;
         + 154:   货 *huò* goods, No. 303.

288   *huà*   话 **word; talk.**

This character is   舌 *shé*, No. 596, tongue, plus radical 149, *yán* speech,
                       No. 799.

         + 85:   活 *huó* to live; alive;
         + 169 and 85: 阔 *kuò* wide; wealthy.

289   *huà*   画(畫) **to draw; to paint.**

This T form   畫 is the phonetic in 劃 T form for *huá* to row,
No. 286, S form: 划;
D. this in turn f.:   書 T form for *shū* book, S form: 书, No. 631.

290   *huàn*   换 **to exchange.**

D. phonetic f.:   免 *miǎn* to avoid, No. 475.

291 *huāng* 荒 wasteland.

+ 61: 慌 *huāng* flurried, and *huang* awfully.

292 *huáng* 皇 emperor.

This character is	王	*wáng* king, No. 706, plus radical 106;
D.f.:	呈	*chéng* to assume a form, or colour, No. 93;
and f.:	臭	*chòu* smelly, No. 105.
D.f. phonetic in:	捏	S form for *niē* to pinch, T form: 揑.

293 *huáng* 黄 yellow.   Radical 201.

D.f.:	莫	*mò* no; not, No. 484;
D.f. phonetic in:	漢	T form for *Hàn* Chinese, No. 269, S form: 汉;

+ 118: 簧 *huáng* reed; a spring;

+ 53: 廣 T form for *guǎng* wide, No. 255, S form: 广;

+ 75: 横 *héng* horizontal, and *hèng* harsh.

Note: 演 *yǎn* to act; to develop, No. 804.

294 *huī* 灰 ash.

Basic: 火 *huǒ* fire, radical 86, see entry No. 301;

+ 46: 炭 *tàn* charcoal;

+ 112 and 46: 碳 *tàn* carbon.

295 *huí* 回 a circle; to return.

D.f.:	画	S form for *huà* to draw, No. 289, T form: 畫.

296 *huǐ* 毁(毀) to destroy.

D. phonetic f. that in:	捏	T form for *niē* to pinch with the fingers,
		S form: 揑.

297 *huì* 汇(匯) converge; remit.

298   *huì*   会(會) to meet together; can; be able to.

+ 120:   绘(繪) *huì* to paint; to draw.

299   *hūn*   婚 to marry; wedding.
Basic: 昏 *hūn* dusk.

300   *hùn*   混 to mix; confuse.
Basic: 昆 *kūn* elder brother; offspring;

D.f.:   皆 *jiē* all; each and every, note this is the phonetic in
the T form   階 *jiē* steps; rank, No. 339, S form: 阶.

301   *huǒ*   火 fire.   Radical 86.

D.f.:   水 *shuǐ* water, radical 85, No. 643;

Note compound of *huǒ*:   灰 *huī* ash, No. 294.
    + 9:   伙 *huǒ* meals; partnership;
    + 1:   灭 S form for *miè* to extinguish, No. 478, T form: 滅;
    + 40:   灾 S form for *zāi* calamity, T form: 災;
    + 115:   秋 *qiū* autumn, No. 555;
    2 × No. 301:   炎 *yán* burning hot, see No. 670;
    2 × No. 301 + 14 form the upper half of the T form for:
        營 *yíng* to seek; a camp, No. 838, S form: 营;
    and for: 勞 *láo* labour, No. 409, S form: 劳;
    and for: 榮 *róng* to flourish, No. 575, S form: 荣.

302   *huò*   或 perhaps.

D. from phonetic in: 感 *gǎn* feel; sense, No. 226;

    + 32:   域 *yù* territory; region.

303   *huò*   货(貨) goods; commodity.

This character is   化 *huà* change, No. 287, plus radical 154;

D. No. 303 f.:   贷(貸) *dài* loan, see entry No. 132 for 代 *dài*;

Note similarity in shape between No. 303 货 and 贸 *mào* trade.

304   *huò*   获(獲) to obtain.

D. the T form phonetic   獲 f. that in: 觀 T form for *guān* to look, No. 251,

S form: 观;

This phonetic is also seen in 護 T form for *hù* to protect, S form: 护, see No. 284.

J

305 *jī*   几(幾) **a small table.**
       jǐ   **how many?; some.**
       + 75:   机(機) *jī* **a machine.**

306 *jī*   击(擊) **to attack.**
       + 170:   陆 S form for *lù* (main)land, No. 447, T form: 陸.

The T form of No. 306   擊 has the radical 64 placed beneath the phonetic;
       D.f.:   繫 T form for *jì* to tie, S form: 系, see also No. 745;
       D.f.:   繁 *fán* numerous, No. 191;
       D.f.:   緊 T form for *jǐn* tight, No. 353, S form: 紧.

307 *jī*   鸡(雞) **chicken.**

The S form is   又 *yòu* again, No. 846, plus radical 196 鸟 *niǎo* a bird.

308 *jī*   积(積) **to amass.**

S form phonetic 只 is S form for *zhǐ* only, No. 902, T form: 祇, and the T form
phonetic 責 is the T form for *zé* duty, No. 875, S form: 责.

309 *jī*   基 **base.**
       Basic: 其 *qí* his, No. 531.

       D.f.:   塞 *sāi* to squeeze in, No. 583;
       D.f.:   赛 *sài* match; competition;
       D.f.:   寨 *zhài* stockade; camp.

310 *jī*   激 **to dash; to arouse.**

       D.f.:   游 *yóu* to swim, No. 844.

       + 120:   缴 *jiǎo* to pay.

311   *jí*   及 **to reach.**

D.f.:   乃 *nǎi* to be; therefore, No. 492.

+ 75:   极(極) *jí* extreme; extremely;

This T form phonetic is   亟 *jí* urgently;

+ 120:   级 *jí* rank; grade;
+ 30:   吸 *xī* to breathe in.

312   *jí*   即 **to approach; even if.**

D.f.:   既 *jì* already; since, No. 317;
D.f. phonetic in: 柳 *liǔ* the willow tree.

+ 118:   節 T form for *jié* joint; section, No. 342, S form: 节;

D. this also f.:   範 T form for *fàn* pattern; model, S form: 范;
Note also: 卿 *qīng* a minister; an official.

313   *jí*   急 **anxious; urgent.**
+ 115:   稳(穩) *wěn* steady; certain;
+ 170:   隐(隱) *yǐn* hidden; latent, No. 833.

314   *jí*   疾 **disease.**

Radical 104, as here, indicates illness, as in 病 *bìng* ill, No. 53.

315   *jí*   集 **to gather together; assemble.**

Note also: 聚 *jù* to assemble, for 取 *qǔ* to get, see No. 559.

316   *jǐ*   己 **oneself.   Radical 49.**

D.f.:   已 *yǐ* to stop, No. 820.

+ 149:   记 *jì* to remember;

	+ 120:	纪 *jì* discipline; epoch;
	+ 46:	岂 S form for *qǐ* (a question particle), T form: 豈;
	+ 156:	起 *qǐ* to rise, No. 534;
	+ 66:	改 *gǎi* to change, No. 220;
	+ 164:	配 *pèi* to marry; mix; allocate, No. 519.
317	*jì*	既 **already; since.**

D.f.:	即 *jí* to approach, No. 312;

	+ 75:	概 *gài* generally, No. 222.
318	*jì*	继(繼) **to continue.**

This phonetic + 69:	断(斷) *duàn* to break, No. 175.

319	*jiā*	加 **to add.**

D.f.:	如 *rú* according to; as if, No. 579.

	+ 75:	架 *jià* frame; rack;
	+ 154:	贺 *hè* congratulate;
	+ 187:	驾 *jià* harness; to drive;

Note also:	嘉 *jiā* good; to praise.

320	*jiā*	夹(夾) **to squeeze.**

D.f.:	来 *lái* to come, No. 406;

	+ 94:	狭(狹) *xiá* narrow.
321	*jiā*	家 **family; home.**
	+ 38:	嫁 *jià* to marry – of a woman.
322	*jiǎ*	甲 **first.**

D.f.:	申 *shēn* to state; express, No. 599;
and f.:	由 *yóu* cause; reason, No. 843.

+ 167:	钾 *jiǎ* potassium;
+ 196:	鸭 *yā* duck;
+ 169:	闸 *zhá* floodgate.

323 *jiǎ*   假 **false.**
    jià   **holiday.**

D. phonetic f.:   段 *duàn* section, No. 174.

| + 142: | 蝦 T form for *xiā* shrimp, S form: 虾, see No. 747; |
| + 173: | 霞 *xiá* morning or evening rosy clouds. |

324 *jiān*   尖 **point; sharp.**

D.f.:   尘 S form for *chén* dust, No. 85, T form: 塵.

325 *jiān*   坚(堅) **firm.**

D.f.:	紧(緊) *jǐn* tight, No. 353;
and f.:	竖(豎) *shù* vertical, see No. 169 for 豆 *dòu*;
and f.:	贤(賢) *xián* virtuous;

These four characters above have an *identical* upper half with different radicals below, and need to be distinguished from a number of others which have an upper half *similar* to that of No. 325 but again with varying radicals underneath.

See for example   监(監) *jiān* pp.69–70, to supervise, No. 327, where other characters with a similar shape are given.

326 *jiān*   兼 **double; concurrently.**

D.f.:   弗 *fú* not, see No. 207: 佛 *fó* Buddha.

+ 53:	廉 *lián* honest and clean;
+ 149:	谦 *qiān* modest;
+ 38:	嫌 *xián* suspicion.

327   *jiān*   监(監) to supervise.

D.f.:   坚(堅) *jiān* firm, No. 325.

+ 167:   鉴(鑒) *jiàn* to reflect;
+ 137:   艦 T form for *jiàn* warship, S form: 舰;
+ 140:   蓝(藍) *lán* blue;
+ 118:   篮(籃) *lán* a basket;

Note similar shape in   盐(鹽) *yán* salt, No. 802;
Note also: 临(臨) *lín* to confront, No. 436.

328   *jiàn*   见(見) to see.   Radical 147.

D.f.:   贝(貝) *bèi* shellfish, radical 154, see also No. 17.

+ 29:   观 S form for *guān* to look at, No. 251, T form: 觀;
+ 113:   视 *shì* to look at;
+ 96:   现 *xiàn* the present, No. 752.

329   *jiàn*   间(間) space in between.
        jiān   between; among.

D.f.:   闻(聞) *wén* to hear; to smell, No. 724;
D.f.:   问(問) *wèn* to ask, No. 725.

+ 118:   简(簡) *jiǎn* simple.

330   *jiàn*   建 to build.
        Same phonetic as: 津 *jīn* a ferry, No. 350.
+ 9:   健 *jiàn* healthy;
+ 167:   键 *jiàn* a key.

331   *jiāng*   将(將) to do; to handle.
        jiàng   a general.
+ 85:   浆(漿) *jiāng* thick liquid; starch;
+ 37:   奖(奬) *jiǎng* to encourage; reward.

332   *jiāng*   姜(薑) ginger.

> Note + 9:   僵 (this one form only) *jiāng* stiff; numb;
>
> Note also: 疆 (this one form only) *jiāng* border.

333   *jiǎng*   讲(講) to speak; tell.

> The S form is 149 +   井 *jǐng* a well, No. 359 in list.
>
> T form phonetic + 85:   溝 T form for *gōu* a ditch, S form: 沟;
>
> T form phonetic + 75:   構 T form for *gòu* to form; compose, S form: 构;
>
> T form phonetic + 154:   購 T form for *gòu* to purchase; buy, S form: 购.

334   *jiāo*   交 to hand over.

> D.f.:   文 *wén* script; language, No. 723.

> + 130:   胶(膠) *jiāo* glue, for 羽 *yǔ* feather, see No. 854;
>
> + 120:   绞 *jiǎo* to twist;
>
> + 159:   较 *jiào* to compare;
>
> + 66:   效 *xiào* effect;
>
> + 75:   校 *xiào* school;
>
> + 30:   咬 *yǎo* to bite.

335   *jiāo*   焦 burnt.

> This character is radical 172 隹 *zhuī* short-tailed birds, rarely used alone, plus the alternative form of radical 86, the four strokes underneath to stand for 火 *huǒ* fire.
>
> This 172 radical is seen in a number of other compound characters with pronunciations similar to *zhuī* such as: 谁 *shuí* who?, No. 642.

> + 112:   礁 *jiāo* a reef; rock;
>
> + 109:   瞧 *qiáo* to look; see.

336   *jiǎo*   角   a horn; an angle.   **Radical 148.**
       jué   **a role.**

     D.f.:   鱼   S form for *yú* fish, radical 195, No. 852, T form: 魚;

     + 142:   触   S form for *chù* to touch, No. 111, T form: 觸;
     + 112:   确   S form for *què* true, No. 563, T form: 確.
     + 30 and 此: 嘴   *zuǐ* mouth, No. 935, for 此 *cǐ* this, see No. 122.

337   *jiào*   叫   **to cry; shout.**

     D.f.:   收   *shōu* to receive, No. 625.

338   *jiào*   教   **to teach.**
       jiāo

339   *jiē*   阶(階) **steps; rank.**

     S form basic: 介   *jiè* to be situated (this one form only), No. 345;
     T form phonetic: 皆   *jiē* all; each and every;
     D. this f.:   昆   *kūn* elder brother, see No. 300: 混 *hùn*.

340   *jiē*   接   **to connect; receive.**

     D.f.:   按   *àn* to press down, see entry No. 5 for 安 *ān* quiet.

341   *jiē*   街   **street.**

This character is radical 144 行 *xíng* to go, No. 774, which has any extra element placed in the centre, here 圭 *guī*, see No. 248, to give No. 341: 街;

     Similarly: 衡   *héng* to weigh; measure;
     And also: 衝   the T form for *chōng* to dash, No. 101, S form: 冲.

342   *jié*   节(節) **joint; part; festival.**

     This T form is   即   *jí* to approach, No. 312, plus radical 118.
     D. T form f.:   筋   *jīn* muscle; sinew;
     and also f.:   範   T form for *fàn* pattern, S form: 范, see also entry
                No. 193 for 犯 *fàn* to violate.

343 *jié*   结 to tie; to settle.
     jiē   to bear (fruit).
     Basic: 吉 *jí* lucky;

D.f.:   古 *gǔ* ancient, No. 243;

     + 75:   桔 *jú* tangerine, alt.form: 橘.

344 *jiě*   解 to separate.
     jiè   to send under guard.
     + 142:   蟹 *xiè* a crab.

345 *jiè*   介 be situated between.
     + 102:   界 *jiè* a boundary;
     + 170:   阶 S form for *jiē* steps, No. 339, T form: 階;
     + 9:   价 S form for *jià* price, T form: 價.

346 *jiè*   借(藉) borrow; make use of.

D. phonetic f. that in: 散 *sǎn* and *sàn* to come loose; disperse, No. 585;

     + 118:   籍 *jí* a book; a register;
     + 142:   蜡 S form for *là* wax; a candle, T form: 蠟;
     + 164:   醋 *cù* vinegar; jealousy;
     + 167:   错 *cuò* complex; mistaken.

347 *jīn*   今 modern; today.

D.f.:   令 *lìng* command, No. 439;

     + 30:   含 *hán* to contain, No. 267;
     + 2 × 96:   琴 *qín* a musical instrument, for 王 *wáng* see No. 706;

348 *jīn*   斤 a half kilo.   Radical 69.

D.f.:   斥 *chì* to scold, seen in 诉 *sù* to tell, No. 653.

     + 162:   近 *jìn* near; close, No. 355;
     + 30:   听 S form for *tīng* to listen to, No. 685, T form: 聽;
     + 75:   析 *xī* to divide; analyse, No. 739;

+ 113:   祈 *qí* to pray;

+ 64:   折 S form for *zhé* to break, No. 886, T form: 摺;

+ 159:   斩 *zhǎn* to cut; note further compounds:

(a) adding radical 85 to this phonetic 渐 *jiàn* gradually; and (b) adding radical 72 to this phonetic 暂 *zàn* temporary.

349   *jīn*   钅(金) metals.   Radical 167.

D.f.:   全 *quán* complete; whole, No. 561;

Note the S form: 鉴 *jiàn* to reflect has two T forms: 鑑 and 鑒, see also No. 327 for 监(監) *jiān* to supervise.

350   *jīn*   津 ferry; ford.

This character is radical 85 added to radical 129: 聿 *yù*, pencil (archaic).

Note the following three frequently used characters with radical 129:

+ 54:   建 *jiàn* to build, No. 330;

+ 118:   筆 T form for *bǐ* a pen, No. 39, S form: 笔;

+ 60:   律 *lü* (fourth tone) law, No. 451.

D.f. radical 129:   隶 S form for *lì* to be subordinate to, T form: 隸, note also use of this phonetic in: 康 *kāng* health, No. 382.

351   *jǐn*   仅(僅) only.

D. T form phonetic f.:   董 *dǒng* to direct, see No. 104 for 重 *chóng* repeat; again.

For other uses of   又 *yòu* again, No. 846, as the S form phonetic, see No. 269;

T form phonetic + 19:   勤 *qín* diligent, No. 550.

352 *jǐn* 尽(盡) **to the greatest extent.**
     jìn **exhausted.**

This character is 尺 *chǐ* a unit of length, No. 98, plus the abbreviated form of radical 15 冰 *bīng* ice, which is also to be seen in the characters 冬 *dōng* winter, No. 165, and 寒 *hán* cold, No. 268.

353 *jǐn* 紧(緊) **tight.**

D. T form f.: 擎 T form for *jī* to attack, No. 306, S form: 击;
and f.: 繁 *fán* numerous, No. 191;
and f.: 堅 T form for *jiān* firm, No. 325, S form: 坚;

    + 154: 贤(賢) *xián* virtuous, see also No. 325;
    + 117 (151): 竖(豎) *shù* vertical.

354 *jìn* 进(進) **to advance; to enter.**
    For 井 *jǐng* a well, see No. 359.

355 *jìn* 近 **near; close to.**
    Basic: 斤 *jīn* a half kilo, No. 348.

356 *jīn* 禁 **bear; endure.**
    jìn **prohibit.**

357 *jīng* 京 **a capital city.**
    + 61: 惊(驚) *jīng* to be frightened; to alarm;
    + 72: 景 *jǐng* view, note + 59: 影 *yǐng* shadow, No. 839;
    + 15: 凉 *liáng* cool.

358 *jīng* 经(經) **pass through; as a result of.**
    + 140: 茎(莖) *jīng* stem of a plant; stalk;
    + 19: 劲(勁) *jìn* strength; energy;
    + 181: 颈(頸) *jǐng* neck;
    + 60: 径(徑) *jìng* footpath; way, means;
    + 159: 轻(輕) *qīng* light;
    + 84: 氢(氫) *qīng* hydrogen (气 *qì* gas, No. 535);
    + 86: 烃(烴) *tīng* hydrocarbon.

359   *jǐng*   井 **a well.**

D.f.:   共 *gòng* common, No. 241;

and f.:   并 *bìng* to combine, No. 52;

and f.:   升 *shēng* to rise, No. 603;

+ 127:   耕 *gēng* to plough, No. 237;

+ 149:   讲 S form for *jiǎng* to speak, No. 333, T form: 講.

+ 162:   进 S form for *jìn* to enter, No. 354, T form: 進.

360   *jìng*   竟 **to complete.**

D.f.:   竞 *jìng* to compete, T form: 競;

and f.:   亮 *liàng* bright, No. 432;

+ 32:   境 *jìng* a border;

+ 167:   镜 *jìng* a mirror.

361   *jìng*   敬 **respect.**

+ 149:   警 *jǐng* alert; police.

362   *jiǔ*   九 **nine.**

+ 116:   究 *jiū* to study carefully;

D.f.:   突 *tū* to dash, No. 694;

+ 159:   轨 *guǐ* rail; track.

363   *jiǔ*   久 **for a long time.**

Note: 畝 T form for *mǔ* a unit of area, S form: 亩,

for   田 *tián* field. See No. 682.

364   *jiǔ*   酒 **alcoholic drink; wine.**

This is radical 164: 酉 *yǒu*, tenth, plus the alt.form of radical 85 水 *shuǐ* water, see also No. 643 and Appendix B;

+ 49:   配 *pèi* to join; distribute, No. 519.

365 *jiù*   旧(舊) old.

366 *jiù*   就 to come near.

367 *jū*   居 to reside.

  + 167:   锯(鋸) *jù* a saw; to cut with a saw;

  + 64:   据(據) *jù* to occupy; seize;

  + 18:   剧(劇) *jù* drama; play.

See also No. 744, for *xì* 戏(戲) also meaning a play or drama, and often found in this sense together with *jù*: 戏剧(戲劇).

368 *jú*   局 chessboard; situation.

369 *jǔ*   举(舉) to lift; raise.

D. T form f. that of: 與 *yǔ* to give; and, No. 853, S form: 与;

  and of: 興 *xīng* to prosper, No. 771, S form: 兴.

370 *jù*   巨 huge.

  D.f.:   臣 *chén* an official, No. 86;

  + 111:   矩 *jǔ* a carpenter's square; rules;

  + 64:   拒 *jù* to resist; refuse;

  + 157:   距 *jù* distance;

  + 85 and 75: 渠 *qú* canal; ditch.

371 *jù*   句 sentence.

  D.f.:   包 *bāo* to wrap; a bundle, No. 24;

  D.f. phonetic in: 约 *yuē* to arrange; approximately, No. 863;

  D.f. phonetic in: 菊 *jú* chrysanthemum;

  D.f.:   旬 *xún* a period of ten days; or of ten years.

  + 94:   狗 *gǒu* dog;

  + *duō* (多): 够(夠) *gòu* enough.

  For   多 *duō* many, see No. 178.

372   *jù*   具 tool.

> D.f.:   其 *qí* his; her; its; their, No. 531;

> + 9:   俱 *jù* all; complete.

373   *juān*   捐 to abandon; to donate.

> D.f.:   损(損) *sǔn* to decrease; to damage;
>
> The basic here is: 员(員) *yuán* a member, No. 861;
>
> D. this phonetic f.:   锁(鎖) *suǒ* a lock; to lock up.

374   *juǎn*   卷 to roll up.
           juàn   a book; file.

           + 31:   圈 *quān* a circle;

> D. the top half of this phonetic f. that of 奉 *fèng* to give, see No. 206 for *fèng* and other examples.
>
> The phonetic in the T form of 勝 *shèng* victory, S form: 胜, is the same as the top half of *juǎn*. See also No. 604 for 生 *shēng* life.

375   *jué*   决(決) to decide.
           + 61:   快 *kuài* fast; happy, No. 401;
           + 32:   块(塊) *kuài* a piece; a lump;

> See No. 257 for   鬼 *guǐ* ghost; spirit.

376   *jué*   觉(覺) to sense; to feel.
           jiào   to sleep.

377   *jué*   绝 to cut off; absolutely.
           Basic: 色 *sè* colour, No. 587.

378   *jūn*   军(軍) armed forces; the army.
           + 64:   挥(揮) *huī* to wave; wipe; command;
           + 光 *guāng*:   辉(輝) *huī* brightness; to shine,
           for   光 *guāng* light, see No. 254;
           + 162:   運 T form for *yùn* movement, S form: 运, for this
                                          S form basic, see No. 866 for 云 *yún* cloud.

K

| 379 | *kǎ* | 卡 to block; to check. |

| 380 | *kāi* | 开(開) to open. |

| D. T form f.: | 聞 T form for *wén* to hear, No. 724, S form: 闻. |

+ 18:	刑 *xíng* punishment, No. 773;
+ 18 and 32:	型 *xíng* mould; model;
+ 59:	形 *xíng* form; shape, No. 775;
+ 112:	研 *yán* to grind; to study, for 石 *shí* stone see No. 614.

| 381 | *kàn* | 看 to see; read; consider. |
| | *kān* | to look after. |

| D.f.: | 着(著) *zhe* with a verb = '-ing', No. 889, also *zhāo* a move; a trick; and *zháo* to touch; and *zhuó* to wear clothes. |

| 382 | *kāng* | 康 health. |
| | Basic: | 隶 S form for *lì* be subordinate to, T form: 隸. |

D.f.:	库(庫) *kù* warehouse, No. 399;
D. the basic phonetic f.:	录 S form for *lù* to record, No. 448, T form: 錄;
and also f. that in:	津 *jīn* ferry; ford, No. 350;
and also f. that in:	唐 *Táng* the Tang dynasty, No. 671.

383	*kàng*	抗 to resist.
	+ 86:	炕 *kàng* a kang – a heatable bed;
	+ 32:	坑 *kēng* a hole; a pit;
	+ 137:	航 *háng* a boat; to navigate.

| 384 | *kǎo* | 考 to give or take a test. |

| D.f. the phonetic in: | 跨 *kuà* a step; stride, No. 400; |
| See also No. 728 for | 污 *wū* dirt, for other similar characters; |

| | + 86: | 烤 *kǎo* to bake; roast. |

| 385 | *kào* | 靠 to lean on; depend on. |

| This character is | 告 *gào* to tell, No. 229, plus |
| | 非 *fēi* wrong, No. 196. |

| 386 | *kē* | 科 a branch of study; an academic department. |
| | Basic: | 斗 *dòu* a struggle, radical 68, No. 168. |

| 387 | *ké* | 壳(殼) a shell; housing. |

| D.f.: | 克 *kè* can; to overcome, No. 389; |
| and also f.: | 亮 *liàng* bright, No. 432. |

388	*kě*	可 can; may.
	+ 30:	呵 *hē* to breathe out;
	+ 9:	何 *hé* what; who;
	+ 85:	河 *hé* river;
	+ 9 and 140:	荷 *hé* lotus, and *hè* to carry;
	+ 170:	阿 *ā* used mainly in transliteration of foreign names;
	+ 30 and 170:	啊 *ā*, *á*, *ǎ*, *à*, *a* (exclamations) oh!; Eh?; what?

| 389 | *kè* | 克 can; be able to; to overcome. |
| | Basic: | 兄 *xiōng* elder brother, No. 778; |

| D.f.: | 壳 *ké* shell, No. 387; |
| and f.: | 亮 *liàng* bright, No. 432. |

390	*kè*	客 visitor; guest.
	Basic:	各 *gè* each; every, No. 234.
	+ 181:	额 *é* forehead.

391   *kè*   课(課) a subject; course; lesson.
       Basic: 果 *guǒ* fruit, No. 262.
       + 75:   棵 *kē* (a measure word), for: a head of cabbage;
       + 181:   颗 *kē* (a measure word), for: beans.

392   *kěn*   肯 agree; be willing.

The upper half of this character is 止 *zhǐ* to stop, radical 77, No. 901,
and the lower half is 月 *yuè* the moon, radical 130, No. 864.

393   *kōng*   空 empty; sky; air.
       kòng   to leave empty or blank.
       + 64:   控 *kòng* to accuse; charge;
       + 130:   腔 *qiāng* cavity; tune; accent.

394   *kǒng*   孔 a hole; Confucius.

395   *kǒng*   恐 fear.

This character is 工 *gōng* work, radical 48, No. 238,
plus: 凡 *fán* every; anyone, No. 190,
plus: 心 *xīn* the heart, radical 61, No. 767.

       minus 61, + 118: 筑 S form for *zhù* to build, T form: 築.

396   *kǒu*   口 the mouth.   Radical 30.
       + 64:   扣 *kòu* to button up; arrest; discount;
       + 76:   吹 *chuī* to blow, No. 117;

       Note also: 嘴 *zuǐ* mouth, No. 935.

397   *kū*   哭 to cry; weep.

398   *kǔ*   苦 bitter; hardship.
       Basic: 古 *gǔ* ancient, No. 243.

399   *kù*   库(庫) warehouse.

       D. T form f.: 康 *kāng* health, No. 382, see also No. 382 for four
                         other similar phonetic shapes.

400   *kuà*   跨 step; stride.

> D. phonetic f.:   考 *kǎo* to give or take a test, No. 384.

401   *kuài*   快 fast; happy.
            + 15 (T + 85):   决(決) *jué* to decide, No. 375;
            + 32:   块(塊) *kuài* piece; lump;

> see No. 257 for: 鬼 *guǐ* ghost, spirit.

402   *kuān*   宽(寬) wide; lenient.

403   *kuǎn*   款 sincere; a sum of money.
            Basic: 欠 *qiàn* to owe, radical 76, No. 541.

404   *kùn*   困 to be hard pressed; to pin down.

> D.f.:   因 *yīn* because of, No. 829;
> D.f. phonetic in: 菌 *jūn* fungus, and *jùn* mushroom.

L

405	lā	拉 to pull.
	Basic:	立 *lì* to stand, radical 117, No. 422.
	+ 30:	啦 *la* (exclamation) really!; or really?
	+ 9:	位 <u>*wèi*</u> place, No. 719.
406	lái	来(來) to come.

| | D.f.: | 夹(夾) *jiā* to squeeze, No. 320; |
| | D.f.: | 米 *mǐ* rice, radical 119, No. 472. |

| 407 | lài | 赖(賴) to rely on. |

| | This character is | 束 *shù* to tie, see No. 656 for 速 *sù* speed, |
| | plus: | 负(負) *fù* to bear; carry, No. 216. |

| 408 | lán | 兰(蘭) orchid. |

Note the basic in T form which is: radical 169 plus 柬 *jiǎn* a card; a note, see No. 83.

	+ 75:	栏(欄) *lán* fence; rail; balustrade;
	+ 86:	烂(爛) *làn* sodden; to rot.
409	láo	劳(勞) work; labour.
	+ 64:	捞(撈) *lāo* to dredge up; to get by improper means; see entries Nos. 301 and 838 for reference to a similar alternation in the S and T
	forms of *yíng*:	营(營) to seek; a camp, No. 838.
410	lǎo	老 old. Radical 125.
411	lè	乐(樂) happy.
	yuè	music.

Note: The use of the same phonetic element of the T form, plus 140, in the T form of 藥 *yào* medicine; drug, S form: 药;
this S form for 'medicine' is 140 plus 约 *yuē* arrange, No. 863.

| 412 | *le*
liǎo and *liào* | 了 (sign of the perfective aspect of the verb.)
to understand; to watch, listed separately as
No. 433. |

| 413 | *léi* | 雷 thunder. |

| D.f.: | 雪 *xuě* snow; |
| and also f.: | 雨 *yǔ* rain, radical 173, No. 855. |

| 414 | *lěi*
léi
lèi | 累 to pile up; to involve.
clusters.
tired. |
| | + 142: | 螺 <u>*luó*</u> spiral shell; snail. |

| 415 | *lèi* | 类(類) kind; category. |

| 416 | *léng* | 棱(稜) edge. |

| D.f. phonetic in: | 酸 *suān* acid, No. 658; |
| D.f. phonetic in: | 滚 *gǔn* to roll, No. 259; |

| | + 170: | 陵 <u>*líng*</u> a hill. |

| 417 | *lí* | 离(離) to leave. |

| D.f.: | 禽 *qín* birds. |

| 418 | *lǐ* | 礼(禮) ceremony; courtesy. |

| Note: | 體 T form for *tǐ* body, No. 679, S form: 体. |

| 419 | *lǐ* | 李 plum. |

D.f.:	季 *jì* season;
and f.:	柔 *róu* soft;
Note also this character + 64:	揉 *róu* to rub.

420   lǐ   里(裏,裡) inside.   **S form is radical 166.**

    + 96:   理 *lǐ* texture; reason;

    + 30:   哩 *lī* (in combinations) sporadic; verbose, *li*
                  (an auxiliary final particle used (a) for emphasis
                  and (b) between items in a list).

    + 32:   埋 *mái* to cover up; bury;

    + 117:   童 *tóng* child, No. 690.

    + 予: 野 *yě* wild, No. 810, for 予 *yǔ* to give see No. 850.

421   lì   力 power.   **Radical 19.**

    D.f.:   万 S form for *wàn* a vast number, No. 705,
                  T form: 萬;

    + 27:   历 S form for *lì* to go through; experience, T form: 歷;

    Note: 励 S form for *lì* to encourage, T form: 勵, and for this
                  T form phonetic, see also entry No. 859 for *yù*: 遇
                  to meet;

    + 116:   穷 S form for *qióng* poor, No. 554, T form: 窮.

422   lì   立 to stand.   **Radical 117.**

    + 119:   粒 *lì* a grain;

    + 64:   拉 *lā* to pull, No. 405;

    + 9:   位 *wèi* a place, No. 719.

423   lì   利 sharp.

    + 93:   犁 *lí* to plough, see also No. 429 for 梁 *liáng* ridge.

424   lián   连(連) link.

    Basic: 车(車) *chē* vehicle, No. 83.

    + 140:   莲 *lián* lotus;

    + 167:   链 *liàn* a chain.

425   lián   联(聯) to unite.

    Basic: 关(關) *guān* to close, No. 250.

426   *liǎn*   脸(臉) face.

D. phonetic in T form from: 輪 T form for *lún* wheel, No. 453, S form: 轮;
and also from phonetic in: 偷 *tōu* to steal, No. 691.

+ 75:   检(檢) *jiǎn* to inspect;
+ 112:   硷(鹼) *jiǎn* alkali, = 碱 *jiǎn* see No. 226;
+ 18:   剑(劍) *jiàn* sword;
+ 118:   签(簽) alt.T form: 籤 see Appendix B, radical 179,
               qiān to sign;
+ 170:   险(險) *xiǎn* danger;
+ 187:   验(驗) *yàn* to examine.

427   *liàn*   练(練) to practise; train.

D. phonetics f.: 东(東) *dōng* east, No. 164 in list, see also No. 83.

+ 86:   炼(煉) *liàn* to refine; temper.

428   *liáng*   良 good; fine.

D.f. phonetic in: 很 *hěn* very, No. 277.

+ 119:   粮(糧) *liáng* grain;
+ 94:   狼 *láng* wolf;
+ 163:   郎 *láng* young man;
+ 85:   浪 *làng* a wave; billow;
+ 38:   娘 *niáng* mother; a young woman.

Note the T form: 鄉 *xiāng* countryside, No. 755, S form: 乡.

429   *liáng*   梁 roof beam; ridge.

D.f.:   黎 *lí* multitude; host;
D.f.:   犁 *lí* plough, see No. 423 for 利 *lì* sharp;
D.f. phonetic in: 楔 *xiē* wedge.

| 430 | *liáng*
liàng | 量 measure.
capacity; quantity. |

| 431 | *liǎng* | 两(兩) two; both. |

	D.f.:	丙 *bǐng* third, see also No. 53 for 病 *bìng* ill;
	D.f.:	内 *nèi* inside, No. 499;
	D.f.:	肉 *ròu* meat; flesh, No. 578.

	+ 159:	辆(輛) *liàng* a measure word, for vehicles;
	+ 9:	俩(倆) *liǎ* the two of us;
	+ 140 and 85:	满(滿) *mǎn* full, No. 460.

| 432 | *liàng* | 亮 bright; light. |

| | D.f.: | 竞 *jìng* to compete, see also No. 360. |

| 433 | *liǎo*

liào

le
+ 9:
+ 162: | 了(瞭) to understand.
了(瞭) to watch from a height.
了 (sign of the perfective – see No. 412.)
僚 *liáo* an official;
辽(遼) *liáo* distant. |

| 434 | *liè*
+ 9:
+ 145:
+ 86: | 列 to arrange.
例 *lì* example;
裂 *liè* split; crack;
烈 *liè* strong; violent. |

| 435 | *lín* | 林 forest. |

| This character is 2 × | 木 *mù* tree, radical 75, No. 487; |

	+ 85:	淋 *lín* pour; drench, and *lìn* strain; filter;
	+ 113:	禁 *jìn* prohibit, No. 356, for 示 *shì* show, see No. 620;
	+ 53:	麻 *má* hemp, radical 200, No. 456;
	+ 103:	楚 *chǔ* clear; neat, No. 110;
	+ 36:	梦 S form for *mèng* dream, No. 471, T form: 夢.

436   *lín*   临(臨) **to face; overlook.**

> D.f.:   监(監) *jiān* to supervise, No. 327;
>
> see also No. 325 for   坚(堅) *jiān* firm, which includes a note on some
>   other similar characters.

437   *líng*   灵(靈) **clever.**

> D.f.:   寻(尋) *xún* to look for, No. 792.

438   *lìng*   另 **other; another.**

+ 18:   别 *bié* to leave; other; another, No. 50;

+ 64:   拐 *guǎi* to turn; to limp.

439   *lìng*   令 **command; to cause.**

> D.f.:   今 *jīn* today, No. 347.

+ 96:   玲 *líng* (in combinations) (a) tinkling, (b) exquisite;

+ 173:   零 *líng* zero;

+ 211:   龄(齡) *líng* age; years;

+ 167:   铃 *líng* bell;

+ 46:   岭(嶺) *lǐng* a mountain range;

+ 181:   领(領) *lǐng* neck; to lead;

+ 15:   冷 *lěng* cold;

+ 163:   邻(鄰) *lín* neighbour;

> Note the use of the same T form phonetic in + 112: 磷 *lín* phosphorus,
> and a similar form in the phonetic of: 瞬 *shùn* wink.

440   *liú*   流 **to flow.**

+ 112:   硫 *liú* sulphur;

+ 103:   疏 *shū* to dredge; sparse.

441   *liú*   留 **to remain.**

+ 85:   溜 *liū* to slide; glide, and *liù* swift current.

442   *liù*   六 **six.**

443 *lóng* 龙(龍) **dragon.**   **Radical 212.**

D.f. phonetic in: 拔 *bá* to pull out, No. 13.

+ 118: 笼(籠) *lóng* cage, and *lǒng* to envelop.

444 *lóu* 楼(樓) **building.**

+ 66: 数(數) *shǔ* to count, No. 635, and *shù* number; figure.

445 *lòu* 漏 **to leak; to reveal.**

D. phonetic f.: 扇 *shān*, to fan, see No. 284 for 户 *hù* door;

The character 露 *lòu* or *lù* also means 'to leak = to reveal' for this character see No. 449 for 路 *lù* road.

446 *lú* 炉(爐) **stove.**

S form basic: 户 *hù* a door, No. 284, radical 63.

447 *lù* 陆(陸) **mainland.**

Note S form of 击 *jī* to attack, No. 306 in list, T form: 擊.

448 *lù* 录(錄) **to record.**

D. S form f.: 隶 *lì* to be subordinate to, see also No. 382.

+ 18: 剥 *bō* (in combinations) to strip of; to deprive;

+ 120: 绿 *lü* (fourth tone) green;

d. this character f.: 缘 *yuán* reason; edge;

+ 84: 氯 *lü* (fourth tone) chlorine.

449 *lù* 路 **road.**

This character is 各 *gè* each, No. 234,

plus radical 157: 足 *zú* foot, No. 934;

+ 173:   露 *lù* dew; to reveal or
                   lòu (in combinations) to appear; show; reveal.

450 *lǚ* (third tone)   旅 to travel.

D.f.:   施 *shī* to carry out; execute, No. 611;

and f.:   族 *zú* race; nationality;

and f: 旋 *xuán* to revolve; return;

note similar phonetic in: 拖 *tuō* to pull.

451 *lǜ* (fourth tone)   律 law; statute.

+ 85:   津 *jīn* a ferry, No. 350.

452 *luàn*   乱(亂) disorder; chaos.

The S form is 舌 *shé* tongue, radical 135, No. 596, plus the alt.form of radical 5, full form: 乙 *yǐ* second, No. 819.

Note the use of radical 135 for the same element of the T form in: (辞)(辭) *cí* diction; take leave.

453 *lún*   轮(輪) wheel.

D. phonetic in T form f.: 臉 T form for *liǎn* face, No. 426, S form: 脸;

and also f. the phonetic in: 偷 *tōu* to steal, No. 691;

+ 9:   伦(倫) *lún* logic;

+ 149:   论(論) *lùn* to discuss.

454 *luó*   罗(羅) a net for catching birds.

D.f.:   岁(歲) *suì* year, No. 662;

D.f.:   梦(夢) *mèng* dream, No. 471.

455 *luò*   落 to fall; drop.

Basic: 各 *gè* each; every, No. 234.

M

456	*má*	麻 hemp; flax. Radical 200.
	+ 30:	嘛 *ma* (a final particle) giving the sense of 'after all';
	+ 112:	磨 *mó* to rub, and *mò* mill; millstones;

| Note: | 麼 T form for *me* what, S form: 么, seen in combinations |
| as in: | 什么(甚麼) *shénme* what?, see also entry No. 602. |

457	*mǎ*	马(馬) horse. Radical 187.
	+ 38:	妈(媽) *mā* ma; mum; mummy;
	+ 30:	吗(嗎) *ma* (a final particle, marking a question);
	+ 112:	码(碼) *mǎ* a sign; a number;
	+ 122 or 2 × 30:	骂(罵) *mà* to curse;
	+ 15:	冯(馮) *Féng* Feng, a surname;
	+ 15 and 61:	憑 T form for *píng* to rely on, No. 526, S form: 凭;
	+ 169:	闯(闖) *chuǎng* to rush, dash.

| 458 | *mǎi* | 买(買) to buy. |

| D.f.: | 实(實) *shí* solid; true, No. 616. |

	+ 24 (+ 33):	卖(賣) *mài* to sell;
	+ 24 (+ 33) and 149:	读(讀) *dú* to read;
	+ 24 (+ 33) and 120:	续(續) *xù* to continue.

| 459 | *mài* | 麦(麥) wheat.   Radical 199. |

| 460 | *mǎn* | 满 full. |
| | Basic: | 两 *liǎng* two; both, No. 431. |

| 461 | *màn* | 慢 slow. |
| | Basic: | 曼 *màn* graceful. |

| 462 | *máng* | 忙 **busy.** |
| | Basic: | 亡 *wáng* to flee; |

| | Note + 61: | 忘 *wàng* forget, No. 708. |

| 463 | *máo* | 毛 **hair.   Radical 82.** |

| | D.f. phonetic in: | 托 *tuō* to hold; entrust, No. 699. |

| | + 127: | 耗 *hào* to consume; cost; |

| | Note also: | 毫 *háo* a writing brush; (not) at all, No. 270; |

| | + 118: | 笔 S form for *bǐ* a pen, No. 39 in list, T form: 筆; |
| | + 44: | 尾 *wěi* tail, No. 715. |

| 464 | *mào* | 冒 **to emit.** |

| | D.f.: | 昌 *chāng* prosperous, see No. 81, 唱 *chàng*, to sing. |

| | + 50: | 帽 *mào* headgear. |

| 465 | *méi* | 没 **as in** 没有 *méiyǒu* **not have; there is not,** |
| | for | 有 *yǒu* to have, see entry No. 845. |

| | D.f.: | 沿 *yán* along, No. 801. |

| | + 64: | 投 *tóu* to throw; |
| | + 149: | 设 *shè* to set up, No. 597. |

466	*měi*	每 **every; each.**
	Basic:	母 *mǔ* mother, No. 486.
	+ 75:	梅 *méi* plum;
	+ 164:	酶 *méi* enzyme; ferment;
	+ 173:	霉 *méi* mould; mildew;
	+ 85:	海 *hǎi* sea, No. 265.

| 467 | *měi* | 美 **beautiful.** |
| | + 167: | 镁 *měi* magnesium. |

| 468 | mén | 门(門) door.   **Radical 169.** |

| | D. T form f.: | 鬥 T form for *dòu* struggle, S form: 斗, No. 168. |

	+ 61:	闷 *mēn* stuffy, and *mèn* bored;
	+ 9:	们 *men* (indicator of the plural);
	+ 187:	闯 *chuǎng* to rush;
	for	马 *mǎ* horse, see No. 457;
	+ 活 *huó*:	阔 *kuò* wide; rich,
	for	活 *huó* live, see No. 288 for 话 *huà* talk;
	+ 9:	闪 *shǎn* to dodge; flash;
	+ 才 *cái*:	闭 *bì* to close,
	for	才 *cái* ability, see No. 60;
	+ 30:	问 *wèn* to ask, No. 725;
	+ 72:	间 *jiàn* space in between and *jiān* between; among, No. 329;
	+ 75:	闲 *xián* idle; spare time;
	+ 128:	闻 *wén* to hear; to smell, No. 724.

469	méng	蒙 **to cover.**
	mēng	**to cheat; deceive.**
	Měng	**the Mongol nationality.**

470	měng	猛 **fierce; violent.**
	Basic:	孟 *mèng* the first month (of a season).
	+ 167:	锰 *měng* manganese.

| 471 | mèng | 梦(夢) **dream.** |

	The S form is	林 *lín* forest, No. 435,
	plus radical 36:	夕 *xī* sunset;
	Note also radical 36 in	罗 S form for *luó* a net, T form: 羅, No. 454.

| 472 | mǐ | 米 rice.   **Radical 119.** |

| | D.f.: | 来 *lái* to come, No. 406. |

| | + 162: | 迷 *mí* to be confused; lost. |

473   *mì*   密 dense; thick; secret.

This character is   必 *bì* to have to, No. 41, plus radicals 40 and 46;
Note also *bì* + 115:   秘 *mì* secret.

474   *mián*   棉 cotton.

D. phonetic f. that in: 線 T form for *xiàn* thread, S form: 线, see No. 540.

+ 167:   锦 *jǐn* brocade.

475   *miǎn*   免 to exempt; avoid.

D.f.:   兔 *tù* hare; rabbit;
note two compounds with this phonetic:
(a) + 162:   逸 *yì* ease; leisure, and
(b) + 14:   冤 *yuān* wrong; injustice;
D.f. phonetic in: 换 *huàn* to exchange, No. 290.

+ 72:   晚 *wǎn* evening; late.

476   *miàn*   面 face; flour.   Radical 176.

D.f.:   而 *ér* and, No. 184.

477   *miáo*   苗 a young plant.

This character is   田 *tián* field, No. 682, plus radical 140.

478   *miè*   灭(滅) to go out; to extinguish.
Basic for S form: 火 *huǒ* fire, No. 301.

D.f.:   灾 S form for *zāi* disaster, T form: 災;
D. phonetic of T form f.:   威 *wēi* might; power, No. 711.

479   *mín*   民 the people.

480   *míng*   名 name.

D.f.:   各 *gè* each; every, No. 234.

481   *míng*   明 bright.

D.f. phonetic in: 棚 *péng* a canopy; a shed, No. 520.

+ 108:   盟 *méng* alliance.

482   *mìng*   命 life; fate; order.

483   *mò*   末 tip; end.

D.f.:   未 *wèi* have not; did not; not, No. 718.

+ 64:   抹 *mǒ* to put on; smear on, and *mò* plaster.

484   *mò*   莫 no one; nothing; no; not.

D.f.:   黄 *huáng* yellow, No. 283;
D.f. phonetic in: 漢 T form for *Hàn* Chinese, No. 269, S form: 汉;
D.f.:   草 *cǎo* grass, see No. 873 for 早 *zǎo* morning.

+ 75:   模 *mó* model; standard and *mú* mould; pattern;
+ 130:   膜 *mó* membrane; film;
+ 64:   摸 *mō* to stroke; feel for.

485   *mǒu*   某 certain; some.
+ 149:   谋 *móu* stratagem; plan;
+ 86:   煤 *méi* coal.

486   *mǔ*   母 mother.

Basic shape for: 每 *měi* each; every, No. 466;
Note also: 毒 *dú* poison, No. 170.

+ 38:   姆 *mǔ* as in: 保姆 *bǎomǔ* nurse.

487   *mù*   木 tree; wood.   Radical 75.

D.f.:   术 S form for *shù* art; skill, No. 637, T form: 術;

D.f.:   本 *běn*, No. 28, root of a plant, No. 36.

2 × 75:   林 *lín* forest; woods, No. 435;

3 × 75:   森 *sēn* full of trees; dark;

+ 59:   杉 *shān* China fir;

+ 109:   相 *xiāng* each other, and *xiàng* looks, No. 756;

+ 9:   休 *xiū* to stop; to rest, No. 780;

+ 40:   宋 *Sòng* the Song dynasty;

+ 53:   床 *chuáng* bed, No. 116;

+ 169:   闲(閑) *xián* idle; leisure, see entry No. 268 for
                               门(門) *mén* door;

+ 66:   枚 *méi* (a measure word), for badges; coins;

+ 167 and 132:   镍 *niè* nickel.

488   *mù*   目 eye.   Radical 109.

+ 85:   泪 S form for *lèi* tear; teardrop, T form: 淚;

Note: 眉 *méi* eyebrow; brow;

+ 75:   相 *xiāng* each other, and *xiàng* looks, No. 756,
                               see also No. 487 for 木 *mù* tree;

+ 少 *shǎo*:   省 *shěng* to save, No. 607,

for   少 *shǎo* few, see No. 595.

489   *mù*   幕 curtain; screen.

D.f.:   幂 *mì* power (in mathematics);

D.f.:   篡 *cuàn* to usurp.

+ 32:   墓 *mù* grave; tomb.

N

| 490 | *ná* | 拿 to hold; take; capture. |

| This character is radical 64: | 合 *hé* to close, No. 274 in list, placed above
手 *shǒu* hand, No. 626. |

| 491 | *nà* | 那 that; in that case. |

| D.f.: | 都 *dōu* all, No. 167; |
| D.f.: | 部 *bù* part; section, No. 59. |

| + 30: | 哪 *nǎ* which; what. |

| 492 | *nǎi* | 乃 to be; therefore. |

| D.f.: | 及 *jí* to reach, No. 311. |

| + 9: | 仍 *réng* to remain; still; yet, No. 573. |

| 493 | *nài* | 耐 to bear; to be patient. |

| This character is plus: | 而 *ér* and, radical 126, No. 184,
寸 *cùn* a unit of length, radical 41, No. 127. |

| 494 | *nán* | 男 male. |

| 495 | *nán* | 南 south. |
| | + 94: | 献 S form for *xiàn* to offer, No. 754, T form: 獻. |

| 496 | *nán*
nàn | 难 (難) difficult.
disaster. |

Note the use of 又 *yòu* again, No. 846, as a phonetic in the S form. The same alternation can be seen in:

| + 85: | 汉 (漢) *Hàn* Chinese, No. 269, |
| and in + 30: | 叹 (嘆) *tàn* to sigh; |

+ 64:　　　　　　摊(攤) *tān* to spread out;

+ 85:　　　　　　滩(灘) *tān* beach; sands;

Apart from the examples given above, the character 又 is also used in other S forms as a phonetic in place of other T form phonetics, viz.:

in:　　　　　仅(僅) *jǐn* only, No. 351,

and in:　　　观(觀) *guān* to look at, No. 251.

497　　*nǎo*　　　　脑(腦) brain.

D.f.:　　　　　　胸 *xiōng* chest.

498　　*nào*　　　　闹(鬧) noisy.

This character is S form, radical 169, T form, radical 191, plus

市 *shì* market, No. 619.

499　　*nèi*　　　　内 inner; within; inside.

D.f.:　　　　　　丙 *bǐng* third, see Nos. 53 and 431;

D.f.:　　　　　　肉 *ròu* flesh, No. 578;

D.f.:　　　　　　闪 *shǎn* to dodge, see No. 468 for 门 *mén* door.

+ 120:　　　　　纳 *nà* to receive; accept;

+ 167:　　　　　钠 *nà* sodium;

+ 167 and 30:　　锅 S form for *guō* pot, No. 260, T form: 鍋.

500　　*néng*　　　能 ability; to be able.

+ 122:　　　　　罷 T form for *bà* to stop, No. 14, S form: 罢;

+ 61:　　　　　　熊 T form for *tài* form, S form: 态 – see No. 669.

501　　*ní*　　　　尼 Buddhist nun.

+ 85:　　　　　　泥 *ní* mud, and *nì* to cover with plaster;

+ 30:　　　　　　呢 *ne* (a final particle), marking a question, and *ní* wool cloth.

502   nǐ   你 you.
       Basic: 尔 S form for ěr you (in classical literature), T form: 爾;
       + 61:   您 _nín_ you (polite; formal);
       + 115:   称 S form for _chēng_ to call, No. 91, T form: 稱.

503   nì   逆 contrary; disobey.

D.f. the phonetic in: 岡 T form for _gāng_ ridge, see No. 227 for _gāng_ firm;
D.f. the phonetic in: 網 T form for _wǎng_ net, No. 707, S form: 网;

       + 130 and 32:   塑 _sù_ to model; mould, No. 657.

504   nián   年 year.

D.f.:   车 S form for _chē_ vehicle, radical 159, No. 83,
                   T form: 車;
D.f.:   东 S form for _dōng_ east, T form: 東, No. 164;
D.f.:   牛 _niú_ ox, radical 93, No. 508.

505   niàn   念 to think of; miss; read aloud.
       + 64:   捻 _niǎn_ to twist with the fingers.

506   niǎo   鸟(鳥) bird.   Radical 196.

D.f.:   乌(烏) _wū_ crow;
D.f.:   岛(島) _dǎo_ island, No. 141.

       + 29:   鸡(雞) _jī_ chicken, No. 307;
       + 30:   鸣(鳴) _míng_ the cry of birds; or animals.

507   níng   宁(寧) peaceful.
       nìng   would rather.
       Basic for S form: 丁 _dīng_ man, No. 162.
       + 64:   拧(擰) _níng_ and _nǐng_ to twist;
       + 154:   贮 T form for _zhù_ to store; save, S form: 贮.

508 *niú*   牛 ox.   **Radical 93.**
Note alt.form of radical 93 seen in 物 *wù* matter, No. 735.

D.f.:   午 *wǔ* noon, No. 731;
D.f.:   年 *nián* year, No. 504.

+ 40:   牢 <u>láo</u> prison;
+ 9:   件 <u>jiàn</u> (a measure word), for a shirt, etc.; a document;
+ 37 and 14:   牵 S form for <u>qiān</u> to lead, T form: 牽.

509 *niǔ*   扭 **to turn round; to twist.**
Basic: 丑 S form for *chǒu* ugly, T form: 醜,
for   鬼 *guǐ* ghost; spirit, radical 194, see No. 257.

D.f.:   互 *hù* mutual, No. 285.

+ 120:   纽 *niǔ* handle; button.

510 *nóng*   农(農) **agriculture; peasant.**

D.f.:   衣 *yī* clothing, radical 145, No. 816.

+ 85:   浓(濃) *nóng* dense.

511 *nòng*   弄 **play with; manage.**

512 *nǔ*   努 **to exert an effort.**
+ 61:   怒 *nù* anger; rage;

D. this character f.:   怨 *yuàn* resentment; enmity.

513 *nü* (third tone)   女 **woman; female.   Radical 38.**
+ 85:   汝 <u>rǔ</u> (in classical Chinese) you.

Note: 妻 *qī* wife, No. 529.

514   *nuǎn*   暖 warm.

D. phonetic f.:   爱 S form for *ài* love, No. 4, T form: 愛.

+ 120:   缓 *huǎn* slow;

+ 64:   援 *yuán* to pull by hand; to hold.

Note: there are no key character entries to the Dictionary for the letter O.

P

515	*pái*	排 arrange; row; line.
	Basic:	非 *fēi* wrong, radical 175, No. 196.

516	*pài*	派 a group; to send.
	+ 130:	脈 T form for <u>*mài*</u> arteries and veins, S form: 脉, see entry No. 840 for 永 *yǒng* forever.

517	*páng*	旁 side.

518	*pāo*	抛 to throw.

519	*pèi*	配 to join; mix; distribute.

This character is
plus:

己 *jǐ* oneself, radical 49, No. 316,

酉 *yǒu* the tenth of the 12 Earthly Branches, radical 164, see entry No. 364 for 酒 *jiǔ* wine.

520	*péng*	棚 canopy; shed.

D. phonetic f.:
and also f.:

明 *míng* bright, No. 481,

册 *cè* volume; book, No. 67.

521	*pí*	皮 skin. **Radical 107.**

D.f.:

支 *zhī* to prop up, No. 897.

+ 64:	披 *pī* to drape over one's shoulders;
+ 60:	彼 *bǐ* that; those; the other;
+145:	被 <u>*bèi*</u> quilt; by (the agent of the passive), No. 33;
+ 85:	波 <u>*bō*</u> wave;
+ 32:	坡 <u>*pō*</u> slope;
+181:	颇 <u>*pō*</u> quite; rather;
+112:	破 <u>*pò*</u> broken.

522	*piàn*	片 a slice. Radical 91.
	piān	film.
	+ 卑 *(bēi)*:	牌 *pái* tablet; signpost, for 卑 *bēi* low, see No. 29.

523	*piào*	票 ticket.
	+ 85:	漂 *piāo* float; *piǎo* bleach; *piào* handsome;
	182:	飘 *piāo* to wave; flutter;
	+ 75:	標 T form for *biāo* a mark; a sign, No. 48, S form: 标.

524	*pǐn*	品 article.

D.f.:	器 *qì* implement, No. 537;
D.f.:	晶 *jīng* brilliant; crystal.

525	*píng*	平 flat; even.

D.f.:	乎 *hū* at; in; from, No. 281.

	+ 149:	评 *píng* comment; criticise;
	+ 140 and 85:	萍 *píng* duckweed.

526	*píng*	凭(憑) to lean against; to rely on.

527	*pǔ*	普 general; universal.

D.f.:	晋 *jìn* to enter; advance;
D.f.:	曾 *céng* once, No. 68.

	+ 149:	谱 *pǔ* a table; chart; register.

Q

528	*qī*	七 seven.
529	*qī*	妻 wife.
530	*qí*	齐(齊) neat. T form is radical 210.

D.f.: 乔 S form for *qiáo* tall, No. 544, T form: 喬.

+ 64: 挤 *jǐ* to squeeze;
+ 18: 剂 *jì* a medicinal preparation; a pill;
+ 85: 济 *jì* to cross a river; to help.

531	*qí*	其 his; he; that; such.

D.f.: 具 *jù* tool, No. 372;
D.f.: 共 *gòng* common; general, No. 241.

+ 130: 期 *qī* a period of time;
+ 76: 欺 *qī* to deceive;
+ 75: 棋 *qí* chess; or any board game;
+ 70 and 14: 旗 *qí* a flag;
+ 32: 基 *jī* base; foundation, No. 30;
+ 69: 斯 s̲ī̲ this, No. 649.

532	*qí*	奇 strange.
	jī	odd (of a number).

+ 187: 骑 *qí* to ride;
+ 40: 寄 *jì* to send;
+ 9: 倚 y̲ǐ̲ to lean on; to rely on.

533	*qǐ*	乞 to beg.
	Basic:	乙 *yǐ* second, No. 819;
	+ 30:	吃 *chī* to eat, No. 96.

534   *qǐ (qi)*   起 to rise; to begin.

This character is   己 *jǐ* oneself, radical 49, No. 316,

plus: 走 *zǒu* to walk; go away, radical 156, No. 931.

535   *qì*   气(氣) gas.   **Radical 84.**

D.f.:   乞 *qǐ* to beg, No. 533.

+ 85:   汽 *qì* vapour; steam;

+ 安: 氨 *ān* ammonia, for 安 *ān* peaceful, see No. 5;

+ 录: 氯 *lü* (fourth tone) chlorine, for 录 *lù* record, see No. 448;

+ phonetic in 经: 氢 *qīng* hydrogen, for 经 *jīng* through, see No. 358;

+ 青: 氰 *qíng* cyanogen, for 青 *qīng* green, see No. 551;

+ 羊: 氧 *yǎng* oxygen, for 羊 *yáng* sheep, see No. 805.

536   *qì*   弃(棄) to abandon.

Note that the shape seen in the phonetic of the T form above is sometimes printed as

in: 葉 T form for *yè* leaf, No. 812, S form: 叶.

537   *qì*   器 implement; utensil.

D.f.:   品 *pǐn* article; product, No. 524.

538   *qiān*   千 thousand.

D.f.:   干 *gān* to do; dry, No. 223;

D.f.:   于 S form for *yú* in; at, T form: 於, No. 849.

+ 162:   迁(遷) *qiān* to move;

+ 120:   纤(纖) *qiàn* a tow line, and *xiān* fine.

539   *qián*   前 front.

+ 18:   剪 *jiǎn* scissors.

540   *qián*   钱(錢) **money.**

     + 85:   浅(淺) *qiǎn* shallow;

     + 78:   残(殘) *cán* deficient; to injure;

     + 120:   线(線) *xiàn* thread.

     For   泉 *quán* a spring, see No. 643.

541   *qiàn*   欠 **to owe.**   **Radical 76.**

     + 30:   吹 *chuī* to blow, No. 117;

     + 15:   次 *cì* order; next; time, No. 123.

     + 29:   欢(歡) *huān* joyous, see also No. 251;

     + 112:   砍 *kǎn* to cut;

     Note: 款 *kuǎn* sincere; a sum of money, No. 403;

     + 159:   软 *ruǎn* soft; weak;

     + 184:   饮 *yǐn* to drink and *yìn* to water animals;

     + 谷: 欲 *yù* desire, No. 858, see this entry also for

              谷 *gǔ* valley.

542   *qiáng*   强(強) **strong.**
        qiǎng   **to make an effort.**

543   *qiáng*   墙(牆) **a wall.**

     D. phonetic f.:   尚 *shàng* still; yet, No. 594.

544   *qiáo*   乔(喬) **tall.**

     D.f.:   齐 S form for *qí* neat, No. 530, T form: 齊.

     + 75:   桥(橋) *qiáo* bridge.

545   *qiǎo*   巧 **skilful.**

     D. phonetic f.:   亏 *kuī* to lose money,
     as seen in: 污 *wū* dirt, No. 728;

     + 75:   朽 *xiǔ* rotten; decayed.

546 *qiē* 切 to cut; slice.
         qiè   to correspond to.

   + 112: 砌 *qì* to build by laying bricks.

547 *qiě* 且 just; for the time being.

   + 40: 宜 *yí* suitable; appropriate;

   D. this f.: 宣 *xuān* to declare, No. 787;

   + 115: 租 *zū* to rent; hire, No. 933, see this entry for further
              compound characters.

548 *qīn* 亲(親) parent; relative.

   D.f.: 辛 *xīn* hot; pungent; bitter, No. 768;

   D.f. phonetic in: 雜 T form for *zá* sundry, S form: 杂, No. 868.

   + 69: 新 *xīn* new, No. 769;

   + 145: 襯 T form for *chèn* lining, No. 89, S form: 衬.

549 *qīn* 侵 to invade.

   + 85: 浸 *jìn* to soak; steep.

550 *qín* 勤 diligent.

   D.f.: 勒 *lè* to rein in,

   for 革 *gé* to change see No. 231.

   + 9: 僅 T form for *jǐn* only, No. 351, S form: 仅.

551 *qīng* 青 blue or green.   Radical 174.

   + 85: 清 *qīng* clear;

   + 61: 情 *qíng* feeling;

   + 72: 晴 *qíng* fine; clear (of weather);

   + 84: 氰 *qíng* cyanogen, for 气 *qì* gas, see No. 535;

   + 149: 请 *qǐng* to request;

   + 119: 精 *jīng* refined;

   + 争: 静 *jìng* quiet, for 争 *zhēng* dispute, see No. 892;

   + 94: 猜 *cāi* to guess.

552   *qīng*   倾 incline.

Basic: 顷 *qǐng* a unit of area; just.

553   *qìng*   庆(慶) celebrate.

D. T form phonetic f. that in: 優 T form for *yōu* excellent, No. 842, S form: 优;

D. S form f.:   床 *chuáng* bed, No. 116;

and f.:   庄 S form for *zhuāng*, village, T form: 莊,
                                   see Nos. 922 and 65.

554   *qióng*   穷(窮) poor.

The S form is   力 *lì* power, No. 421, plus radical 116;

D. this S form f.:   究 *jiū* to study, see No. 362 for 九 *jiǔ* nine.

555   *qiū*   秋 autumn.

This character is   火 *huǒ* fire, No. 301, plus radical 115;

+ 61:   愁 *chóu* worry; be anxious.

556   *qiú*   求 to beg; request.

+ 96:   球 *qiú* sphere; ball;

+ 66:   救 *jiù* to rescue; save.

557   *qū*   区(區) area; district.

D.f.:   凶 *xiōng* fierce, No. 777.

+ 187:   驱(驅) *qū* to drive;

+ 76:   欧(歐) *ōu* Europe.

558   *qū*   趋(趨) to hasten; to tend towards.

+ 172:   雏(雛) *chú* young (of birds);

+ 皮: 皱(皺) *zhòu* wrinkle; crease,

for   皮 *pí* skin, see No. 521.

559   *qǔ*   取 **to get.**

This character is:	耳 *ěr* ear, No. 185, radical 128, plus 又 *yòu* again, No. 846;
Note:	聚 *jù* to assemble.

560   *qù*   去 **to go away; to leave.**

+ 122:   罢 S form for *bà* to stop, No. 14, T form: 罷;

+ 1:   丢 *diū* to lose; mislay;

+ 85:   法 *fǎ* the law, No. 188;

+ 26:   却(卻) *què* to step back; however;

This character + 130:   脚(腳) *jiǎo* foot.

561   *quán*   全 **complete; whole.**

D.f.:   金 *jīn* metals, radical 167, No. 349.

+ 64:   拴 *shuān* to tie; fasten.

562   *quē*   缺 **to be short of.**

This character is seen (+ 15) in:	缶 *fǒu* a jar, radical 121, plus the phonetic 决 *jué* to decide, No. 375.
D.f.:	卸 *xiè* to unload.

Note the following two compound characters with radical 121:

+ 64 and 20:   掏 *tāo* to pull out, No. 673, and

+ 116:   窑(窯) *yáo* a kiln.

563   *què*   确(確) **true; reliable.**

S form basic: 角 *jiǎo* an angle, radical 148, No. 336.

564   *qún*   群(羣) **crowd; group.**

Basic: 君 *jūn* monarch; gentleman;

+ 163:   郡 *jùn* prefecture;

+ 9 and minus radical 30:   伊 *yī* he or she.

R

565   *rán*   然 correct.

> D.f.:   热 *rè* heat, No. 568 in list, T form: 熱;
> D.f.:   熟 *shú* ripe; familiar, No. 633.

   + 86:   燃 *rán* to burn; ignite.

566   *ràng*   让(讓) to yield; allow.

> S form basic: 上 *shàng* upper, No. 593;
> D. T form phonetic f.:   囊 *náng* bag; pocket.

   + 30:   嚷 *rāng* and *rǎng* to shout;
   + 167:   镶 *xiāng* inlay.

567   *rào*   绕(繞) to wind; coil.
          + 85:   浇(澆) *jiāo* to pour liquid; to sprinkle;
          + 86:   烧(燒) *shāo* to burn; to cook;
          + 72:   晓(曉) *xiǎo* dawn; to know.

568   *rè*   热(熱) heat.
          Basic: 执 S form for *zhí* to hold, No. 899, T form: 執.

> D.f.:   然 *rán* correct, No. 565;
> D.f.:   熟 *shú* ripe; familiar, No. 633.

569   *rén*   人 man; human being.   Radical 9.
Compounds usually have this radical in its alt.form: 仅(僅) *jǐn* only, No. 351.

> D.f.:   入 *rù* to enter, No. 580.

   + 149:   认(認) *rèn* to know, note 忍 *rěn* to bear, No. 571;
   + 131:   卧 T form for *wò* to lie, S form: 卧, No. 727;
   + 27:   仄 *zè* narrow.

570   *rén*   仁 benevolence.

571   *rěn*   忍 to bear; endure.

D.f.:   忽 *hū* to neglect; suddenly;

and f.:   勿 *wù* not, see entry No. 735 for 物 *wù* matter.

Basic: 刃 *rèn* the edge of a knife;

D. this f.:   刀 *dāo* knife; sword, No. 140.

+ 149:   認 T form for *rèn* to recognise, S form: 认, No. 569.

572   *rèn*   任 to appoint.

D. phonetic f.:   王 *wáng* king, No. 706.

573   *réng*   仍 to remain; still.
      Basic: 乃 *nǎi* to be, No. 492.

D.f.:   及 *jí* to reach, No. 311.

+ 64:   扔 *rēng* to throw.

574   *rì*   日 the sun; day.   Radical 72.

D.f.:   曰 *yuē* to say; to name.

575   *róng*   荣(榮) to flourish.

Note that the upper half of this character varies between the S and T forms in the same way as does 劳(勞) *láo* labour, No. 409.

576   *róng*   绒 fine hair; down.

D. phonetic f. that in: 械 *xiè* tool; instrument;

and f.:   武 *wǔ* military, No. 732;

and f.:   式 *shì* type; style, No. 622;

+ 154:   贼 *zéi* thief; traitor.

577	*róng*	容 to hold; contain.
	+ 85:	溶 *róng* to dissolve;
	+ 86:	熔 *róng* to melt; smelt.

| 578 | *ròu* | 肉 meat; flesh.   (See note on radical 130 in Appendix B.) |

	D.f.:	内 *nèi* inner; within, No. 499;
	D.f.:	丙 *bǐng* third, see No. 53 for 病 *bìng* ill;
	D.f.:	两 *liǎng* two; both, No. 431.

| 579 | *rú* | 如 according to; like. |

| | D.f.: | 加 *jiā* to add, No. 319. |

| 580 | *rù* | 入 to enter.   Radical 11. |

| | D.f.: | 人 *rén* man, No. 569; |
| | D.f.: | 八 *bā* eight, No. 11. |

581	*ruò*	若 like; seem.
	+ 149:	诺 <u>*nuò*</u> to promise.
582	*ruò*	弱 weak; feeble.

S

| 583 | *sāi* | 塞 to fill in; squeeze in. |
| | *sài* | a place of strategic importance. |

D.f.:	基 *jī* base, No. 309;
Basic:	其 *qí* his, No. 531;
D.f.:	赛 *sài* match; competition;
D.f.:	寨 *zhài* stockade;
D.f.:	寒 *hán* cold, No. 268;

| 584 | *sān* | 三 three. |

| 585 | *sǎn* | 散 to come loose; dispersed. |
| | *sàn* | to break up; to disperse. |

| D.f. phonetic in: | 借 *jiè* to borrow, No. 346. |

| + 64: | 撒 *sā* to let go, and *sǎ* to scatter; sprinkle. |

| D. this f.: | 撤 *chè* to remove, No. 84. |

586	*sǎo*	嫂 sister-in-law.
	+ 104:	瘦 *shòu* thin; emaciated;
	+ 137:	艘 *sōu* a measure word, for ships.

| 587 | *sè* | 色 colour. Radical 139. |
| | + 120: | 绝 *jué* to cut off; absolutely, No. 377. |

| 588 | *shā* | 杀(殺) to kill. |

| D.f.: | 希 *xī* hope, No. 738. |

| 589 | *shān* | 山 mountain. Radical 46. |
| | + 9: | 仙 *xiān* celestial being; immortal. |

590   *shàn*   善 good.

> D.f.:   害 *hài* evil, No. 266.

591   *shāng*   伤(傷) wound; injury.

> D. phonetic in S form f.:   方 *fāng* square, No. 194.
>
> D. T form phonetic f. that in: 腸 T form for *cháng* intestines, S form: 肠,
>   see No. 77.

592   *shāng*   商 to discuss; consult.

> D.f. phonetic in: 滴 *dī* to drip, No. 151.

593   *shàng*   上 upper; upward; previous.

    + 149:   让 S form for *ràng* to give way, No. 566, T form: 讓.

594   *shàng*   尚 still; yet.

> D.f. phonetic in: 墙 *qiáng* a wall, No. 543.

    + 9:   倘 *tǎng* if; in case;
    + 158:   躺 *tǎng* to lie down;
    + 156:   趟 *tàng* (a measure word), for number of times done.

595   *shǎo*   少 few; less.

> D.f.:   小 *xiǎo* small, radical 42, No. 763.

    + 167:   钞 *chāo* a bank-note; paper money;
    + 86:   炒 *chǎo* stir-fry;
    + 115:   秒 *miǎo* a second;
    + 38:   妙 *miào* wonderful; excellent;
    + 85:   沙 *shā* sand; granulated;
    + 120:   纱 *shā* yarn;
    + 112:   砂 *shā* sand; grit;
    + 109:   省 *shěng* economise; save, No. 607.

596   *shé*   舌 the tongue.   **Radical 135.**

Note: 舍 *shě* to abandon, and *shè* a shed;
This character + 30:   啥 *shà* what;

+ 160:   辞(辭) *cí* diction; to decline;
+ 66:   敌(敵) *dí* enemy, see No. 151 for 滴 *dī* drip;
+ 18:   刮(颳) *guā* scrape; blow, see No. 203 for 風 wind;
+ 149:   话 *huà* word; talk, No. 288;
+ 85:   活 *huó* to live; alive; work;
+ 85 and 169: 阔 *kuò* wide; rich;
+ 162:   适(適) *shì* fit; proper;
+ 99:   甜 *tián* sweet, see No. 224 for 甘 *gān* sweet.

597   *shè*   设 **to set up; establish.**
Basic: 殳 *shū* an ancient bamboo weapon, radical 79;

D.f. phonetic in: 沿 *yán* along, No. 801.

+ 130:   股 *gǔ* thigh; a share;
+ 85:   没 *méi* no; not, No. 465;
+ 64:   投 *tóu* to throw;
+ 60:   役 *yì* labour; service;

Note: 殷 *yīn* abundant; ardent, see also No. 9.
Note: 殿 *diàn* a hall; a palace.

598   *shè*   社 **society.**
Basic: 土 *tǔ* soil; earth, No. 696, radical 32.

599   *shēn*   申 **to state; explain.**

D.f.:   甲 *jiǎ* first, No. 322;
D.f.:   由 *yóu* cause; from, No. 843.

+ 9:   伸 *shēn* to stretch; extend;
+ 120:   绅 *shēn* gentry;

+ 113:	神 *shén* god; spirit; mind;
+ 40:	审(審) *shěn* careful; to examine;
+ 38 and 40:	婶(嬸) *shěn* aunt,

Basic for these T forms:	番 *fān* occasion, No. 189.

600	*shēn*	身 body.　Radical 158.
	+ 41:	射 *shè* to shoot; to fire;

Note:	躲 *duǒ* to hide; avoid, No. 180.

601	*shēn*	深 deep.
	+ 64:	探 *tàn* to explore; sound out,

D. this f.	採 T form for *cǎi* to pick; select, No. 62, S form: 采.

602	*shén*	什(甚) what?
	shèn	甚 what?, and very; extremely.

The first form is 十 *shí* ten, No. 613, plus radical 9.
This character is usually seen in combination, as in 什么(甚麼) *shénme* what?,
see also entry No. 456 for 麻 *má* hemp.

603	*shēng*	升 to rise; hoist.

D.f.:	井 *jǐng* a well, No. 359.

604	*shēng*	生 to give birth to; life.　Radical 100.
	+ 118:	笙 *shēng* sheng (a reed pipe wind instrument);
	+ 130:	胜(勝) *shèng* victory, see also No. 374;
	+ 72:	星 *xīng* star, No. 772;
	+ 61:	性 *xìng* nature; sex, No. 776;
	+ 38:	姓 *xìng* surname; family name.

Note:	產 T form for *chǎn*, to bear; produce, S form: 产, No. 75.

| 605 | *shēng* | 声(聲) sound; voice. |

| 606 | *shéng* | 绳(繩) rope. |

The S form is   电 *diàn* electricity, No. 157, plus radicals 30 and 120.

| 607 | *shěng* | 省 economise; a province. |

This character is   少 *shǎo* few, No. 595,
plus: 目 *mù* eye, radical 109, No. 488.

| 608 | *shī* | 尸 a corpse.   Radical 44. |

D.f.:   户 *hù* a door; household, No. 284.

+ 82:   尾 <u>wěi</u> tail, No. 715,
for: 毛 *máo* hair, see No. 463.

609	*shī*	失 to lose.
	+ 157:	跌 <u>diē</u> to fall;
	+ 162:	迭 <u>dié</u> to alternate; repeatedly;

D. this f.:   送 *sòng* to deliver; to accompany, No. 652;

+ 167:   铁 S form for <u>tiě</u> iron, No. 684, T form: 鐵.

| 610 | *shī* | 师(師) teacher; master. |

D. right-hand element f.:   市 *shì* market, No. 619;
and f.:   巾 *jīn* a cloth, see also No. 57 for 布 *bù* cloth.
The left-hand element of the T form is seen also in 追 *zhuī* to pursue, No. 924;

+ 118:   筛(篩) <u>shāi</u> sieve;

The right-hand element + 184 very closely resembles 饰 *shì* decorations;
to adorn.

611   *shī*   施 **to execute; carry out.**

D.f.:   旅 *lü* (third tone) to travel, No. 450;

and f.:   旋 *xuán* to revolve; return;

and f.:   族 *zú* race; nationality.

+ 64:   拖 *tuō* to pull; to delay.

612   *shī*   湿(濕) **wet.**

Basic: 显(顯) *xiǎn* obvious, No. 750.

613   *shí*   十 **ten.   Radical 24.**

+ 149:   计 *jì* to count;

+ 9:   什 *shén* what?, No. 602;

+ 30:   叶 S form for *yè* leaf, No. 812, T form: 葉;

+ 167:   针 *zhēn* needle;

+ 85:   汁 *zhī* juice.

614   *shí*   石 **stone.   Radical 112.**

+ 46:   岩 S form for *yán*, rock; cliff, T form: 巖, see also No. 800;

+ 开 *kāi*:   研 *yán* to grind; to study, for *kāi* open, see No. 380.

615   *shí*   时(時) **time.**

Basic for S form: 寸 *cùn* very small, radical 41, No. 127;

Basic for T form: 寺 *sì* temple.

+ 149:   诗 *shī* poetry;

+ 93:   特 *tè* special, No. 676;

+ 64:   持 *chí* to hold; grasp, No. 97;

+ 118:   等 *děng* class; to wait, No. 149;

+ 60:   待 *dāi* to stay, and *dài* to deal with.

616	*shí*	实(實) solid; true.

	D.f..:	买(買) *mǎi* to buy, No. 458.

617	*shí*	饣(食) to eat; food. Radical 184.
	+ 123:	養 T form for *yǎng* raise; foster, No. 806, S form: 养.

618	*shǐ*	使 to send; to cause; to use.
	Basic:	吏 *lì* an official; mandarin.

	D.f.:	史 *shǐ* history;
	Note: + 187	驶 *shǐ* to drive;
	D.f.:	更 *gēng* to change, No. 236.

619	*shì*	市 market.

	D.f.:	布 *bù* cloth; to announce, No. 57;
	D.f. right-hand element in:	师(師) *shī* teacher; master, No. 610;
	D.f. right-hand element in:	肺 *fèi* lungs, No. 197.

	+ 169 (S) or 191 (T):	闹(鬧) *nào* noisy, No. 498.

620	*shì*	示 to show. Radical 113.
	+ 75:	标 S form for *biāo* a mark; a sign, No. 48, T form: 標;
	+ 170:	际 S form for *jì* border, T form: 際, see No. 73;
	+ 40:	宗 *zōng* ancestor, No. 929.
	+ 2 × 75:	禁 *jīn* to bear and *jìn* prohibit, No. 356, see also No. 435.

621	*shì*	世 lifetime; an era; the world.

622	*shì*	式 type; style.

	D.f.:	武 *wǔ* military, No. 732.

	+ 149:	试 *shì* to try; test.

623	*shì*	事 matter; affair.

624   shì   是 correct; to be.

+ 32:   堤 dī dyke; embankment;

+ 64:   提 tí to carry; to raise, No. 677;

+ 181:   题 tí topic, No. 678.

625   shōu   收 to receive.

D.f.:   叫 jiào to cry out; to shout, No. 337.

626   shǒu   手 hand.   Radical 64.

627   shǒu   守 to guard; keep watch.

This character is   寸 cùn a unit of length, No. 127, plus radical 40.

628   shǒu   首 head; first.   Radical 185.

+ 162:   道 dào way; doctrine, No. 143;

+ 162 and 41:   導 T form for dǎo to lead; guide, S form: 导.

629   shòu   寿(壽) longevity; life.

D.f.:   夺 S form for duó to seize, No. 179, T form: 奪.

+ 118:   筹(籌) chóu a chip; a counter;

+ 85:   涛(濤) tāo great waves; billows;

+ 167:   铸(鑄) zhù casting; founding.

630   shòu   受 to receive.

D.f.:   爱 S form for ài love, No. 4, T form: 愛.

+ 64:   授 shòu to award; to teach.

631   shū   书(書) book; to write.

D. T form phonetic f.:   畫 T form for huà to draw, No. 289, S form 画.

632   shū   叔 uncle.

+ 109:   督 dū to supervise.

633	*shú* *shóu*	熟 ripe; familiar.

	D.f.:	热 S form for *rè* heat, No. 568, T form: 熱

634	*shǔ*	属(屬) category; to belong to.

Note that part of the T form phonetic is: 蜀 *Shǔ* Sichuan, see also No. 111 for 触(觸) *chù*, to touch.

635	*shǔ* *shù*	数(數) to count. a number; a figure.
	+ 75:	楼(樓) *lóu* a building, No. 444.

636	*shǔ*	鼠 mouse; rat. Radical 208.

	D.f. phonetic in:	蠟 T form for *là* wax, S form: 蜡, see No. 346.

637	*shù*	术(術) art; skill.
	Basic for S form:	木 *mù* tree; wood, No. 487.
	+ 162:	述(述) *shù* to state; relate.

638	*shù*	树(樹) tree.

639	*shuā*	刷 brush.

	D.f.:	制 S form for *zhì* to manufacture, No. 909, T form: 製.

640	*shuài* *lü* (fourth tone)	率 to lead; command. rate; proportion.

	D.f.:	傘 T form for *sǎn* umbrella, S form: 伞.

641	*shuāng*	双(雙) two; both.

	The S form is 2 ×	又 *yòu* again, No. 846.

642   *shuí*   谁 **who?**

Basic: 隹 *zhuī*, radical 172, see note in No. 335.

+ 9 and 46:   催 *cuī* to urge on;

+ 32:   堆 *duī* to pile up; a heap;

+ 85:   淮 *Huái* the Huaihe River;

+ 86:   焦 *jiāo* burnt, No. 335;

+ 30:   售 *shòu* to sell;

+ 64:   推 *tuī* to push, No. 697;

+ 61:   惟 *wéi* only; but;

+ 30:   唯 *wéi* only; alone;

+ 120:   维 *wéi* to tie up; to safeguard;

Note: 雄 *xióng* male; a hero, No. 779;

+ 167:   锥 *zhuī* an awl;

+ 15:   准 *zhǔn* to allow; standard, No. 925.

643   *shuǐ*   水 **water.   Radical 85.**

D.f.:   火 *huǒ* fire, radical 86, No. 301;

D.f.:   永 *yǒng* forever, No. 840.

+ 112:   泵 *bèng* a pump;

+ 15:   冰 *bīng* ice, radical 15 (see Appendix B and No. 352);

+ 48:   汞 *gǒng* mercury, see also No. 238;

+ 44:   尿 *niào* urine;

+ 106:   泉 *quán* spring; fountain;

Note this + 130:   腺 *xiàn* a gland,

and also + 120:   線 T form for *xiàn* thread, S form 线, see No. 540.

644   *shùn*   顺 **along.**

Basic: 川 *chuān* river, radical 47;

D. this basic form f.: 州 *zhōu* an administrative area, No. 913.

+ 162:   巡 *xún* to patrol, note alt.form for radical 47;

+ 149:   训 *xùn* to lecture; a model.

645 *shuō* 说 to speak.

+ 115: 税 <u>*shuì*</u> tax;

+ 130: 脱 <u>*tuō*</u> to shed (skin); to escape;

+ 169: 阅 <u>*yuè*</u> to read; to review.

646 *sī* 丝(絲) silk. **Radical 120.**

D.f.: 兹 <u>*zī*</u> this, No. 926,

note similar phonetic in: 顯 T form for *xiǎn* obvious, No. 750, S form: 显.

647 *sī* 私 private.

648 *sī* 思 to think.

D.f.: 息 *xī* breath, No. 740;

D.f.: 意 *yì* meaning; idea, No. 828.

+ 141: 慮 T form for <u>*lǜ*</u> (fourth tone) to ponder, S form: 虑, see also entry No. 767 for 心 *xīn* heart.

649 *sī* 斯 this.

This character is 其 *qí* his, No. 531, plus radical 69.

+ 64: 撕 *sī* to tear; to rip.

650 *sǐ* 死 to die.

651 *sì* 四 four.

D.f.: 匹 *pǐ* be equal to;

D.f.: 西 *xī* west, No. 737.

652 *sòng* 送 to deliver; to accompany.

D.f.: 迭 *dié* to alternate; repeatedly, see also No. 609 for 失 *shī* to lose;

D.f.: 遂 *suì* to satisfy, see also No. 176 for 队(隊) *duì* team; group;

D.f.: 逐 *zhú* to pursue.

653   *sù*   诉(訴) **to tell.**

D. this phonetic   斥 *chì* to scold f.: 斤 *jīn* half kilo, No. 348.

+ 64:   拆 *chāi* to tear open;

D. this from: 折 *zhé* to break; snap, No. 886.

654   *sù*   肃(肅) **solemn.**
+ 140:   萧(蕭) *xiāo* desolate; dreary;
+ 120:   繡 T form for *xiù* to embroider, S form: 绣.

655   *sù*   素 **white; plain.**

D.f.:   索 *suǒ* rope; to search.

656   *sù*   速 **fast; speed.**
Basic: 束 *shù* to bind; tie;

D.f. phonetic in: 刺 *cì* thorn; splinter, No. 124.

+ 38 and 66:   嫩 *nèn* tender; delicate;

Note also: 赖 *lài* to rely on, No. 407.

657   *sù*   塑 **model; mould.**

Note: 逆 *nì* contrary; disobey, No. 503.

658   *suān*   酸 **acid; sour.**

D. phonetic f. that in: 棱 *léng* edge, No. 416,
and from that in: 滚(滾) *gǔn* to roll, No. 259.

+ 75:   梭 *suō* shuttle.

659   *suàn*   算 **calculate.**

660   *suī*   虽(雖) although.

661   *suí*   随(隨) to follow.

Note use of T phonetic: 隋 *Suí* the Sui dynasty.

662   *suì*   岁(歲) year; age.

D. the S form f.:   罗 S form for *luó* a net, No. 454, T form: 羅.

663   *suō*   缩 to contract; to shrink.

This character adds to   百 *bǎi* hundred, No. 16, radicals 9,120 and 40.

664   *suǒ*   所 place.

T

| 665 | *tā* | 它(牠) it. |

666	*tā*	他 he.
	Basic:	也 *yě* also, No. 809.
	+ 38:	她 *tā* she.

| 667 | *tà* | 踏 to step on. |

> D. this phonetic f.: 泉 *quán* fountain, see No. 643 for 水 *shuǐ* water.

| 668 | *tái* | 台(臺) platform; stage. |

> D. T form f.: 喜 *xǐ* happy, No. 743.

	+ 130:	胎 *tāi* foetus;
	+ 64:	抬 *tái* to lift;
	+ 38:	始 *shǐ* beginning;
	+ 85:	治 *zhì* to rule; to treat disease, No. 907.

| 669 | *tài* | 太 highest; too. |
| | + 61: | 态(態) *tài* form; appearance, |

> note basic for T form: 能 *néng* ability; can, No. 500.

670	*tán*	谈(談) to talk; chat.
	Basic:	炎 *yán* scorching hot;
	This is 2 ×	火 *huǒ* fire, No. 301.
	+ 85:	淡 *dàn* light; pale;
	+ 84:	氮 *dàn* nitrogen, for 气 *qì* gas, see No. 535;

> Note the following two characters with similar sound and related meaning:
> 炭 *tàn* charcoal,
> and 碳 *tàn* carbon, both listed in entry No. 294 for:
> 灰 *huī* ash.

671 *Táng* 　　唐 the Tang dynasty.

D.f.: 　　康 *kāng* health, No. 382.

+ 32: 　　塘 *táng* dyke; embankment;
+ 119: 　　糖 *táng* sugar.

672 *táng* 　　堂 a hall.

D.f.: 　　當 T form for *dāng* equal, No. 138, S form: 当;

D.f.: 　　党 S form for *dǎng* political party, No. 139,
　　　　　　　 T form: 黨;

D.f.: 　　赏 *shǎng* to reward, see also entry No. 78
　　　　　　　 for reference to 偿(償) *cháng* repay.

673 *tāo* 　　掏 to draw out.

For other uses of 缶 radical 121, see No. 562 for 缺 *quē* to lack.

674 *táo* 　　逃 to escape; flee.
+ 75: 　　桃 *táo* peach;
+ 64: 　　挑 <u>*tiāo*</u> to choose, and <u>*tiǎo*</u> to push; poke;
+ 157: 　　跳 <u>*tiào*</u> to jump;
+ 38: 　　姚 <u>*Yáo*</u> a surname.

675 *tào* 　　套 sheath; cover.

676 *tè* 　　特 special.
Basic: 　　寺 *sì* a temple, see also entry No. 615 for *shí* time:
　　　　　　　 时(時).

677 *tí* 　　提 to carry; to lift.
Basic: 　　是 *shì* to be, No. 624.
+ 32: 　　堤 *dī* dyke; embankment;
+ 181: 　　题 *tí* topic, No. 678.

678   *tí*   題 topic.

       Basic: 是 *shì* to be, No. 624, see also No. 677 above.

679   *tǐ*   体(體) body.

Basic for S form:	本 *běn* root of a plant, No. 36;
Note T form phonetic in	禮 T form for *lǐ* courtesy, No. 418, S form: 礼.
D. No. 679 f.:	休 *xiū* to stop; to rest, No. 780.

680   *tì*   替 take the place of; for.

       D.f.:   赞 *zàn* to support; praise, No. 871.

       + 85:   潜 S form for *qián* latent; hidden, T form: 潛.

Note use of this T form phonetic in: 蠶 T form for *cán* silkworm; S form: 蚕, see entry No. 103 for 虫 *chóng* insect.

681   *tiān*   天 heaven; sky.

       D.f. phonetic in: 跃 S form for *yuè* to leap; jump, T form: 躍.

       + 85 and 61:   添 *tiān* to add; increase;

       + 142:   蚕 S form for *cán* silkworm, T form: 蠶, see also entry
                             No. 103 for 虫 *chóng* insect.

682   *tián*   田 field.   Radical 102.
       + 140:   苗 *miáo* seedling, No. 477;
       + 8:   亩 S form for *mǔ* mu (a unit of area), T form: 畝,

note: the right-hand element of this T form 久 is *jiǔ* for a long time, No. 363;

       + 120:   细 *xì* thin; fine, No. 746.

683   *tiáo*   条(條) twig.

       D. S form f.:   务 S form for *wù* affair, No. 734, T form: 務.

684   *tiě*   铁(鐵) iron.

Phonetic in S form is   失 *shī* to lose, No. 609.

+ 157:   跌 *diē* to fall;

+ 162:   迭 *dié* to alternate; repeatedly,

D. this f.:   送 *sòng* to deliver; accompany, No. 652,

and f.:   选 S form for *xuǎn* to select, No. 789, T form: 選.

685   *tīng*   听(聽) to listen; to hear.

S form basic: 斤 *jīn* a half kilo, radical 69, No. 348;
The right-hand element of the T form is seen also in 德 *dé* virtue, No. 146.

686   *tíng*   停 to stop.
Basic: 亭 *tíng* pavilion; kiosk,

D. this f.:   享 *xiǎng* to enjoy, No. 758.

687   *tǐng*   挺 straight; quite.
Basic: 廷 *tíng* court of a feudal ruler,

D. this f.:   延 *yán* to prolong; postpone, No. 798;

+ 53:   庭 *tíng* front yard; law court.

688   *tōng*   通 through.
+ 75:   桶 *tǒng* bucket;
+ 104:   痛 *tòng* pain;
+ 19:   勇 *yǒng* brave;
+ 85:   涌 *yǒng* to well up.

689   *tóng*   同 same.

D.f.:   司 *sī* to take charge of, see also entry No. 121;
D.f.:   向 *xiàng* direction, No. 760.

+ 118:	筒	*tǒng* tube; a tube-shaped object;
+ 167:	铜	*tóng* copper;
+ 85:	洞	*dòng* hole; cavity.

690   *tóng*   童 **child.**

This character is plus:	里	*lǐ* inside, radical 166, No. 420,
	立	*lì* to stand, radical 117, No. 422.
D. No. 690 f.:	章	*zhāng* chapter, No. 880;

+ 64:	撞	*zhuàng* to run into; collide with, No. 923.

691   *tōu*   偷 **to steal.**

D. phonetic f. that in:	臉	T form for *liǎn* face, No. 426, S form: 脸,
and also f. that in:	輪	T form for *lún* wheel, No. 453, S form: 轮.

+ 159:	输	*shū* to transport;
+ 61:	愈	*yù* to heal; the more . . . the more.

692   *tóu*   头(頭) **head; hair; first.**

The T form is	豆	*dòu* beans, No. 169, plus radical 181.

693   *tòu*   透 **penetrate.**

Basic: 秀 *xiù* elegant; excellent, No. 782.

D.f.:	委	*wěi* to entrust; a committee, No. 716.

694   *tū*   突 **to dash forward.**

D.f.:	究	*jiū* to study, see No. 362 for 九 *jiǔ* nine.

695   *tú*   图(圖) **map.**

The S form is	冬	*dōng* winter, No. 165, plus radical 31.

| 696 | *tǔ* | 土 earth; soil.   **Radical 32.** |

| | D.f.: | 士 *shì* bachelor; scholar, radical 33. |

	+ 30:	吐 *tǔ* to spit and *tù* to vomit;
	+ 75:	杜 *dù* to shut out; prevent;
	+ 42:	尘 S form for *chén* dust, No. 85, T form: 塵;
	+ 64 and 72:	捏 S form for *niē* to pinch, T form: 捏;
	+ 53:	庄 S form for *zhuāng* village, T form: 莊, see No. 922;

Note two other uses of this as a phonetic in the S forms of characters:

| | + 130: | 脏 S form for *zāng* dirty, T form: 髒,
S form for *zàng* the internal organs,
T form: 臟, see also entry No. 65 for 藏 *cáng*
to hide; |
| | + 75: | 桩 S form for *zhuāng* stake; pile, T form: 樁, see also
entry No. 119 for 春 *chūn* spring. |

| 697 | *tuī* | 推 to push; shove. |
| | See No. 642 for: | 谁 *shuí* who?, for other compounds with this phonetic. |

| | D.f.: | 拖 *tuō* to pull; delay, see also entry No. 611 for
施 *shī* to execute; carry out. |

698	*tuì*	退 to move back; retreat.
	See No. 277 for:	很 *hěn* very, for other compounds with this phonetic.
	+ 130:	腿 *tuǐ* leg.

| 699 | *tuō* | 托 to hold; to entrust. |

| | D. phonetic f.: | 毛 *máo* hair, No. 463. |

W

700	*wā*	挖 to dig.
701	*wǎ*	瓦 a tile.　**Radical 98.**
	wà	to tile.

D.f.:　五 *wǔ* five, No. 730.

+ 并 *bìng* to combine, No. 52: 瓶 *píng* bottle; vase;

+ 次 *cì* order, No. 123: 瓷 *cí* porcelain.

702　*wài*　外 outer; foreign.

D.f.:　处 *chǔ* to get along with, and *chù* place, No. 109.

703　*wán*　完 whole; complete.

Basic:　元 *yuán* first; principal, No. 860.

+ 96:　玩 *wán* to have fun; joke;

+ 170:　院 *yuàn* courtyard; court.

704　*wǎn*　碗 bowl.

Minus 112 and 40, + 61:　怨 *yuàn* resentment;

D. this character f.:　怒 *nù* anger, see No. 512 for 努 *nǔ* to exert effort.

705　*wàn*　万(萬) ten thousand; a myriad.

D. S form f.:　力 *lì* power, No. 421;

and f.:　五 *wǔ* five, No. 730;

T form 萬 is radical 140 plus the phonetic for 遇 *yù* meet, No. 859.

+ 27 and 19:　励(勵) *lì* to encourage;

+ 162:　迈(邁) *mài* step; stride.

706	*wáng*	王 king. **Radical 96. (See note in Appendix B.)**
	+ 85:	汪 *wāng* to accumulate (of a liquid);
	+ 72:	旺 *wàng* prosperous; flourishing;
	+ 30:	呈 *chéng* to assume; to present, No. 93;
	+ 106:	皇 *huáng* emperor, No. 292;
	+ 27 and 75:	框 *kuāng* to frame and *kuàng* a frame;
	+ 27 and 118:	筐 *kuāng* a basket;
	+ 94:	狂 *kuáng* mad;
	2 × No. 706 + 今:	琴 *qín* musical instruments, for 今 *jīn* today, see No. 347;
	+ 85 and 169:	润 *rùn* moist; sleek;
	Note:	玉 *yù* jade;
	Note also:	宝 S form for *bǎo* treasure, No. 25, T form: 寶.

707	*wǎng*	网(網) net.

D. phonetic in T form f. that in: 剛 T form for *gāng* firm, No. 227, S form: 刚;

D. phonetic in T form f. that in: 逆 *nì* contrary; disobey, No. 503.

708	*wàng*	忘 to forget.
	Basic:	亡 *wáng* to flee.
	+ 61 on the left:	忙 *máng* busy, No. 462.

709	*wàng*	望 to gaze; to hope.

710	*wēi*	危 danger.
	+ 130:	脆 *cuì* fragile; brittle.

711	*wēi*	威 might; power.

D.f. phonetic in: 滅 T form for *miè* to extinguish, No. 478, S form: 灭.

712	*wēi*	微 tiny.

D.f.: 徵 T form for *zhēng* to journey; proof, S form: 征,

for 正 *zhèng* straight, see No. 894.

| 713 | *wéi*
 wèi | 为(為) to act.
 for. |

| | D.f.: | 办 S form for *bàn* to do, No. 21, T form: 辦. |

| | + 9: | 伪(偽) *wěi* false; fake. |

| 714 | *wéi*
 + 9:
 + 120: | 围(圍) to enclose.
 伟(偉) *wěi* big; great;
 纬(緯) *wěi* latitude; |

| | Note: | 韩(韓) *Hán* a surname; Korea. |

| 715 | *wěi* | 尾 tail. |

| | This character is <br> plus: | 毛 *máo* hair, No. 463,
 尸 *shī* corpse, No. 608. |

| 716 | *wěi* | 委 to entrust. |

| | D.f.: | 秀 *xiù* to flower; elegant, No. 782, see also No. 693. |

| | + 194:
 + 111: | 魏 *Wèi* a surname; the Kingdom of Wei;
 矮 *ǎi* short, No. 3. |

| 717 | *wèi* | 卫(衛) to guard. |

| 718 | *wèi* | 未 not. |

| | D.f.: | 末 *mò* tip; end, No. 483. |

| | + 30:
 + 38: | 味 *wèi* taste; flavour;
 妹 *mèi* younger sister; sister. |

| 719 | *wèi*
 Basic:
 + 64: | 位 place.
 立 *lì* to stand, radical 117, No. 422.
 拉 *lā* to pull, No. 405. |

720	*wèi*	胃 stomach.

D.f.:	畏 *wèi* fear; respect, see also entry No. 721.

+ 149:	谓 *wèi* to say; call.

721	*wèi*	喂 hello!; to feed.
	Basic:	畏 *wèi* fear; respect, see also entry No. 720.

722	*wēn*	温 warm.

723	*wén*	文 writing. Radical 67.

D.f.:	交 *jiāo* to hand over, No. 334;
D. also f. phonetic in:	刘 S form for *Liú* Liu, a surname, T form: 劉.

+ 120:	纹 *wén* veins; wrinkles;
+ 126:	斋 *zhāi* to fast, for 而 *ér* and, see No. 184.

724	*wén*	闻(聞) to hear; to smell.

This character is	门(門) *mén* door, No. 468, plus 耳 *ěr* ear, No. 185.
D. T form f.:	開 T form for *kāi* to open, No. 380, S form: 开;
D.f.:	间(間) *jiàn* space in between, No. 329;
D.f.:	闲(閑) *xián* idle, for 木 *mù* tree; wood, see No. 487.

725	*wèn*	问(問) to ask.

This character is	门(門) *mén* door, No. 468, plus 口 *kǒu* mouth, No. 396.
D.f.:	间(間) *jiàn* space in between, No. 329,
and also f.:	闻(聞) *wén* to hear; to smell, No. 724.

726	*wǒ*	我 I.
	+ 9:	俄 *é* very soon; Russian;
	+ 196:	鹅 *é* goose;
	+ 184:	饿 *è* hunger;
	+ 30:	哦 *ó* and *ò* What!; Oh!

727   *wò*   臥(卧) **to lie.**

The S form is   臣 *chén* official, No. 85, plus 卜 *bǔ* divination, see No. 55;

The T form is   臣 plus 人 *rén* man, No. 569.

728   *wū*   污(汙) **dirt.**

Basic: 亏 S form for *kuī* to lose; luckily, T form: 虧.

D. phonetic f. that in: 巧 *qiǎo* skilful, No. 545;

and in: 朽 *xiǔ* rotten.

Note similarities in: 考 *kǎo* to take or give a test, No. 384;

and in: 夸 the phonetic in 跨 *kuà* step, No. 400;

Note also: 号 S form for *hào* name; number, No. 272, T form: 號;

and: 与 S form for *yǔ* to give, No. 853, T form: 與.

729   *wú*   无(無) **nothing; not.   S form is radical 71.**

D. T form f.:   舞 *wǔ* dance, No. 733.

+ 64:   抚(撫) *fǔ* to comfort; to nurture.

730   *wǔ*   五 **five.**

D.f.:   瓦 *wǎ* tile, No. 701;

D.f.:   万 S form for *wàn* ten thousand, No. 705, T form: 萬.

+ 30:   吾 *wú* I or we;

+ 9:   伍 *wǔ* five (used on cheques etc.);

+ 149 and 30:   语 *yǔ* language, No. 856.

731   *wǔ*   午 **noon.**

D.f.:   牛 *niú* ox, No. 508.

+ 149:   许 *xǔ* to praise; to permit.

732   *wǔ*   武 military.

D.f.:   式 *shì* type; style, No. 622;

D.f. phonetic in: 绒 *róng* fine hair; down, No. 576;

D.f. phonetic in: 械 *xiè* tool.

+ 154:   赋 *fù* to bestow on.

733   *wǔ*   舞 dance.

D.f.:   無 T form for *wú* not, No. 729, S form: 无.

734   *wù*   务(務) affair.

D. S form f.:   条 S form for *tiáo* twig, No. 683, T form: 條.

+ 173:   雾(霧) *wù* fog.

735   *wù*   物 matter.

Basic: 勿 *wù* not.

+ 61:   忽 *hū* to neglect; suddenly;

D. this f.:   忍 *rěn* to bear; to endure, No. 571;

D. also f. phonetic in: 葱 *cōng* onion.

736   *wù*   误(誤) mistake.

Basic: 吴(吳) *Wú* the Kingdom of Wu; Wu, a surname.

X

737   *xī*   西 **west.** **Radical 146.**

D.f.:   四 *sì* four, No. 651.

+ 75:   栖 *xī* to perch;

+ 85:   洒 S form for *sǎ* to sprinkle, T form: 灑;

+ 72:   晒 S form for *shài* to shine upon, T form: 曬;

The phonetic in these T forms is 麗 T form for *lì* beautiful, S form: 丽.

738   *xī*   希 **hope.**

D.f.:   杀 S form for *shā* to kill, No. 588, T form: 殺.

+ 86:   烯 *xī* alkene;

+ 115:   稀 *xī* rare; sparse.

739   *xī*   析 **to divide; analyse.**

Basic: 斤 *jīn* a half kilo, No. 348;

+ 64:   折 S form for *zhé* to break, No. 886, T form: 摺.

740   *xī*   息 **breath.**

D.f.:   思 *sī* to think, No. 648.

741   *xí*   习(習) **to practise.**

Note: 羽 *yǔ* feather, No. 854.

742   *xǐ*   洗 **to wash.**

Basic: 先 *xiān* first, No. 749;

+ 40:   宪 S form for *xiàn* constitution, T form: 憲;

+ 162:   选 S form for *xuǎn* to choose, No. 789, T form: 選.

743   *xǐ*   喜 happy.

D.f.:   臺 T form for *tái* platform, No. 668, S form: 台.

744   *xì*   戏(戲) play; drama.
Basic: 戈 *gē* an ancient weapon, radical 62, see also No. 884.

745   *xì*   系(係)(繫) system.
jì   to tie; fasten.

D.f. phonetic in: 悉 *xī* all; to know;
D.f. phonetic in: 溪 *xī* a small stream.

+ 子: 孫 T form for <u>*sūn*</u> grandson, S form: 孙,
for   子 see note in entry No. 927,
for   小 *xiǎo* small, see entry No. 763.

746   *xì*   细(細) thin; fine.

This character is   田 *tián* field, No. 682, plus radical 120.

747   *xià*   下 below; next.
+ 142:   虾 S form for *xiā* shrimp, T form: 蝦,

for T form phonetic see No. 323 for 假 *jiǎ* false;

+ 30:   吓 S form for *xià* to frighten, T form: 嚇,

for T form phonetic: 赫 *hè* grand, see No. 100 for 赤 *chì* red; bare.

748   *xià*   夏 summer.

D.f.:   复 *fù* duplicate, No. 218.

749   *xiān*   先 first; earlier.
+ 40:   宪 S form for *xiàn* constitution, T form: 憲;
+ 85:   洗 <u>*xǐ*</u> to wash, No. 742;
+ 162:   选 S form for <u>*xuǎn*</u> to choose, No. 789, T form: 選.

750   *xiǎn*   显(顯) obvious.

Basic for S form: 业 S form for *yè* business, No. 811, T form: 業;
Note also: 亚 S form for *yà* inferior, No. 796, T form: 亞.

+ 85:   湿(濕) *shī* wet, No. 612.

751   *xiàn*   县(縣) county.
           + 61:   悬(懸) *xuán* to hang.

752   *xiàn*   现(現) the present.
           Basic: 见(見) *jiàn* to see, radical 147, No. 328.

753   *xiàn*   陷 a trap.

754   *xiàn*   献(獻) to offer.

This S form is   南 *nán* south, No. 495, plus radical 94.

755   *xiāng*   乡(鄉) countryside.

This T form is   乡+郎 *láng* your, see No. 428 for 良 *liáng* good.

756   *xiāng*   相 each other.
           xiàng   appearance.

This character is   木 *mù* tree; wood, radical 75, No. 487,
plus: 目 *mù* eye, radical 109, No. 488.

+ 118:   箱 *xiāng* chest; box;
+ 85:   湘 *Xiāng* another name for Hunan; a river in Hunan;
+ 61:   想 *xiǎng* to think, No. 759;
+ 173:   霜 *shuāng* frost.

757   *xiāng*   香 fragrant.   Radical 186.
           Note: 香港 *xiāng gǎng* Hong Kong,
           for   港 *gǎng* port; Hong Kong, see No. 241 共 *gòng*
                                common.

758   *xiǎng*   享 to enjoy.

D.f. phonetic in: 厚 *hòu* thick, No. 279;

and f. that in: 哼 *hēng* to snort; hum;

and f. that in: 停 *tíng* to stop, No. 686.

+ 164:   醇 *chún* mellow wine; alcohol;

+ 163:   郭 *guō* the outer wall of a city; Guo, a surname.

759   *xiǎng*   想 to think.
Basic: 相 *xiāng* each other, No. 756.

760   *xiàng*   向 direction.

D.f.:   同 *tóng* same, No. 689.

+ 30:   响 S form for *xiǎng* sound, T form: 響.

761   *xiàng*   象 elephant; appearance.
+ 9:   像 *xiàng* likeness;
+ 予: 豫 *yù* pleased; comfort,
for   予 *yú* I, see entry No. 850.

762   *xiāo*   消 disappear.

D. this phonetic f.:   员 *yuán* member, No. 861;

+ 18:   削 *xiāo* to pare; peel;

+ 167:   销 *xiāo* to melt (metal); to sell;

D. this f.:   锁 *suǒ* lock;

+ 75:   梢 *shāo* tip; top (of a tree);

+ 115:   稍 *shāo* a little;

+ 44:   屑 *xiè* bits; scraps;

+ 156:   趙 T form for *Zhào* Zhao, a surname, S form: 赵.

763   *xiǎo*   小 small.   Radical 42.

+ 子: 孙 S form for *sūn* grandson, T form: 孫,

for   孑 *jié* lonely, see note in entry No. 927;

+ 32:   尘 S form for *chén* dust, T form: 塵, No. 85;

+ 37:   尖 *jiān* point; sharp, No. 324;

+ 106, 115 and 59:   穆 *mù* solemn, see also No. 15.

764   *xiào*   笑 smile.

765   *xiě*   写(寫) to write.

Basic for S form: 与 S form for *yǔ* to give, T form: 與, No. 853.

766   *xiè*   谢(謝) to thank.

Basic: 射 *shè* shoot, for 身 *shēn* body, see No. 600.

767   *xīn*   心 heart.   Radical 61.

+ 140:   芯 *xīn* (lamp)wick and *xìn* (rock)core;

+ 141:   虑 S form for *lü* (fourth tone) to consider, T form: 慮;

+ 85 and 141:   滤 S form for *lü* (fourth tone) to filter, T form: 濾;

+ 48 and 凡: 恐 *kǒng* fear, No. 395,

for   凡 *fán* anyone, see entry No. 190.

768   *xīn*   辛 hot; pungent.   Radical 160.

+ 167:   锌 *xīn* zinc.

769   *xīn*   新 new.

770   *xìn*   信 trust; a letter.

This character is 言 *yán* speech, radical 149, No. 799, plus radical 9.

771   *xīng*   兴(興) to prosper.
          xìng   mood; interest.

D.f.:   举(舉) *jǔ* to lift, No. 369.
D. T form f.: 與 T form for *yǔ* to give, S form: 与, No. 853.

772   *xīng*   星 star.

This character is 生 *shēng* life, No. 604 in list, plus radical 72.

+ 164:   醒 *xǐng* to come round.

773   *xíng*   刑 punishment.

This character is 开 S form for *kāi* to open, No. 380, plus radical 18.

+ 32:   型 *xíng* mould; type.

774   *xíng*   行 to go; to do.   Radical 144.
          háng   line; profession.

Note: with this radical the phonetic is sometimes placed in the centre:
e.g.:   衝 T form for *chōng* to dash, S form: 冲, No. 101;
             街 *jiē* street, No. 341;
             衡 *héng* to weigh; measure.

775   *xíng*   形 form.

This character is 开 S form for *kāi* to open, No. 380, plus radical 59.
D.f.:   影 *yǐng* shadow, No. 839, see No. 357 for 景 *jǐng* view.

776   *xìng*   性 nature.

This character is 生 *shēng* life, No. 604, plus radical 61.

777   *xiōng*   凶 **fierce.**

D.f.:   风 S form for *fēng* the wind, No. 203, T form: 風;
D.f.:   区 S form for *qū* area, No. 557, T form: 區;

+ 130 and 20:   胸 *xiōng* chest; thorax;
Note: 赵 S form for *Zhào* Zhao, a surname, T form: 趙,
                                   see No. 762.

778   *xiōng*   兄 **elder brother.**
+ 24:   克 *kè* can; to overcome, No. 389;
+ 15 (T form + 85):   况(況) *kuàng* condition; situation;
+ 113:   祝 *zhù* to express good wishes.

779   *xióng*   雄 **male.**
Basic: 隹 see entry No. 642 for 谁 *shuí* who?

780   *xiū*   休 **to stop; to rest.**
Basic: 木 *mù* tree; wood, No. 487;

D.f.:   体 S form for *tǐ* body, T form: 體, No. 679;
Basic for this S form: 本 *běn* the root or stem of a plant, No. 36.

781   *xiū*   修 **to repair.**

D. the phonetic f.:   参 *cān* to join, No. 63;
and f. phonetic in: 趁 *chèn* to take advantage of, No. 90.

782   *xiù*   秀 **elegant; excellent.**

D.f.:   委 *wěi* to entrust, No. 716.

+ 120:   绣 S form for *xiù* to embroider, T form: 繡,

the phonetic for this T form 肅 is the T form for *sù* solemn, No. 654, S form: 肃;

+ 162:   透 *tòu* to penetrate, No. 693.

| 783 | *xū* | 须(鬚) must; have to; beard. |

| | D. S form f.: | 颜 *yán* face; colour. |

| 784 | *xū* | 虚 void; empty. |

| | This character is | 业 S form for *yè* occupation, T form: 業, No. 811, plus 141 虍 = 虎 *hǔ* tiger, No. 283. |

| 785 | *xū* | 需 need. |

| | This character is plus: | 而 *ér* and, No. 184, radical 126, 雨 *yǔ* rain, No. 855, radical 173; |

| | + 9: | 儒 *rú* Confucianism. |

| 786 | *xù* | 畜 to raise (domestic animals). |

| | This character is plus: | 玄 *xuán* black, No. 788, radical 95, 田 *tián* field, No. 682, radical 102; |

| | + 140: | 蓄 *xù* to store up. |

| 787 | *xuān* | 宣 to declare. |

| | D. phonetic f. that in: and f. that in: D. No. 787 also f.: | 担 S form for *dān* to carry, No. 136, T form: 擔, 恒 *héng* permanent; 宜 *yí* suitable, see No. 547 for 且 *qiě* just. |

| 788 | *xuán* | 玄 black.   Radical 95. |

| | D.f. phonetic in: | 幼 *yòu* young, No. 848. |

| | + 57: | 弦 *xián* bowstring; string; |
| | + 102: | 畜 *xù* to raise (domestic animals), No. 786. |

| 789 | *xuǎn* | 选(選) to select; elect. |

| | Basic for S form: | 先 *xiān* earlier; first, No. 749. |
| | D. S form f.: | 迭 *dié* to alternate, see No. 684 for 铁 *tiě* iron. |

790	*xué*	学(學) to study.
791	*xuè*	血 blood. Radical 143.
792	*xún*	寻(尋) to look for.

| | D. S form f.: | 灵 S form for *líng* clever, No. 437, T form: 靈, |
| | D. T form f.: | 尊 *zūn* senior; respect, No. 939. |

| 793 | *xùn* | 讯(訊) to interrogate. |

| | D. phonetic f.: | 丑 S form for *chǒu* ugly, T form: 醜, see No. 257, |
| | and also f.: | 凡 *fán* anyone, No. 190. |

| | + 85: | 汛 *xùn* flood. |

Y

794   yā   压(壓) **to press down.**

795   yá   牙 **tooth.**

+ 30:   呀 *yā* Oh!
                    ya ya (a particle of emphasis).

+ 140:   芽 *yá* bud; sprout;

+ 172:   雅 *yǎ* proper; elegant;

+ 116:   穿 *chuān* to pierce; penetrate, No. 112.

796   yà   亚(亞) **inferior.**

D. S form f.:   业 S form for *yè* business, No. 811, T form: 業;
Note also: 显 S form for *xiǎn* obvious, No. 750, T form: 顯.

+ 61:   恶(惡) *ě* disgusting, and *è* evil;
+ 33:   壶(壺) *hú* kettle; pot.

797   yān   烟(煙) **smoke; tobacco.**

The S form phonetic: 因 is *yīn* because of, No. 829.

+ 30:   咽 *yān* pharynx, and *yàn* to swallow.

This character, in the meaning 'to swallow', has also a traditional form, using,
after radical 30, instead of 因 the phonetic 燕.
This phonetic is a character in its own right: 燕 *yàn* the swallow (the bird).

798   yán   延 **to prolong.**

D.f.:   廷 *tíng* the court of a feudal ruler, see entry No. 687.

799   yán   讠(言) **speech.   Radical 149.**

D. T form f.:   音 *yīn* sound, No. 831;

+ 舌: 话(話) *huà* word; talk, No. 288,

for   舌 *shé* tongue, see No. 596.

+ 9:   信 *xìn* trust; a letter, No. 770;

+ 162:   這 T form for *zhè* this, S form: 这, No. 888.

800   *yán*   严(嚴) **tight; strict.**

D. S form f.:   产 S form for *chǎn* to give birth to, No. 75, T form: 產;

Note: 敢 *gǎn* to dare, No. 225, is the phonetic in the
                     T form: 嚴.

+ 46:   巖 T form for *yán* cliff, S form: 岩, see No. 614.

801   *yán*   沿 **along.**
          yàn   **water's edge.**

D.f.:   没 *méi* not, No. 465 in list, and d. also f. such
                     compounds

with this phonetic as   设 *shè* to establish, see entry No. 597 for list;

+ 137:   船 *chuán* boat, No. 113;

+ 167:   铅 *qiān* lead.

802   *yán*   盐(鹽) **salt.**
          See No. 327: 监(監) *jiān* to supervise, for a list of similar characters.

803   *yǎn*   眼 **the eye.**
          See No. 277: 很 *hěn* very, for other characters with this phonetic.

804   *yǎn*   演 **to develop; to act.**

Note similar phonetic in: 黄 *huáng* yellow, No. 293.

805   *yáng*   羊 **sheep.   Radical 123.**

+ 85:   洋 *yáng* vast; foreign; Western;

+ 84:   氧 *yǎng* oxygen;

+ 75:   样(樣) *yàng* appearance; type;

+ 195:   鲜 *xiān* fresh, and *xiǎn* little; rare;

+ 149:   详 *xiáng* detailed;

+ 113:	祥 *xiáng* auspicious; lucky;	
+ 86 and 116:	窯 T form for *yáo* kiln, S form: 窑, see No. 562;	
+ 108:	盖 *gài* a lid; to cover, No. 221.	

806   *yǎng*   养(養) **to provide for.**

Note: the T form includes 食 *shí* food, radical 184, No. 617.

807   *yáo*   摇 **to shake.**

Note: this phonetic includes 缶 *fǒu* a jar, radical 121; for other characters which include this radical see entry No. 562 for 缺 *quē* to lack.

808   *yào*   要 **to wish.**
      yāo   **to demand.**
      + 130:   腰 *yāo* the waist.

809   *yě*   也 **also.**
      + 85:   池 *chí* a pool;
      + 32:   地 *dì* the earth, No. 152;
      + 9:   他 *tā* he, No. 666;
      + 38:   她 *tā* she,
      + 93:   牠 T form for *tā* it, S form: 它, No. 665.

810   *yě*   野 **wild.**

This character is 里 *lǐ* inside, No. 420, plus 予 *yǔ* to give, No. 850.

811   *yè*   业(業) **business; occupation.**

D. S form f.:	亚 S form for *yà* inferior, No. 796, T form: 亞;	
D.f. phonetic in:	碰 *pèng* to bump into;	
D. this phonetic f.:	并 *bìng* to combine, No. 52;	
D. T form f.:	叢 T form for *cóng* a thicket, S form: 丛, see No. 125;	
and also f. phonetic in:	撲 T form for *pū* to pounce, S form: 扑 No. 55.	

      + 72:   显 S form for *xiǎn* obvious, No. 750, T form: 顯.

812   *yè*   叶(葉) leaf.

> The S form is: 十 *shí* ten, No. 613, plus 口 *kǒu*, No. 396, mouth, for note on the T form phonetic see also No. 536.

813   *yè*   页(頁) page; leaf.   **Radical 181.**

814   *yè*   夜 night.
        + 85:   液 *yè* liquid; juice.

815   *yī*   一 one.   **Radical 1.**

816   *yī*   衣 clothing.   **Radical 145.**

> D.f.:   农 S form for *nóng* agriculture, No. 510, T form: 農.

        + 9:   依 *yī* to depend on.

817   *yī*   医(醫) doctor.

818   *yí*   疑 doubt.
        + 64:   擬 T form for <u>*nǐ*</u> to draft, S form: 拟,
        for   以 *yǐ* to use, see entry No. 821;
        + 15:   凝 <u>*níng*</u> to congeal.

819   *yǐ*   乙 second.   **Radical 5.**
        + 9:   亿(億) *yì* a hundred million;
        + 61:   忆(憶) *yì* to recall; recollect;

> The phonetic in these T forms is 意 *yì* meaning; wish, No. 828;

        + 140:   艺(藝) *yì* skill;
        + 135:   乱(亂) <u>*luàn*</u> disorder; chaos, No. 452;
        + 14:   乞 <u>*qǐ*</u> to beg, No. 533.

820   *yǐ*   已 to stop; already.

> D.f.:   己 *jǐ* oneself, No. 316.

821	*yǐ*	以 **to use.**
	+ 64:	拟 S form for *nǐ* to draft, T form: 擬; the T form phonetic 疑 is *yí* doubt, No. 818;
	+ 9:	似 *sì* similar.
822	*yì*	义(義) **justice.**

D. S form f.: 叉 *chā* fork;

	+ 9:	仪(儀) *yí* appearance; ceremony;
	+ 149:	议(議) *yì* opinion.
823	*yì*	亦 **also.**

D.f.: 赤 *chì* red; bare, No. 100.

+ 162 (alt.form + 157): 迹(跡) *jī* trace.

| 824 | *yì* | 异(異) **different; strange.** |

D. S form f.: 导 S form for *dǎo* to lead, T form: 導, see No. 143;
T form + 124: 翼 *yì* wing, for 羽 *yǔ* feather, see No. 854.

825	*yì*	译(譯) **to translate.**
	+ 165:	释(釋) *shì* to explain;
	+ 85:	泽(澤) *zé* pool; pond;
	+ 64:	择(擇) *zé* to select.
826	*yì*	易 **easy.**

D.f. phonetic in: 場 T form for *cháng* a level open space, No. 77, S form: 场.

	+ 154:	赐 *cì* grant; favour;
	+ 157:	踢 *tī* to kick;
	+ 167:	锡 *xī* tin.

827   *yì*   益 benefit.

D.f.:   盖 S form for *gài* a lid; to cover, No. 221, T form: 蓋;
D.f.:   盒 *hé* a box; a case, No. 275.

828   *yì*   意 meaning; idea.

D.f.:   思 *sī* to think, No. 648;
D.f.:   息 *xī* breath; news, No. 740.

+ 9:   億 T form for *yì* a hundred million, S form: 亿;
+ 61:   憶 T form for *yì* to recall, S form: 忆, see No. 819.

829   *yīn*   因 because of.

D.f.:   困 *kùn* to be hard pressed, No. 404;
D.f.:   闪 *shǎn* to dodge; flash past, see also No. 468.

+ 61:   恩 *ēn* kindness, No. 182;
+ 86:   烟 S form for *yān* smoke; tobacco, No. 797, T form: 煙;
+ 30:   咽 *yān* pharynx, and *yàn* swallow, see No. 797.

830   *yīn*   阴(陰) shade; hidden.

The S form is   月 *yuè* the moon; a month, No. 864, plus radical 170;
D. S form f.:   阳 S form for *yáng* the sun, T form: 陽, see No. 77.

831   *yīn*   音 sound.   Radical 180.

D.f.:   言 *yán* speech, radical 149, No. 799.

+ 72:   暗 *àn* dark, No. 7;
+ 勺: 韵 S form for *yùn* musical sound, T form: 韻,
for   勺 *yún* even, see No. 867; for 員 *yuán* member,
                                see No. 861.

832   *yǐn*   引 to attract.

This character is   弓 *gōng* a bow, No. 239, plus radical 2.

833   *yǐn*   隐(隱) concealed.
        Basic for S form: 急 *jí* anxious; urgent, No. 313;
        + 115:   稳(穩) <u>*wěn*</u> steady; certain.

834   *yìn*   印 seal; print.

D.f. the phonetic in: 迎 *yíng* to go to meet, No. 837.

835   *yīng* and *yìng*   应(應) to answer; ought.

836   *yīng*   英 hero.
        + 72:   映 *yìng* reflect;
        + 115:   秧 <u>*yāng*</u> seedling.

837   *yíng*   迎 to go to meet.

D. phonetic f.:   印 *yìn* seal; print, No. 834.

        + 9:   仰 <u>*yǎng*</u> to look up to;
        + 64:   抑 <u>*yì*</u> to restrain.

838   *yíng*   营(營) to seek; a camp.
        Basic: 吕(呂) *Lü* (third tone) Lu, a surname, see also No. 114.

To this basic, this character adds radicals 14 and 140 in the S form and 14 and 2 × 86 in the T form. For similar alternations between S and T forms see Nos. 301, 409 and 575.

839   *yǐng*   影 shadow.
        Basic: 景 *jǐng* scene, see also No. 357 for 京 *jīng* capital.

D.f.:   形 *xíng* form; shape, No. 775.

840   *yǒng*   永 forever.

D.f.:   水 *shuǐ* water, No. 643.

        + 130:   脉 S form for <u>*mài*</u> vein, T form: 脈, see also No. 516.

841   *yòng*   用 to use.   **Radical 101.**

D.f.:   甩 *shuǎi* to swing.

+ 64:   拥(擁) *yōng* to embrace.

842   *yóu*   尤 outstanding.

D.f. phonetic in: 伏 *fú* to bend over, No. 210.

+ 9:   优 S form for *yōu* excellent, T form: 優, see No. 553;
+ 94:   犹 S form for *yóu* just as; like, T form: 猶.

843   *yóu*   由 cause.

D.f.:   甲 *jiǎ* first, No. 322;
D.f.:   申 *shēn* to state; explain, No. 599.

+ 85:   油 *yóu* oil;
+ 167:   铀 *yóu* uranium;
+ 165:   釉 *yòu* glaze;
+ 64:   抽 *chōu* to take out;
+ 44:   届(屆) *jiè* to fall due;
+ 53:   庙 S form for *miào* temple, T form: 廟, see No. 82;
+ 159:   轴 *zhóu* axle; shaft.

844   *yóu*   游 to swim; to travel.

D.f.:   激 *jī* to dash; to arouse, No. 310.

845   *yǒu*   有 to have.

846   *yòu*   又 again.   **Radical 29.**

D.f.:   叉 *chā* fork.

+ 196:   鸡 S form for *jī* chicken, No. 307, T form: 雞;
+ 9:   仅 S form for *jǐn* only, No. 351, T form: 僅;

+ 38:	奴	*nú* bondservant; slave, see also No. 512;
+ 128:	取	*qǔ* to take, No. 559;
+ 75:	权	S form for *quán* right, T form: 權, see No. 251;
× 3 + 75:	桑	*sāng* mulberry
Note also:	叠	S form for *dié* pile up; fold, T form: 疊;
+ 32:	圣	S form for *shèng* sacred; saint, T form: 聖;
× 2:	双	S form for *shuāng* two, No. 641, T form: 雙.

847   *yòu*   右 **the right side.**

D.f.:	友	*yǒu* friend, see also No. 13 for 拔 *bá* pull out;
D.f.:	石	*shí* stone, radical 112, No. 614;
D.f.:	左	*zuǒ* the left side, No. 940.

848   *yòu*   幼 **young.**

D. left-hand element f.:	玄	*xuán* black, No. 788.

849   *yú*   于 (於) **in; at.**

D. S form f.:	干	*gān* to do; dry, No. 223;
D. also f.:	千	*qiān* thousand, No. 538.

850   *yú*   予 **I.**
    yǔ   **to give; grant.**

D.f.:	子	*zǐ* son; child, No. 927.

+ 象:	豫	*yù* pleased, for 象 *xiàng* elephant, see No. 761;
+ 181:	预	*yù* in advance;
+ 53:	序	*xù* order; sequence;
+ 166:	野	*yě* open country; wild, No. 810, see also No. 420.

851   *yú*   余(餘) surplus.

D.f. phonetic in: 茶 *chá* tea, No. 71.

+ 170:   除 *chú* to get rid of; except, No. 108;

+ 85:   涂 *tú* to smear on;

+ 162:   途 *tú* way; route;

+ 68:   斜 *xié* oblique; tilted;

+ 60:   徐 *xú* slowly; gently.

852   *yú*   鱼 fish.   Radical 195.

D.f.:   角 *jiǎo* horn; angle, No. 336.

+ 85:   渔(漁) *yú* fishing;

+ 72:   鲁 *lǔ* stupid;

+ 140 and 115:   蘇 T form for *sū* to revive, S form: 苏 see No. 21.

853   *yǔ*   与(與) to give; with.
            yù   to take part in.

D. T form f.:   舉 T form for *jǔ* to raise, No. 369, S form: 举;

and from: 興 T form for *xīng* prosper, No. 771, S form: 兴;

D. S form f. phonetic in: 污 *wū* dirt, No. 728;

S form + 14:   写 S form for *xiě* to write, No. 765, T form: 寫.

854   *yǔ*   羽 feather.   Radical 124.

+ 66:   翅 *chì* wing;

+ 130 and phonetic of 趁   膠 T form for *jiāo* glue, S form: 胶, see No. 334,

for   趁 *chèn* to take advantage of, see entry No. 90;

+ 63:   扇 *shān* to fan, and *shàn* a fan;

+ 106:   習 T form for *xí* to practise, No. 741, S form: 习;

+ 異: 翼 *yì* wing, 異 is T form for *yì* strange, No. 824,
                     S form: 异;

+ 157 and 172:   躍 T form for *yuè* leap; jump, S form: 跃;

+ 106 and 64:   摺 T form for *zhé* to break, No. 886, S form: 折.

| 855 | *yǔ* | 雨 rain.   **Radical 173.** |
| | + 102: | 雷 *léi* thunder, |

| | D. this f.: | 雪 *xuě* snow. |

| | + 126: | 需 *xū* to need; needs, No. 785. |

856	*yǔ*	语(語) language.
	Basic:	吾 *wú* I or we, see also No. 730 for 五 *wǔ* five;
	+ 61:	悟 *wù* to realise; awaken.

| 857 | *yù* | 育 to rear; educate. |

858	*yù*	欲 desire.
	Basic:	谷 *gǔ* valley, radical 150;
	for	欠 *qiàn* to owe, see No. 541.
	+ 145:	裕 *yù* abundant; affluent;
	+ 9:	俗 *sú* custom; vulgar.

859	*yù*	遇 to meet.
	+ 61:	愚 *yú* foolish; stupid;
	+ 40:	寓 *yù* to reside; live;
	+ 9:	偶 *ǒu* image; idol;
	+ 162 and 140:	邁 T form for *mài* step; stride, S form: 迈;
	+ 140:	萬 T form for *wàn* ten thousand, No. 705, S form: 万;
	This plus 27 and 19:	勵 T form for *lì* encourage, S form: 励, see also No. 421.

860	*yuán*	元 first.
	+ 31:	园(園) *yuán* garden;
	+ 162:	远 S form for *yuǎn* distant, T form: 遠,

| | D. this T form f.: | 達 T form for *dá* No. 129, S form: 达; |

	+ 170 and 40:	院 *yuàn* courtyard;
	+ 41 and 14:	冠 *guān* a hat; crown, and *guàn* to precede;
	+ 40:	完 *wán* intact; whole, No. 703;
	+ 96:	玩 *wán* to play; joke.

861 *yuán* 员(員) member.

D.f. phonetic in: 捐 *juān* to abandon; contribute, No. 373.

+ 31: 圆 *yuán* round;

+ 64: 损 *sǔn* to lose; damage;

+ 180: 韻 T form for *yùn* musical sound, S form: 韵,
see also entry No. 867 for 勺 *yún* even.

862 *yuán* 原 primary; original.

+ 85: 源 *yuán* source; cause;

+ 61: 愿 S form for *yuàn* hope; be willing, T form: 願.

863 *yuē* 约(約) to arrange.

D. phonetic f.: 包 *bāo* to wrap; a bundle, No. 24;

D. phonetic f.: 句 *jù* sentence, No. 371;

D. phonetic f.: 勺 *yún* even, No. 867.

+ 140: 药 S form for *yào* medicine, T form: 藥, see also
notes in entry No. 411 for 乐 *lè* happy;

+ 30: 哟 *yō* and *yo* Oh! and Ho!

864 *yuè* 月 the moon; a month.   Radical 130.
(See note in Appendix B on the number given to this radical.)

+ 170: 阴 S form for *yīn* the moon, No. 830, T form: 陰;

+ 77: 肯 *kěn* be willing, No. 392, for 止 *zhǐ* to stop,
see No. 901.

865 *yuè* 越 to exceed.

D. phonetic f.: 成 *chéng* to become, No. 92.

866 *yún* 云(雲) cloud.

The upper part of the T form is 雨 *yǔ* rain, radical 173, No. 855.

+ 162: 运(運) *yùn* movement; transport,

the phonetic for this T form 軍 is T form for *jūn* No. 378, army, S form: 军;

+ 44:	层(層)	*céng* layer; storey, see also entry No. 68;
+ 19:	动(動)	*dòng* to move, No. 166;
+ 72:	昙(曇)	*tán* covered with clouds.

867   *yún*   勻 **even**.

D.f. phonetic. in: 约 *yuē* to arrange, No. 863.

+ 180:	韵	S form for *yùn* musical sound, T form: 韻,
for:	音	*yīn* sound, see entry No. 831;
+ 32:	均	*jūn* equal; all.

Z

868　　*zá*　　　　　杂(雜) sundry.

869　　*zài*　　　　　再 again.

870　　*zài*　　　　　在 to exist; at.
　　　　　+ 140:　　　　茬 *chá* stubble.

871　　*zàn*　　　　　赞(贊) to praise.

D. T form f. phonetic in:　　潜 T form for *qián* latent, S form: 潜 see No. 680.

　　　　　+ 167:　　　　鑽 T form for *zuān* and *zuàn* drill, S form: 钻,
　　　　　for　　　　　占 *zhàn* to occupy, see entry No. 879.

872　　*zāo*　　　　　遭 to meet with; suffer.
　　　　　Basic:　　　　曹 *cáo* a surname.
　　　　　+ 75:　　　　槽 *cáo* a trough.

873　　*zǎo*　　　　　早 (early) morning.

D.f.:　　　　旱 *hàn* drought, see No. 223 for 干 *gān* dry;

　　　　　+ 140:　　　　草 *cǎo* grass;

D. this f.:　　　莫 *mò* no; not, No. 484.

874　　*zé*　　　　　则 standard.
　　　　　+ 9:　　　　侧 *cè* side;
　　　　　+ 85:　　　　测 *cè* to survey; measure.

875　　*zé*　　　　　责(責) duty.
　　　　　+ 115:　　　　積 T form for *jī* to amass, No. 308, S form: 积;
　　　　　+ 120:　　　　绩(績) *jī* achievement;
　　　　　+ 9:　　　　债(債) *zhài* debt.

876	*zěn*	怎 why; how.
	+ 86:	炸 *zhá* to fry, and *zhà* to explode;
	+ 116:	窄 *zhǎi* narrow;
	+ 9:	作 *zuò* to do, No. 942.
877	*zhā*	扎 to prick.
	zhá	to pitch (a tent).
	+ 159:	轧 *zhá* to roll (steel), and *yà* to run over.
878	*zhǎn*	展 open up; spread out.

D.f. phonetic in: 振 *zhèn* to shake, No. 891.

| 879 | *zhàn* | 占(佔) to occupy. |
| | *zhān* | to practise divination. |

D. S form f.:   贞 *zhēn* loyal; faithful;

	+ 85:	沾 *zhān* to moisten;
	+ 62:	战(戰) *zhàn* war;
	+ 117:	站 *zhàn* to stand;
	+ 53:	店 *diàn* shop, No. 158;
	+ 119 or 202:	粘 or 黏 *nián* sticky; glutinous, or *zhān* glue;

D. radical 202 f. phonetic in: 漆 *qī* paint;

	+ 154:	贴 *tiē* to paste; stick on;
	+ 167:	钻(鑽) *zuān* and *zuàn* drill, see also entry No. 871.
880	*zhāng*	章 chapter.

D.f.:   童 *tóng* child, No. 690.

881	*zhǎng*	掌 palm.
	+ 64:	撑(撐) *chēng* to prop up.
882	*zhàng*	丈 husband; measure of length (3¹/₃ metres).
	+ 9:	仗 *zhàng* weaponry; to rely on.

883   *zhāo*   招 to beckon.

　　Basic: 召 *zhào* to summon.

　　+ 72 and 86:   照 *zhào* to shine, No. 885;

　　+ 156:   超 *chāo* to exceed.

884   *zhǎo*   找 to look for.

　　Basic: 戈 *gē* an ancient weapon, radical 62;

　　D.f. phonetic in: 代 *dài* to replace; dynasty, No. 132.

　　+ 9:   伐 *fá* to fell;

　　+ 9 and 169:   阀 *fá* a powerful person; a valve;

　　+ 29:   戏 S form for *xì* play; drama, No. 744, T form: 戲.

885   *zhào*   照 to shine.

　　Basic: 召 *zhào* to summon, see entry No. 883.

886   *zhē*   折 to roll over.

　　zhé   折(摺) to break, for T form see note in No. 854.

　　Basic: 斤 *jīn* a half kilo, radical 69, No. 348.

　　D.f.:   拆 *chāi* to tear open, see No. 653 for 诉 *sù* to tell.

　　+ 85:   浙 *Zhè* Zhejiang Province;

　　+ 75:   析 *xī* to divide; analyse, No. 739.

887   *zhě*   者 (indicates a person performing an action.)

　　D.f.:   孝 *xiào* filial piety; mourning.

　　+ 149:   诸 *zhū* all, see No. 916 for other uses of this phonetic;

　　+ 163:   都 *dōu* all, No. 167.

888   *zhè*   这(這) this.

　　The T form is   言 *yán* speech, No. 799, plus radical 162;
　　The S form phonetic is seen in 刘 S form for *Liú* Liu, a surname, see No. 723.

889 zhe   着(著) (indicates continuing action.)
zhāo   a move; a trick.
zháo   to touch; to burn.
zhuó   to wear.

D.f.:   看 *kàn* to see; to read, No. 381.

890 zhēn   真 true.

D.f.:   直 *zhí* straight, No. 900.

+ 167:   镇 *zhèn* to press down;
+ 32:   填 *tián* to fill; to stuff.

891 zhèn   振 to shake.

D. phonetic f.:   展 *zhǎn* to open up; spread out, No. 878.

+ 173:   震 *zhèn* to shock; quake;
+ 72:   晨 *chén* morning.

892 zhēng   争(爭) to struggle; argue.
+ 109:   睁 *zhēng* to open the eyes;
+ 15 (T form + 85): 净(淨) *jìng* clean;
+ 174:   静(靜) *jìng* quiet, for 青 *qīng* green, see No. 551.

893 zhěng   整 whole.
Basic: 正 *zhèng* straight, No. 894.

894 zhèng   正 straight.
zhēng   the first month of the lunar year.

D.f. phonetic in: 钙 *gài* calcium.

+ 60:   征(徵) *zhēng* to go on a journey;

D. T form f.:   微 *wēi* tiny, No. 712;

+ 104:   症(癥) *zhēng* and *zhèng* illness;
+ 149:   证(證) *zhèng* proof,

	登	*dēng* to ascend, see No. 148;
for		
+ 66:	政	*zhèng* politics, No. 895;
+ 不:	歪	*wāi* askew; crooked, for 不 *bù* not, see No. 56.

| 895 | *zhèng* | 政 politics. |
| | Basic: | 正 *zhèng* straight, No. 894. |

| 896 | *zhī* | 之 (sign of the genitive.) |
| | + 140: | 芝 *zhī* as in 芝加哥 Zhījiāgē Chicago. |

| 897 | *zhī* | 支 to prop up.   Radical 65. |

| D.f.: | 皮 *pí* skin, No. 521. |

+ 75:	枝	*zhī* branch; twig;
+ 124:	翅	*chì* wing;
+ 64:	技	*jì* skill;
+ 77:	歧	*qí* fork; branch;
+ 30:	吱	*zī* and *zhī* to creak; squeak; chirp.

| 898 | *zhī* | 知 to know. |
| | + 72: | 智 *zhì* wisdom. |

| 899 | *zhí* | 执(執) to grasp. |

The left-hand element of the T form is 幸 *xìng* good fortune, see entry No. 768, and it is seen also in 報 T form for *bào* report, No. 27, S form: 报.

+ 32:	垫	S form for *diàn* to fill up; to pad; T form: 墊;
+ 86:	热	S form for *rè* heat, No. 568, T form: 熱;
+ 19:	势	S form for *shì* power; force, T form: 勢.

| 900 | *zhí* | 直 straight. |

| D.f.: | 真 *zhēn* true, No. 890. |

+ 9:	值	*zhí* value;
+ 75:	植	*zhí* to plant; grow;
+ 122:	置	*zhì* to place; put.

901	*zhǐ*	止 to stop. Radical 77.
	+ 64:	扯 *chě* to pull;
	+ 130:	肯 *kěn* to be willing to, No. 392.

902	*zhǐ*	只(祇) only.
	zhī	只(隻) single; one only.
	+ 120:	织 S form for *zhī* to weave, T form: 織;
	+ 128:	职 S form for *zhí* duty, T form: 職, see also No. 185;
	+ 115:	积 S form for *jī* to amass, No. 308, T form: 積,
	for	責 T form for *zé* duty, S form: 责, see No. 875;
	+ 149:	识 S form for *shí* to know, T form: 識.

903	*zhǐ*	纸(紙) paper.
	Basic:	氏 *shì* family name; surname, radical 83.

D. this f. phonetic in: 低 *dī* low, No. 150.

904	*zhǐ*	指 finger; to point at.
	zhī	as in: 指甲 *zhījia*, nail;
	zhí	as in: 指头 *zhítou*, finger; toe.
	+ 130:	脂 *zhī* fat; grease;
	+ 164:	酯 *zhǐ* ester.

905	*zhì*	至 until. Radical 133.
	+ 66:	致 *zhì* to send;
	+ 40:	室 *shì* a room;
	+ 64 and 44:	握 *wò* to hold; grasp;
	+ 44:	屋 *wū* house; room.

| 906 | *zhì* | 志(誌) will; aspiration. |

The S form is   士 *shì* bachelor; scholar, radical 33, plus radical 61.

907	*zhì*	治 to rule; treat a disease.
	Basic:	台 S form for *tái* platform, No. 668, T form: 臺.

908 *zhì* 质(質) nature; character.

The T form is 2 × radical 69: 斤 *jīn* a half kilo, No. 348, plus radical 154.

909 *zhì* 制(製) to make; manufacture.

D. S form f.: 刷 *shuā* brush, No. 639.

910 *zhōng* 中 centre.
  zhòng   to hit.
  + 61: 忠 *zhōng* loyal; devoted;
  + 167: 钟(鐘) *zhōng* bell; clock,

T form phonetic 童 is *tóng* child, No. 690;

  + 115: 种(種) *zhǒng* species, and *zhòng* grow,

T form phonetic 重 is *zhòng* heavy, No. 912;

  + 9: 仲 *zhòng* second;
  + 15 or 85: 冲 S form for *chōng*, to dash, No. 101, T form: 衝.

911 *zhòng* 众(眾) many; a crowd.

912 *zhòng* 重 weight; heavy.
  chóng   repeat; again. Listed separately as No. 104.
  + 115: 種 T form for *zhǒng* species, and *zhòng* grow,
        S form: 种;
  + 140: 董 *dǒng* to direct; supervise;
  + 61 and 140: 懂 *dǒng* to understand; to know;
  + 19: 動 T form for *dòng* to move, S form: 动, No. 166.

913 *zhōu* 州 prefecture.

D.f.: 川 *chuān* river, see entry No. 644 for 顺 *shùn* along.

  + 85: 洲 *zhōu* continent.

914   *zhōu*   周(週) all around.

+ 149:   调 *diào* transfer, and *tiáo* to mix, see No. 160.

915   *zhū*   朱(硃) vermilion.

+ 96:   珠 *zhū* pearl;

+ 75:   株 *zhū* trunk of a tree;

+ 78:   殊 *shū* different.

916   *zhū*   诸(諸) all; various.

Basic: 者 *zhě* (a person performing an action), No. 887;

+ 94:   猪 S form for *zhū* pig, T form: 豬, using
              radical 152;

+ 86:   煮 *zhǔ* to boil; cook;

+ 140:   著 *zhù* outstanding;

+ 9 and 149: 储 *chǔ* to store up;

+ 32:   堵 *dǔ* to stop up;

+ 122:   署 *shǔ* a government office;

+ 140 and 122: 薯 *shǔ* potato.

917   *zhú*   竹 bamboo.   Radical 118.

This is the full form of radical 118 when used as a character on its own. It is
more usually seen in its short form as part of a compound character,

as in: 笔(筆) *bǐ* a pen, No. 39.

918   *zhǔ*   主 host.

D.f.:   圭 *guī* ceremonial jade, see entries Nos. 204
             and 248;

+ 64:   拄 *zhǔ* to lean on (a stick etc.);

+ 9:   住 *zhù* to live; reside;

+ 85:   注(註) *zhù* to pour; concentrate;

+ 187:   驻 *zhù* to halt; stay;

+ 75:   柱 *zhù* post; pillar;

+ 60:   往 *wǎng* to go; towards, and *wàng* to; towards.

919   *zhù*   助 to help.

This character is   且 *qiě* just, No. 547, plus radical 19, see also No. 933.

+ 167:   锄 *chú* hoe; to hoe.

920   *zhuā*   抓 to seize.

D. phonetic f.:   瓜 *guā* melon, No. 247;

+ 巴: 爬 *pá* to crawl; climb, for 巴 *bā* hope, see No. 12.

921   *zhuān*   专(專) special; expert.

D. T form f. phonetic in: 博 *bó* rich, No. 54.

+ 112:   砖(磚) *zhuān* brick;

+ 159:   转(轉) *zhuǎn* turn, and *zhuàn* revolve;

+ 9:   传(傳) *zhuàn* commentaries on classics and *chuán* to pass on;

+ 31:   團 T form for *tuán* round, S form: 团, for 才 *cái* ability, see No. 60.

922   *zhuāng*   装(裝) to dress up; pretend.
           Basic: 壮(壯) *zhuàng* strong.

The basic form is: 爿 *pán* slit bamboo, radical 90, plus radical 33, 士 *shì* bachelor. For radical 33 see Appendix B and entry No. 696 for 土 *tǔ* earth; soil, radical 32. Distinguish radical 33: 士 from radical 32: 土.

D.f.:   状(狀) *zhuàng* form; shape.

+ 140:   莊 T form for *zhuāng* village, S form: 庄, see No. 65,

this S form + 75:   桩 S form for *zhuāng* stake; pile, T form: 椿, see No. 119.

923   *zhuàng*   撞 to bump into.
           Basic: 童 *tóng* child, No. 690;

D.f.:   章 *zhāng* chapter, No. 880.

924   *zhuī*   追 to pursue.

This phonetic is seen also in 師 T form for *shī* teacher, S form: 师, No. 610.

925   *zhǔn*   准 (準) to allow.
          Basic for S form: 隹 *zhuī* (radical 172), as seen in 谁 *shuí* who, No. 642;
          + 85:   淮 *Huái* the Huaihe River.

926   *zī*   兹 (茲) this.

          D.f.:   丝 (絲) *sī* silk, No. 646.

          + 112:   磁 (磁) *cí* magnetism.

927   *zǐ*   子 son; child.   Radical 39.

          zi   one of a group, as: 帽子 *màozi* a cap.

          D.f.:   予 *yú* I, and *yǔ* to grant, No. 850.

          + 9:   仔 *zǐ* young (of animals, fowls);
          + 119:   籽 *zǐ* seed;
          + 40:   字 *zì* word; character;
          + 115:   季 *jì* season;
          + 75:   李 *lǐ* plum, No. 419;

Note use of a rare character similar to 子: 孑 *jié* lonely, in: 孙 (孫) *sūn* grandson.
See also references in Nos. 745 and 763.

928   *zì*   自 oneself.   Radical 132.

          D.f.:   目 *mù* eye, No. 488.

          + 30:   咱 *zán* we.

929   *zōng*   宗 ancestor.

          This character is   示 *shì* to show, radical 113, No. 620, plus radical 40.
          D.f.:   宋 *Sòng* the Song dynasty; Song, a surname,
                                        see No. 487.

          + 120:   综 *zōng* to sum up.

930 *zǒng* 总 (總) assemble; always.

931 *zǒu* 走 to walk; go.   **Radical 156.**

+ 卜: 赴 *fù* to go to, for 卜 *bǔ* divination, see No. 55;

+ 51: 赶 *gǎn* to catch up with, for 干 *gān*, see No. 223;

+ 49: 起 *qǐ* to rise, No. 534, for 己 *jǐ* oneself, see No. 316;

+ 60: 徒 *tú* on foot; a follower.

932 *zòu* 奏 to play (music).

D.f.: 奉 *fèng* to give with respect, No. 206.

+ 15 (T form + 85): 凑 (湊) *còu* to collect; move closer.

933 *zū* 租 to rent.

Basic: 且 *qiě* just, No. 547.

+ 170: 阻 *zǔ* to hinder;

+ 120: 组 *zǔ* to organise; form;

+ 113: 祖 *zǔ* grandfather; ancestor;

+ 119: 粗 *cū* thick; coarse;

+ 38: 姐 *jiě* (elder) sister;

+ 40: 宜 *yí* suitable, see also No. 547;

+ 19: 助 *zhù* to help, No. 919.

934 *zú* 足 foot.   **Radical 157.**

+ 9: 促 *cù* hurried; to urge on;

+ 64: 捉 *zhuō* to clutch; grasp;

+ 各: 路 *lù* road, No. 449, for 各 *gè* each, see No. 234.

935 *zuǐ* 嘴 mouth.

This character is 此 *cǐ* this, No. 122,

plus radical 30: 口 *kǒu*, the mouth, No. 396,

and radical 148: 角 *jiǎo* a horn, and *jué* a role, No. 336.

936 *zuì* 最 the most (indicates the superlative).

937   *zuì*   罪 **crime; guilt.**

     Basic: 非 *fēi* wrong, No. 196.

938   *zuì*   醉 **drunk.**

     Basic: 卒 *zú* soldier; private.

     + 124:   翠 *cuì* emerald green;

     + 112:   碎 *suì* to break to pieces; smash.

939   *zūn*   尊 **senior; to respect.**

     D.f.:   尋 T form for *xún* to look for, No. 792, S form: 寻.

     + 162:   遵 *zūn* to abide by; obey;

     + 157:   蹲 *dūn* to squat on the heels.

940   *zuǒ*   左 **the left side.**

     D.f.:   右 *yòu* the right side, No. 847.

941   *zuò*   坐 **to sit; take a seat.**

     + 53:   座 *zuò* a seat; a place.

942   *zuò*   作 **to do.**
     zuō
     zuó

     + 72:   昨 *zuó* yesterday;

     + 61:   怎 *zěn* why?; how?, No. 876;

     + 86:   炸 *zhá* to fry, and *zhà* to explode;

     + 116:   窄 *zhǎi* narrow.

943   *zuò*   做(作) **to make; produce.**

Appendix A: Notes on the choice of Chinese characters included in the Dictionary

As mentioned in the Introduction, the characters presented as the 943 key characters in the Dictionary have been chosen on the basis of usefulness, defined as frequency of use. As a beginner learning to read the Chinese characters I started to notice and make my own list of the frequently repeated elements in a number of compound characters. These elements were clearly of a phonetic nature, since the pronunciation of the many compounds was often (although not always) identical or similar. My provisional list of key phonetic elements consisted of approximately 900 items.

One of the textbooks I used was the Chinese reader course by John DeFrancis and his colleagues.[1] The vocabulary used in this course was based strictly on a character frequency count carried out by Chén Hèqín (1928) had shown that the most frequently used 1,200 characters of the count comprise 91.3 per cent of the texts analysed. These 1,200 characters were almost exclusively the only ones used in the three books of the course.[2] Not surprisingly there was a close correspondence between the characters in my provisional list and those used in the DeFrancis textbooks, and therefore by extension also with the first 1,200 characters in Chén Hèqín's frequency count. (I mention below one important difference in my approach which reduced the list from 1,200 in length to a provisional figure of 920–930.)

A second and decisive use of a frequency count became possible with the appearance in 1990 of the wide-ranging work done by Liu Yuan and his colleagues.[3] This provides a count of the number of times a particular character is used (a 'usage number') over the body of the material analysed.[4] When DeFrancis' vocabulary and my tentative list were collated with the 1990 count, almost without exception no character had a 'usage number' under 200.

---

[1] *Beginning Chinese Reader* (1966), *Intermediate Chinese Reader* (1967) and *Advanced Chinese Reader* (1968), by John DeFrancis, with the assistance of Teng Chia-yee and Yung Chih-sheng, Yale University Press for Seton Hall University.

[2] In the Preface to the *Beginning Chinese Reader*, particularly on pages xvii–xix, DeFrancis gives details of the frequency count used and of the reasons for introducing a very small number of extra characters into the reading course.

[3] *Dictionary of Usage Frequency of Modern Chinese Words*, 现代汉语常用词词频词典(音序部分). *Xiàndài Hànyǔ chángyòngcí cídiǎn (yīnxù bùfen)*. Principal editor: Liu Yuan (刘源). Publishers: 宇航出版 (*Yǔháng chūbǎn*). Beijing, 1990.

[4] The Foreword to the above *Dictionary of Usage Frequency* states: 'The statistical survey (on which the Dictionary is based) . . . covers more than 70,000 words and over 20 million characters . . . gathered from many fields' Qian Weichang, p.2.

Since frequency is the most important factor in deciding on the useful-ness of learning one character rather than another I used the minimum count of 200 in the 1990 list not only to decide which key characters to include, but also which cross-references to list.

As mentioned, the approach in this Dictionary is not only to take into account the frequency of use of the characters chosen, but also to group them in 'phonetic families'. Adding this notion of the phonetic to the importance of frequency of use results in a reduction in the number of entries. Consider this example: the DeFrancis course includes the following four very useful characters: 交 较 校 效; these are: *jiāo* (to hand over), *jiào* (to compare), *xiào* (school) and *xiào* (effect). The basic phonetic common to these four (and other) characters is clearly the first one: 交 and this character appears as entry No. 334 in the Dictionary, the other three appearing only as cross-references, together with the number indicating which radical is added to the basic phonetic in each case to form the compound character, in this instance: + 159, + 75 and + 66.[5]

Although this approach seems to me to bring very clear advantages in memorising a number of closely related characters, it also brings with it a number of problems of presentation. Two of these problems I mention below, together with the solutions I propose.

(1) The basic phonetic shape may sometimes not exist as a separate character or, if it does exist, is not in frequent use. I have usually here taken a compound character in frequent use as the key character, although I sometimes print the basic shape where I consider it might be helpful: see for instance entry No. 248, key: *guà* 挂, basic: *guī* 圭 (a rare character).

(2) The basic phonetic exists as a character in frequent use, but some compounds are equally (or more) frequent in use and are therefore given as a separate entry, particularly in those cases where the sound differs from the basic phonetic:

thus entry No. 162 is *dīng* 丁, but *dǎ* 打 has a separate entry (No. 130);

similarly No. 33 is *bèi* 被, whereas the basic sounds *pí* 皮 (No. 515);

possibly more debatable are the decisions, usually on the same grounds, to give separate entries where the sound is similar or even identical: both *gè* 各, No. 234 and *kè* 客, No. 390; both *bēi* 背, No. 30, and *běi* 北, No. 31; both *ān* 安, No. 5, and *àn* 案, No. 6.

In applying the criteria mentioned above, particularly that of frequency of use, this Dictionary of 943 key characters aims to present all the most useful phonetics in the language. It also attempts to include every character in the *Dictionary of Usage Frequency* which has a usage number of 200 or over, if not as a key character, then in the cross-references.

[5] For a discussion of the various attempts to count the number of phonetics in the Chinese language, see John DeFrancis: *The Chinese Language: Fact and Fantasy*, University of Hawaii, 1948, especially pp.93–95. The numbers there mentioned range from 862 to 1,348.

Appendix B

The 214 radicals, numbered as in the traditional count used in the Kang Xi dictionary, are detailed below with comments and examples where appropriate.

The numbers of those used more frequently are printed in larger type.

Radicals which are also key characters in the Dictionary are printed in bold, and the number in the Dictionary is given, thus radical No. 1 appears also as a key character in the Dictionary as No. 815.

For those radicals which have both simplified and traditional forms both are given, the simplified form first, followed by the traditional form in brackets. There are 24 of these radicals and for their use in compound characters please refer to the supplementary note on p. 205.

Examples are also given of the use of alternative or abbreviated forms.

No.	Character	Pinyin	Meaning	Usage number[1]	Comments and examples
1	一	yī	one	146,721	No. 815 in Dictionary.
2	丨	gǔn	a vertical stroke	0	Added to 弓 = 引 yǐn (to attract), see entry No. 832 in Dictionary.
3	丶	zhú	a dot	0	Added to 又 = 叉 chā (a fork), see entry No. 846 in Dictionary.
4	丿	piē	a stroke to the left	0	Seen as part of 乃 nǎi (to be), No. 492 in Dictionary.
5	乙	yǐ	second	4,473	Note alt.form in 乱(亂) luàn (disorder), No. 452 in Dictionary.
6	亅	jué	a barb	0	Seen in 事 shì (affair), No. 623.
7	二	èr	two	3,615	No. 186 in Dictionary.
8	亠	tóu	above	0	Seen in 六 liù (six), No. 442.
9	人	rén	man	39,972	No. 569 in Dictionary. Note alt.form in compounds: e.g. 倘 tǎng (if; in case), see No. 594 in Dictionary.

[1] An indication of the frequency of usage. See Appendix A p. 190. A usage number 0 indicates that the character does not appear in the frequency list, edited by Liu Yuan, mentioned on p. 190.

No.	Character	Pinyin	Meaning	Usage number	Comments and examples
10	儿	rén	man	0	Seen in 元 yuán (first), No. 860.
11	入	rù	to enter	8,687	No. 580 in Dictionary.
12	八	bā	eight	10,654	No. 11 in Dictionary.
13	冂	jiōng	a desert	0	Seen now only in combinations, e.g. 同 tóng (same), No. 689.
14	冖	mì	cover	0	Seen now only in combinations, e.g. 军(軍) jūn (military), No. 378.
15	冰	bīng	ice	726	Two alt.forms are seen in compound characters viz.: (a) 冲 chōng (to rush), No. 101, or (b) 冬 dōng (winter), No. 165.
16	几	jǐ	some	13,685	No. 305 in Dictionary.
17	凵	kǎn	holder	0	Seen now only in combinations, e.g. 凶 xiōng (fierce), No. 777.
18	刀	dāo	knife	1,366	No. 140. Note the alt.form, always seen on the right in compound characters, e.g. 刻 kè (to carve), see No. 219.
19	力	lì	power	7,925	No. 421 in Dictionary.
20	勹	bāo	a parcel	0	This radical is the upper element of 包 bāo (wrap), No. 24.
21	匕	bǐ	a spoon	30	Seen in 比 bǐ (to compare), No. 38.
22	匚	fāng	a box	0	Seen in 匪 fěi (bandit), see No. 196.
23	匸	xǐ	a box	0	Seen in 医 yī (doctor), No. 817.

No.	Character	Pinyin	Meaning	Usage number	Comments and examples
24	十	*shí*	ten	36,452	No. 613 in Dictionary.
25	卜	*bǔ*	to divine	222	See No. 55 in Dictionary.
26	卪巳	*jié*	festival	0	Seen now only as one element in compound characters as in: 节 *jié* (festival), No. 342.
27	厂	*hàn*	a cliff	0	Seen in 厅 *tīng* (a hall), see No. 162.
28	厶	*sī*	private	15	Seen in 私 *sī* (private), No. 647.
29	又	*yòu*	again	26,230	No. 846 in Dictionary.
30	口	*kǒu*	mouth	3,594	No. 396 in Dictionary.
31	囗	*wéi*	an enclosure	0	Seen in 囚 *qiú* (to imprison).
32	土	*tǔ*	earth	3,085	No. 696 in Dictionary.
33	士	*shì*	bachelor	990	See No. 696 in Dictionary.
34	夂	*zhì*	to follow	0	Seen only as one element in a few compound characters e.g. 峰 *fēng* (summit), see No. 205.
35	夊	*suī*	moving slowly	0	Seen only as one element in a few compound characters e.g. 夏 *xià* (summer), see No. 748.
36	夕	*xī*	sunset	130	Seen in 梦(夢) *mèng* (dream), No. 471 in Dictionary.
37	大	*dà*	big	30,880	No. 131 in Dictionary.
38	女	*nǚ* (Third tone)	woman	2,066	No. 513 in Dictionary.
39	子	*zǐ*	son	6,453	No. 927 in Dictionary.
40	宀	*mián*	roof	0	Seen in: 穴 *xué* (cave), see No. 11.

No.	Character	Pinyin	Meaning	Usage number	Comments and examples
41	寸	cùn	very small	1,002	No. 127 in Dictionary.
42	小	xiǎo	small	19,870	No. 763 in Dictionary.
43	尢兀尣	wāng	lame	0	Seen in 尤 yóu (outstanding), No. 842.
44	尸	shī	a corpse	195	No. 608 in Dictionary.
45	屮	chè	plants sprouting	0	Seen in phonetic of: 逆 nì (disobey), No. 503 in Dictionary.
46	山	shān	mountain	3,730	No. 589 in Dictionary.
47	川	chuān	river	621	See No. 644, and note alt.form for radical 47 in some compounds e.g. 巡 xún (to patrol).
48	工	gōng	labour	2,951	No. 238 in Dictionary.
49	己	jǐ	oneself	442	No. 316 in Dictionary.
50	巾	jīn	napkin	239	See No. 57 for 布 bù (cloth).
51	干	gān	to do	4,170	No. 223 in Dictionary.
52	幺	yāo	one; small	21	Seen (plus radical 19) in 幼 yòu (young), No. 848 in Dictionary.
53	广	ān	covering	0	This radical is identical to the S form of guǎng (wide), No. 255 in Dictionary: 广, T form: 廣.
54	廴	yǐn	to move on	0	Seen in 建 jiàn (to build), No. 330.
55	廾	gǒng	hands joined	0	Seen in 弊 bì (fraud), see No. 40.
56	弋	yì	a dart	107	Seen in 式 shì (type), No. 622.
57	弓	gōng	a bow	803	No. 239 in Dictionary.
58	彐彑	jì	a pig's head	0	Seen in 寻(尋) xún (to seek), No. 792.

No.	Character	Pinyin	Meaning	Usage number	Comments and examples
59	彡	shān	feathers	0	Seen in 杉 shān (China fir), see No. 487.
60	彳	chì	a step with the left foot	0	Seen in 待 dāi (to stay), see No. 97.
61	心	xīn	heart	4,318	No. 767 in Dictionary; note alt.form of radical seen in 忙 máng (busy), No. 462 in Dictionary.
62	戈	gē	a spear	199	Seen in 找 zhǎo (look for), No. 884.
63	户	hù	a door	1,702	No. 284 in Dictionary.
64	手	shǒu	hand	5,665	No. 626 in Dictionary; note alt.form of radical 64 seen in most compounds e.g. 打 dǎ (strike), No. 130.
65	支	zhī	a branch	2,602	No. 897 in Dictionary.
66	攴 攵	pǔ	to tap	0	Seen in 敲 qiāo (to knock), see No. 228, note the commoner alt.form seen in 故 gù (incident), see No. 243.
67	文	wén	writing	3,452	No. 723 in Dictionary.
68	斗	dòu	struggle	1,142	No. 168 in Dictionary.
69	斤	jīn	a half kilo	3,031	No. 348 in Dictionary.
70	方	fāng	square	4,243	No. 194 in Dictionary.
71	无	wú	not	9,174	No. 729 in Dictionary.
72	日	rì	the sun	17,024	No. 574 in Dictionary.
73	曰	yuē	to speak	1,357	Seen in 曷 hé (how), the basic phonetic for the characters listed in entry No. 273 for 喝 hē (to drink).
74 (130)	月	yuè	the moon	8,281	No. 864 in Dictionary (for a special note on the number given to this radical see entry for radical 130 on p. 200).

No.	Character	Pinyin	Meaning	Usage number	Comments and examples
75	木	*mù*	tree	3,479	No. 487 in Dictionary.
76	欠	*qiàn*	to owe	273	No. 541 in Dictionary.
77	止	*zhǐ*	to stop	1,038	No. 901 in Dictionary.
78	歹	*dǎi*	evil	17	Seen in 残 *cán* (deficient), see No. 540.
79	殳	*shū*	a spear	198	See No. 597 for 设 *shè* (set up).
80	毋	*wú*	not	85	D.f. 母 *mǔ* (mother), No. 486.
81	比	*bǐ*	to compare	11,127	No. 38 (see also radical 21, p.194).
82	毛	*máo*	hair	4,114	No. 463 in Dictionary.
83	氏	*shì*	a family	1,904	Seen in 纸 *zhǐ* (paper), No. 903.
84	气	*qì*	gas	3,925	No. 535 in Dictionary.
85	水	*shuǐ*	water	18,930	No. 643 in Dictionary. Note the alt.form in compounds, e.g. 汁 *zhī* (juice), see No. 613.
86	火	*huǒ*	fire	1,854	No. 301 in Dictionary. Note also alt.form seen for example in: 焦 *jiāo* (burnt), No. 335.
87	爪	*zhǎo* or *zhuǎ*	claw	24 or 142	Seen in 爬 *pá* (to crawl), see No. 12.
88	父	*fù*	father	764	No. 214 in Dictionary.
89	爻	*yáo*	intertwine	0	Seen in 爽 *shuāng* (bright; frank).
90	爿	*pán*	slit bamboo	8	Seen in 将(將) *jiāng* (to handle), No. 331.
91	片	*piàn*	a slice	3,476	No. 522 in Dictionary.
92	牙	*yá*	tooth	426	No. 795 in Dictionary.
93	牛	*niú*	ox	1,587	No. 508 in Dictionary.

No.	Character	Pinyin	Meaning	Usage number	Comments and examples
94	犬	*quǎn*	dog	71	This radical is more generally seen in its alt.form, e.g. 犹(猶) *yóu* (just as), see No. 842.
95	玄	*xuán*	black	198	No. 788 in Dictionary.
96	王	*wáng*	king	4,127	No. 706 in Dictionary[2].
97	瓜	*guā*	melon	442	No. 247 in Dictionary.
98	瓦	*wǎ*	tile	832	No. 701 in Dictionary.
99	甘	*gān*	sweet	271	No. 224 in Dictionary.
100	生	*shēng*	life	8,722	No. 604 in Dictionary.
101	用	*yòng*	to use	40,684	No. 841 in Dictionary.
102	田	*tián*	field	2,201	No. 682 in Dictionary.
103	疋	*pǐ*	be equal to	0	Seen in 定 *dìng* (to fix), No. 163.
104	疒	*nì*	disease	0	Seen in 病 *bìng* (disease), No. 53.
105	癶	*bò*	back to back	0	Seen in 登 *dēng* (to ascend), No. 148.
106	白	*bái*	white	3,878	No. 15 in Dictionary.
107	皮	*pí*	skin	1,616	No. 521 in Dictionary.
108	皿	*mǐn*	utensil	33	Seen in 盆 *pén* (basin), see No. 199.
109	目	*mù*	eye	1,411	No. 488 in Dictionary.
110	矛	*máo*	a spear	96	Seen in 矜 *jīn* (pity).
111	矢	*shǐ*	an arrow	90	Seen in 矮 *ǎi* (short), No. 3 in Dictionary.
112	石	*shí*	stone	2,686	No. 614 in Dictionary.

[2] Although Mathews gives this radical as 玉, pronounced *yù* and meaning jade, he also lists an alt.form, 王, which is identical to the character for king, and under which *all* the characters in his dictionary are listed. For this reason in this Dictionaryradical No. 96 refers only to 王 *wáng* (king), see entry No. 706.

No.	Character	Pinyin	Meaning	Usage number	Comments and examples
113	示	*shì*	show	3,532	No. 620 in Dictionary; note the alt.form of this radical seen in compound characters, e.g. 神 *shén* (god).
114	内	*rǒu*	footprint	0	Seen in 愚 *yú* (stupid), see No. 859.
115	禾	*hé*	crops	154	Seen in 秆 *gǎn* (stalk), see No. 223.
116	穴	*xué*	cave	362	Seen in 究 *jiū* (study), No. 362.
117	立	*lì*	to stand	3,409	No. 422 in Dictionary.
118	竹	*zhú*	bamboo	839	No. 917 in Dictionary. Note this radical appears in compound characters in its short form, e.g. 笔 *bǐ* (a pen).
119	米	*mǐ*	rice	5,517	No. 472 in Dictionary.
120	丝(絲)	*sī*	silk	2,055	No. 646 in Dictionary; note alt.form in S form compound characters: e.g. 纱 *shā* (yarn), see No. 595.
121	缶	*fǒu*	a jar	0	Seen in 缺 *quē* (to lack), No. 562.
122	网(網)	*wǎng*	a net	1,171	No. 707 in Dictionary. This radical is usually placed above the phonetic and has the following alt.form seen in: 置 *zhì* (to put), see No. 900.
123	羊	*yáng*	sheep	934	No. 805 in Dictionary.
124	羽	*yǔ*	feather	201	No. 854 in Dictionary.
125	老	*lǎo*	old	7,484	No. 410 in Dictionary.
126	而	*ér*	and	44,153	No. 184 in Dictionary.
127	耒	*lěi*	plough	0	Seen in 耕 *gēng* (plough), No. 237.

No.	Character	Pinyin	Meaning	Usage number	Comments and examples
128	耳	*ěr*	ear	982	No. 185 in Dictionary.
129	聿	*yù*	pencil	23	Seen in 津 *jīn* (a ford), No. 350.
130 (74)	肉 月	*ròu*	flesh	1,102	No. 578 in Dictionary[3].
131	臣	*chén*	an official	685	No. 86 in Dictionary.
132	自	*zì*	oneself	6,124	No. 928 in Dictionary.
133	至	*zhì*	until	6,914	No. 905 in Dictionary.
134	臼	*jiù*	mortar	26	Seen in 旧 (舊) *jiù* (old), No. 365.
135	舌	*shé*	tongue	362	No. 596 in Dictionary.
136	舛	*chuǎn*	error	0	Seen in 瞬 *shùn* (wink), see No. 439.
137	舟	*zhōu*	boat	250	Seen in 船 *chuán* (boat), No. 113.
138	艮	*gěn*	tough	0	Seen in 很 *hěn* (very), No. 277.
139	色	*sè*	colour	4,097	No. 587 in Dictionary.
140	草 艹	*cǎo*	grass	1,952	See No. 873 for 早 *zǎo* (morning)[4].
141	虍	*hū*	tiger	0	Seen in 虎 *hǔ* (tiger), No. 283.
142	虫	*chóng*	insect	1,551	No. 103 in Dictionary.
143	血	*xuè*	blood	1,134	No. 791 in Dictionary.

[3] Although the first of these two forms (肉) is given as radical 130 it appears only in 4 of the 168 characters listed in Mathews' dictionary under this radical, being replaced in all other cases by the second, alternative form (月) which is identical to radical 74. In this Dictionary the term 'radical 130' applies only to this second, alternative form. The same occurs in L. Wieger's book *Chinese Characters*, Dover Publications, New York, 1965, where in the list for radical 130 only 5 of the 178 characters listed actually contain the form 肉, being replaced in all other cases by the form 月.

[4] In all compound characters only the alt.form 艹 is used.

No.	Character	Pinyin	Meaning	Usage number	Comments and examples
144	行	*xíng*	to walk	4,548	No. 774 in Dictionary.
145	衣	*yī*	clothing	778	No. 816; note alt.form in compounds, e.g. 衬 *chèn* (lining), see No. 127.
146	西	*xī*	west	2,964	No. 737 in Dictionary.
147	见(見)	*jiàn*	to see	6,533	No. 328 in Dictionary.
148	角	*jiǎo*	a horn	5,050	No. 336 in Dictionary.
149	讠(言)	*yán*	speech	2,817	No. 799 in Dictionary.
150	谷	*gǔ*	valley	986	See entry No. 858 for 欲 *yù* (desire).
151	豆	*dòu*	beans	577	No. 169 in Dictionary.
152	豕	*shǐ*	pig	10	Seen in 猪 T form for *zhū* (pig), the S form is 猪, see entry No. 916.
153	豸	*zhì*	insect	0	Seen in 豹 *bào* (leopard).
154	贝(貝)	*bèi*	shellfish	342	Seen in 败 *bài* (to be defeated), No. 17.
155	赤	*chì*	red	370	No. 100 in Dictionary.
156	走	*zǒu*	to walk	9,583	No. 931 in Dictionary.
157	足	*zú*	foot	1,302	No. 934 in Dictionary.
158	身	*shēn*	body	2,025	No. 600 in Dictionary.
159	车(車)	*chē*	vehicle	3,265	No. 83 in Dictionary.
160	辛	*xīn*	hot	339	No. 768 in Dictionary.
161	辰	*chén*	morning	74	Seen in 晨 *chén* (morning), see No. 891.
162	辶	*chūo*	walking	0	Seen in 边(邊) *biān* (side), No. 43.
163	邑 阝	*yì*	region	78	In compound characters this radical appears only in the alt.form, and on the right, as in 部 *bù* (part), No. 59.

No.	Character	Pinyin	Meaning	Usage number	Comments and examples
164	酉	*yǒu*	tenth	13	Seen in 酒 *jiǔ* (wine), No. 364.
165	采	*biàn*	to separate	0	Seen in 釉 *yòu* (glaze), see No. 843.
166	里	*lǐ*	inside	26,650	No. 420 in Dictionary.
167	钅(金)	*jīn*	metal	3,131	No. 349 in Dictionary.
168	长(長)	*cháng*	long	8,536	No. 76 in Dictionary.
169	门(門)	*mén*	door	4,078	No. 468 in Dictionary.
170	阜阝	*fù*	a mound	41	In compound characters this radical appears only in the alt.form, and on the left, e.g. 限 *xiàn* (limit), see No. 277 in Dictionary.
171	隶	*dài*	to reach to	0	Seen in 逮 *dǎi* (to seize).
172	隹	*zhuī*	short-tailed birds	0	Seen in 焦 *jiāo* (burnt), No. 335.
173	雨	*yǔ*	rain	1,473	No. 855 in Dictionary.
174	青	*qīng*	green	2,238	No. 551 in Dictionary.
175	非	*fēi*	wrong	4,671	No. 196 in Dictionary.
176	面	*miàn*	face	7,131	No. 476 in Dictionary.
177	革	*gé*	leather	409	No. 231 in Dictionary.
178	韦(韋)	*wéi*	hides	0	Seen in 圍 T form for *wéi* (to enclose), S form: 围 see No. 714 in Dictionary.
179	韭	*jiǔ*	leeks	17	Seen in 籤 T form for *qiān* (to sign), S form: 签, see No. 426 in Dictionary.
180	音	*yīn*	sound	2,710	No. 831 in Dictionary.
181	页(頁)	*yè*	leaf	1,530	No. 813 in Dictionary. This radical is always placed on the right.
182	风(風)	*fēng*	wind	3,007	No. 203 in Dictionary.

No.	Character	Pinyin	Meaning	Usage number	Comments and examples
183	飞(飛)	*fēi*	to fly	1,624	No. 195 in Dictionary.
184	饣(食)	*shí*	food	1,952	No. 617 in Dictionary.
185	首	*shǒu*	head	1,313	No. 628 in Dictionary.
186	香	*xiāng*	fragrant	1,167	No. 757 in Dictionary.
187	马(馬)	*mǎ*	horse	3,465	No. 457 in Dictionary.
188	骨	*gǔ*	bone	928	No. 244 in Dictionary.
189	高	*gāo*	tall	13,169	No. 228 in Dictionary.
190	髟	*biāo*	hair	0	Seen in 髯 *rán* (whiskers).
191	鬥	*dòu*	struggle	1,142	T form for No. 168, S form: 斗.
192	鬯	*chàng*	sacrificial wine	0	Seen in 鬱, T form for *yù* (gloomy), S form: 郁.
193	鬲	*gé*	pot	0	Seen in 隔 *gé* (to separate), No. 232.
194	鬼	*guǐ*	spirit	553	No. 257 in Dictionary.
195	鱼(魚)	*yú*	fish	3,646	No. 852 in Dictionary.
196	鸟(鳥)	*niǎo*	bird	482	No. 506 in Dictionary.
197	卤(鹵)	*lǔ*	salt	77	Seen in 鹹 T form for *xián* (salt), S form: 咸, see reference in No. 226.
198	鹿	*lù*	a deer	90	Seen in 塵 T form for *chén* (dust), S form: 尘, No. 85 in Dictionary.
199	麦(麥)	*mài*	wheat	892	No. 459 in Dictionary.
200	麻	*má*	hemp	570	No. 456 in Dictionary.
201	黄	*huáng*	yellow	2,668	No. 293 in Dictionary.
202	黍	*shǔ*	millet	35	Seen in 黏 *nián* (sticky), see No. 879.
203	黑	*hēi*	black	2,538	No. 276 in Dictionary.

No.	Character	Pinyin	Meaning	Usage number	Comments and examples
204	黹	*zhǐ*	embroidery	0	Seen in 黻 *fú* (an embroidered robe).
205	黾(黽)	*mǐn*	a toad	0	Seen in 鼋(鼋) *yuán* (soft-shelled turtle).
206	鼎	*dǐng*	cooking vessel	149	Seen in 鼐 *nài* (an incense tripod).
207	鼓	*gǔ*	drum	717	No. 245 in Dictionary.
208	鼠	*shǔ*	mouse	225	No. 636 in Dictionary.
209	鼻	*bí*	nose	220	No. 37 in Dictionary.
210	齐(齊)	*qí*	neat	1,493	No. 530 in Dictionary.
211	齿(齒)	*chǐ*	tooth	1,000	No. 99 in Dictionary.
212	龙(龍)	*lóng*	dragon	790	No. 443 in Dictionary.
213	龟(龜)	*guī*	tortoise	103	
214	龠	*yuè*	a flute	0	Seen in 龥 T form for *yù* (to implore), S form: 吁.

Supplementary note to Appendix B. The Radicals

For the 24 radicals which have both S and T forms (viz. Nos: 120, 122, 147, 149, 154, 159, 167, 168, 169, 178, 181, 182, 183, 184, 187, 195, 196, 197, 199, 205, 210, 211, 212, 213), both forms are given when they occur as key characters in the Dictionary but otherwise, in the Dictionary, and in the pinyin index, the practice is followed of giving only the S form, unless the subsequent T form character shows a further variation.

Thus, for example, entry No. 185, for 耳 *ěr* (ear), when giving important compounds with three of the radicals listed above reads as follows:

+ 184: 饵 *ěr* (cakes), S form, omitting 餌 T form;

+ 30 and 159: 辑 *jí* (to edit), S form, omitting 輯 T form;

+ 169: 闻 *wén* (to hear), S form, omitting 聞 T form.

These 24 radicals are as follows

120: 丝(絲); 122: 网(網); 147: 见(見); 149: 讠(言); 154: 贝(貝); 159: 车(車);
167: 钅(金); 168: 长(長); 169: 门(門); 178: 韦(韋); 181: 页(頁); 182: 风(風);
183: 飞(飛); 184: 饣(食); 187: 马(馬); 195: 鱼(魚); 196: 鸟(鳥); 197: 卤(鹵);
199: 麦(麥); 205: 黾(黽); 210: 齐(齊); 211: 齿(齒); 212: 龙(龍); 213: 龟(龜)

A number of radicals have alternative forms which are detailed with examples on pages 192–204. The following 12 occur frequently:

Radical 9 人, with alt.form 倘; Radical 18 刀, with alt.form 刻;

Radical 61 心, with alt.form 忙; Radical 64 手, with alt.form 打;

Radical 85 水, with alt.form 汁; Radical 86 火, with alt.form 焦;

Radical 94 犬, with alt.form 犹; Radical 113 示, with alt.form 神 (D. this f. alt.form of Radical 145 as in 衬 – see below); Radical 118 竹, with alt.form 笔; Radical 122 网, with alt.form 置; Radical 145 衣, with alt.form 衬.

Pinyin index for the Dictionary

For each of the Dictionary's 2,108 characters the number of the entry (No.) and the Radical (R) under which it can be found are given below. (See also p. 277 for a note on the allocation of the simplified characters to one of the traditional 214 radicals.)

A

1	ā	阿	proper name	No.388,R170.
2	ā á ǎ à a	啊	oh!; eh?; what?	No.388,R30.
3	āi	哎	oh!; look out!	No.1,R30.
4	āi ái	挨	approach; suffer	No.2,R64.
5	āi	埃	dust	No.2,R32.
6	āi ài	唉	OK; what?; alas!	No.2,R30.
7	ǎi	矮	short; low	No.3,R111.
8	ài	爱(愛)	love	No.4,R87 (61).
9	ān	安	peaceful	No.5,R40.
10	ān	氨	ammonia	No.5,R84.
11	ǎn	俺	I; we	No.157,R9.
12	àn	按	press down	No.5,R64.
13	àn	胺	amine	No.5,R130.
14	àn	案	table; case	No.6,R75.
15	àn	暗	dark	No.7,R72.
16	àn	岸	bank; shore	No.223,R46.
17	āo	凹	concave	No.8,R17.
18	āo áo	熬	boil	No.9,R86.
19	ào	奥	profound	No.10,R37.

B

20	bā	八	eight	No.11,R12.
21	bā	巴	hope earnestly	No.12,R49.
22	bā ba	吧	crack!; let us!	No.12,R30.
23	bǎ bà	把	hold; handle	No.12,R64.

24	*bà*	爸	dad	No.12,R88.
25	*bá*	拔	pull out	No.13,R64.
26	*bà*	罢(罷)	stop	No.14,R122 (122).
27	*bà*	坝(壩)	dam	No.17,R32 (32).
28	*bái*	白	white	No.15,R106.
29	*bǎi*	百	hundred	No.16,R106.
30	*bǎi*	摆(擺)	put	No.14,R64 (64).
31	*bài*	败	be defeated	No.17,R66.
32	*bài*	拜	do obeisance	No.18,R64.
33	*bān*	班	class; team	No.19,R96.
34	*bān*	斑	spot; speck	No.19,R67.
35	*bān*	般	sort; kind	No.20,R137.
36	*bān*	搬	remove	No.20,R64.
37	*bān*	扳	pull; turn	No.192,R64.
38	*bǎn*	版	edition	No.192,R91.
39	*bǎn*	板(闆)	board	No.192,R75 (169).
40	*bàn*	办(辦)	to do	No.21,R19 (160).
41	*bàn*	半	half	No.22,R24.
42	*bàn*	拌	mix	No.22,R64.
43	*bāng*	邦	nation	No.23,R163.
44	*bāng*	帮(幫)	help	No.23,R50 (50).
45	*bàng*	棒	cudgel	No.206,R75.
46	*bāo*	包	wrap	No.24,R20.
47	*bāo*	胞	afterbirth	No.24,R130.
48	*báo*	薄	thin	No.54,R140.
49	*bǎo*	保	protect	No.26,R9.
50	*bǎo*	堡	fort	No.26,R32.
51	*bǎo*	饱	be full	No.24,R184.
52	*bǎo*	宝(寶)	treasure	No.25,R40.
53	*bào*	抱	embrace	No.24,R64.
54	*bào*	刨	to plane	No.24,R18.
55	*bào*	报(報)	report	No.27,R64 (32).
56	*bào*	暴	violent	No.28,R72.
57	*bào*	爆	explode	No.28,R86.
58	*bēi*	杯	glass	No.56,R75.
59	*bēi*	卑	low	No.29,R24.
60	*bēi bèi*	背	carry; back	No.30,R130.
61	*běi*	北	north	No.31,R21.

62	*bèi*	辈	lifetime	No.196,R159.
63	*bèi*	贝	shellfish	No.17,R154.
64	*bèi*	备(備)	prepare	No.32,R102 (9).
65	*bèi*	被	quilt	No.33,R145.
66	*bèi*	倍	times	No.34,R9.
67	*bēn bèn*	奔	rush	No.35,R37.
68	*běn*	本	root	No.36,R75.
69	*běn*	苯	benzol	No.36,R140.
70	*bèng*	泵	a pump	No.643,R112.
71	*bī*	逼	to force	No.213,R162.
72	*bí*	鼻	nose	No.37,R209.
73	*bǐ*	比	compare	No.38,R81.
74	*bǐ*	笔(筆)	pen	No.39,R118 (118).
75	*bǐ*	彼	that; other	No.521,R60.
76	*bì*	毕(畢)	accomplish	No.38,R81 (102).
77	*bì*	币(幣)	currency	No.40,R50 (50).
78	*bì*	闭	close	No.60,R169.
79	*bì*	弊	fraud	No.40,R55.
80	*bì*	必	must; have to	No.41,R61.
81	*bì*	避	avoid	No.42,R162.
82	*bì*	壁	wall	No.42,R32.
83	*bì*	臂	the arm	No.42,R130.
84	*biān*	边(邊)	side	No.43,R162 (162).
85	*biān*	编	organise	No.44,R120.
86	*biǎn*	扁	flat	No.44,R63.
87	*biàn*	变(變)	change	No.45,R29 (149).
88	*biàn*	便	convenient	No.46,R9.
89	*biàn*	辨	differentiate	No.47,R160.
90	*biàn*	辩	argue	No.47,R160.
91	*biàn*	遍	everywhere	No.44,R162.
92	*biāo*	标(標)	mark; sign	No.48,R75 (75).
93	*biāo*	彪	young tiger	No.283,R59.
94	*biǎo*	表	surface; a watch	No.49,R145.
95	*bié biè*	别	leave; don't!	No.50,R18.
96	*bīng*	兵	weapons	No.51,R12.
97	*bīng*	冰	ice	No.643,R15.
98	*bìng*	并(並)	combine	No.52,R1.
99	*bǐng*	丙	third	No.53,R1.

100	*bǐng*	柄	handle	No.53,R75.
101	*bǐng*	饼	cake	No.52,R184.
102	*bǐng*	炳	bright	No.53,R86.
103	*bìng*	病	ill; disease	No.53,R104.
104	*bō*	剥	deprive	No.448,R18.
105	*bō*	播	sow	No.189,R64.
106	*bō*	拨(撥)	move	187,R64 (64).
107	*bō*	波	wave	No.521,R85.
108	*bó*	博	rich	No.54,R24.
109	*bó*	薄	slight	No.54,R140.
110	*bó*	伯	uncle	No.15,R9.
111	*bó*	泊	to moor	No.15,R85.
112	*bǔ*	补(補)	amend	No.55,R145 (145).
113	*bǔ*	捕	seize	No.55,R64.
114	*bǔ*	卜	divination	No.55,R25.
115	*bù*	不	no; not	No.56,R1.
116	*bù*	布	cloth	No.57,R50.
117	*bù*	步	step	No.58,R77.
118	*bù*	部	part	No.59,R163.

C

119	*cā*	擦	rub; wipe	No.73,R64.
120	*cāi*	猜	guess	No.551,R94.
121	*cái*	才	ability	No.60,R64.
122	*cái*	材	material	No.60,R75.
123	*cái*	财	wealth	No.60,R154.
124	*cái*	裁	cut	No.61,R145.
125	*cǎi*	采(採)	select	No.62,R165 (64).
126	*cǎi*	彩	colour	No.62,R59.
127	*cài*	菜	vegetables	No.62,R140.
128	*cān*	参(參)	join	No.63,R28 (28).
129	*cán*	蚕(蠶)	silkworm	No.681,R142 (142).
130	*cán*	残(殘)	injure	No.540,R78 (78).
131	*cāng*	仓(倉)	storehouse	No.64,R9 (9).
132	*cáng*	藏	hide	No.65,R140.
133	*cāo*	操	grasp	No.66,R64.
134	*cáo*	曹	you; a surname	No.872,R73.

135	cáo	槽	trough	No.872,R75.
136	cǎo	草	grass	No.873,R140.
137	cè	策	plan	No.124,R118.
138	cè	侧	side	No.874,R9.
139	cè	测	survey	No.874,R85.
140	cè	册(冊)	volume	No.67,R13 (1).
141	céng	曾	once	No.68,R73.
142	céng	层(層)	layer	No.68,R44 (44).
143	chā	叉	fork	No.846,R29.
144	chā chà	差	difference	No.69,R48.
145	chā	插	insert	No.70,R64.
146	chá	茬	stubble	No.870,R140.
147	chá	茶	tea	No.71,R140.
148	chá	查	check	No.72,R75.
149	chá	察	examine	No.73,R40.
150	chāi	拆	tear open	No.653,R64.
151	chái	柴	firewood	No.122,R75.
152	chān	掺	mix	No.63,R64.
153	chān	搀	mix	No.63,R64.
154	chán	缠(纏)	tangle	No.74,R120 (120).
155	chǎn	产(產)	produce	No.75,R117 (100).
156	chǎn	铲(鏟)	shovel	No.75,R167 (167).
157	chāng	昌	prosperous	No.81,R72.
158	cháng / chǎng	场(場)	open space / meeting place	No.77,R32 (32). / No.77.
159	cháng	长(長)	long	No.76,R4 (168).
160	cháng	尝(嘗)	taste	No.78,R42 (30).
161	cháng	常	often	No.79,R50.
162	cháng	肠(腸)	intestines	No.77,R130 (130).
163	chǎng	厂(廠)	factory	No.80,R27 (53).
164	chàng	唱	sing	No.81,R30.
165	chāo	超	exceed	No.883,R156.
166	chāo	钞	banknote	No.595,R167.
167	cháo	朝	court; towards	No.82,R74.
168	cháo	潮	tide	No.82,R85.
169	chǎo	炒	stir-fry	No.595,R86.
170	chē	车(車)	vehicle	No.83,R159 (159).
171	chě	扯	pull	No.901,R64.

172	*chè*	撤	remove	No.84,R64.
173	*chén*	尘(塵)	dust	No.85,R42 (32).
174	*chén*	臣	official	No.86,R131.
175	*chén*	晨	morning	No.891,R72.
176	*chén*	沉	deep	No.87,R85.
177	*chén*	沈	deep	No.87,R85.
178	*chén*	陈(陳)	explain	No.88,R170 (170).
179	*chèn*	衬(襯)	lining	No.89,R145 (145).
180	*chèn*	趁	use advantage	No.90,R156.
181	*chēng*	撑	prop up	No.881,R64.
182	*chēng*	称(稱)	name	No.91,R115 (115).
183	*chéng*	成	become	No.92,R62.
184	*chéng*	诚	honest	No.92,R149.
185	*chéng*	城	wall	No.92,R32.
186	*chéng*	盛	fill	No.92,R108.
187	*chéng*	呈	assume	No.93,R30.
188	*chéng*	程	rule	No.93,R115.
189	*chéng*	承	bear	No.94,R64.
190	*chéng*	乘	ride	No.95,R4.
191	*chī*	吃	eat	No.96,R30.
192	*chí*	持	hold	No.97,R64.
193	*chí*	池	pool	No.809,R85.
194	*chí*	迟(遲)	slow	No.98,R162 (162).
195	*chǐ*	齿(齒)	tooth	No.99,R211 (211).
196	*chǐ*	尺	ruler	No.98,R44.
197	*chì*	赤	bare	No.100,R155.
198	*chì*	翅	wing	No.854,R124.
199	*chōng*	充	full	No.102,R10.
200	*chōng*	冲(衝)	rush	No.101,R15 (144).
	chòng		towards	No.101.
201	*chóng*	虫(蟲)	insect	No.103,R142.
202	*chóng*	重	repeat	No.104,R166.
203	*chōu*	抽	take out	No.843,R64.
204	*chóu*	愁	worry	No.555,R61.
205	*chóu*	筹(籌)	a chip	No.629,118 (118).
206	*chǒu*	丑(醜)	ugly	No.509,R1 (164).
207	*chòu*	臭	foul	No.105,R132.
208	*chū*	出	go out	No.106,R17.

209	chū	初	beginning	No.107,R18.
210	chú	锄	hoe	No.919,R167.
211	chú	雏(雛)	young	No.558,R172 (172).
212	chú	除	except	No.108,R170.
213	chǔ chù	处(處)	get along with place	No.109,R25 (141).
214	chǔ	楚	clear	No.110,R75.
215	chǔ	储	store up	No.916,R9.
216	chù	触(觸)	touch	No.111,R148 (148).
217	chuān	川	river	No.644,R47.
218	chuān	穿	penetrate	No.112,R116.
219	chuán	传(傳)	pass on	No.921,R9 (9).
220	chuán	船	boat	No.113,R137.
221	chuàn	串	string together	No.114,R2.
222	chuāng	窗	window	No.115,R116.
223	chuāng chuàng	创(創)	wound start	No.64,R18 (18). No.64.
224	chuáng	床	bed	No.116,R53.
225	chuǎng	闯	rush	No.457,R169.
226	chuī	吹	blow	No.117,R30.
227	chuí	锤	hammer	No.118,R167.
228	chuí	垂	hang down	No.118,R33.
229	chūn	春	spring	No.119,R72.
230	chún	醇	alcohol	No.758,R164.
231	chún	纯	simple	No.120,R120.
232	cì	刺	thorn	No.124,R18.
233	cí	磁	magnetism	No.926,R112.
234	cí	雌	female	No.122,R172.
235	cí	辞(辭)	diction	No.596,R160 (160).
236	cí	瓷	porcelain	No.123,R98.
237	cí	词	word	No.121,R149.
238	cǐ	此	this	No.122,R77.
239	cì	赐	grant	No.826,R154.
240	cì	次	time	No.123,R76.
241	cōng	葱	onion	No.735,R140.
242	cóng cōng	从(從)	from (used in combination): calm, plentiful	No.125,R9 (60). No.125.
243	cóng	丛(叢)	thicket	No.125,R1 (29).

244	*còu*	凑(湊)	collect	No.932,R15 (85).
245	*cū*	粗	thick	No.933,R119.
246	*cù*	醋	vinegar	No.346,R164.
247	*cù*	促	urge on	No.934,R9.
248	*cuàn*	篡	usurp	No.489,R118.
249	*cuī*	催	urge on	No.642,R11.
250	*cuì*	脆	fragile	No.710,R130.
251	*cuì*	翠	green	No.938,R124.
252	*cūn*	村(邨)	village	No.127,R75 (163).
253	*cún*	存	exist	No.126,R39.
254	*cùn*	寸	very small	No.127,R41.
255	*cuò*	错	complex	No.346,R167.

D

256	*dā*	搭	build	No.128,R64.
257	*dā & dá*	答	answer	No.128,R118.
258	*dá*	达(達)	reach	No.129,R162 (162).
259	*dǎ*	打	strike	No.130,R64.
260	*dà*	大	big	No.131,R37.
261	*dāi*	呆	blank	No.26,R75.
262	*dāi*	待	stay	No.615,R60.
	dài		deal with	No.615.
263	*dài*	戴	put on	No.134,R62.
264	*dài*	带(帶)	belt	No.133,R50 (50).
265	*dài*	代	replace	No.132,R9.
266	*dài*	贷	loan	No.132,R154.
267	*dài*	袋	bag	No.132,R145.
268	*dān*	担(擔)	carry	No.136,64 (64).
269	*dān*	丹	red	No.190,R3.
270	*dān*	单(單)	single	No.135,R24 (30).
271	*dǎn*	胆(膽)	courage	No.136,R130 (130).
272	*dàn*	氮	nitrogen	No.670,R84.
273	*dàn*	但	but	No.136,R9.
274	*dàn*	淡	pale	No.670,R85.
275	*dàn*	弹(彈)	bullet	No.135,R57 (57).
276	*dàn*	蛋	egg	No.137,R142.
277	*dāng*	当(當)	ought	No.138,R79 (102).
	dàng		treat as	No.138.

278	*dǎng*	挡(擋)	ward off	No.138,R64 (64).
279	*dǎng*	党(黨)	party	No.139,R10 (203).
280	*dàng*	档(檔)	shelves	No.138,R75 (75).
281	*dāo*	刀	knife	No.140,R18.
282	*dǎo*	倒	fall	No.142,R9.
	dào		pour	No.142.
283	*dǎo*	岛(島)	island	No.141,R46 (46).
284	*dǎo*	导(導)	lead	No.143,R49 (41).
285	*dào*	到	arrive	No.142,R18.
286	*dào*	稻	rice	No.144,R115.
287	*dào*	道	road	No.143,R162.
288	*dào*	盗	steal	No.123,R108.
289	*dé*	德	virtue	No.146,R60.
290	*dé*	得	obtain	No.145,R60.
	de		particle of possibility	No.145.
291	*de*	的	particle of possession	No.147,R106.
292	*de*	地	adverbial indicator	No.152,R32.
290	*děi*	得	must	No.145.
293	*dēng*	灯(燈)	lamp	No.148,R86 (86).
294	*dēng*	登	ascend	No.148,R105.
295	*děng*	等	wait	No.149,R118.
296	*dèng*	邓(鄧)	a name	No.148,R163 (163).
297	*dī*	堤	dyke	No.624,R32.
298	*dī*	低	low	No.150,R9.
299	*dī*	滴	drip	No.151,R85.
300	*dí*	敌(敵)	enemy	No.151,R135 (66).
301	*dǐ*	抵	support	No.150,R64.
302	*dǐ*	底	base	No.150,R53.
303	*dì*	地	earth	No.152,R32.
304	*dì*	蒂	base of a fruit	No.154,R140.
305	*dì*	第	indicates ordinal	No.153,R118.
306	*dì*	帝	emperor	No.154,R50.
307	*dì*	弟	younger brother	No.153,R57.
308	*dì*	递(遞)	hand over	No.153,R162 (162).
309	*diǎn*	碘	iodine	No.155,R112.
310	*diǎn*	点(點)	a drop	No.156,R86 (203).
311	*diǎn*	典	dictionary	No.155,R12.
312	*diàn*	垫(墊)	fill up; pad	No.899,R32 (32).

313	*diàn*	电(電)	electricity	No.157,R73&2 (173).
314	*diàn*	店	shop	No.158,R53.
315	*diàn*	殿	palace	No.241,R79.
316	*diào*	掉	fall	No.161,R64.
317	*diào*	吊	hang	No.159,R30.
318	*diào*	调	transfer	No.160,R149.
319	*diē*	跌	fall	No.609,R157.
320	*diē*	爹	dad	No.178,R88.
321	*dié*	迭	alternate	No.609,R162.
322	*dié*	叠(疊)	fold	No.846,R29 (102).
323	*dīng*	丁	man	No.162,R1.
324	*dīng*	盯	stare at	No.162,R109.
325	*dīng & dìng*	钉	nail	No.162,R167.
326	*dǐng*	顶	top of the head	No.162,R181.
327	*dìng*	锭	tablet	No.163,R167.
328	*dìng*	定	fix	No.163,R40.
329	*dìng*	订	agree on	No.162,R149.
330	*diū*	丢	lose	No.560,R1.
331	*dōng*	东(東)	east	No.164,R1 (75).
332	*dōng*	冬	winter	No.165,R15.
333	*dǒng*	董	supervise	No.104,R140.
334	*dǒng*	懂	understand	No.104,R61.
335	*dòng*	动(動)	move	No.166,R19 (19).
336	*dòng*	冻(凍)	freeze	No.164,R15 (15).
337	*dòng*	洞	hole	No.689,R85.
338	*dōu*	都	all	No.167,R163.
339	*dǒu*	抖	tremble	No.168,R64.
340	*dǒu* *dòu*	斗(鬥)	a measure struggle	No.168,R68 (191). No.168.
341	*dòu*	豆	beans	No.169,R151.
338	*dū*	都	capital	No.167,R163.
342	*dū*	督	supervise	No.632,R109.
343	*dú*	毒	poison	No.170,R80.
344	*dú*	独(獨)	alone	No.103,R94 (94).
345	*dú*	读(讀)	read	No.458,R149 (149).
346	*dǔ*	堵	stop up	No.916,R32.
347	*dù*	杜	prevent	No.696,R75.
348	*dù*	度	degree	No.171,R53.

349	*dù*	渡	cross	No.171,R85.
350	*duān*	端	end	No.172,R117.
351	*duǎn*	短	short	No.173,R111.
352	*duàn*	锻	forge	No.174,R167.
353	*duàn*	段	section	No.174,R79.
354	*duàn*	断(斷)	break	No.175,R69 (69).
355	*duī*	堆	heap	No.642,R32.
356	*duì*	队(隊)	team	No.176,R170 (170).
357	*duì*	对(對)	opposite	No.177,R29 (41).
358	*dūn*	吨(噸)	ton	No.120,R30 (30).
359	*dūn*	蹲	squat	No.939,R157.
360	*dùn*	顿	pause	No.120,R181.
361	*duō*	多	many	No.178,R36.
362	*duó*	夺(奪)	seize	No.179,R37 (37).
363	*duǒ*	躲	hide	No.180,R158.
364	*duǒ*	朵	measure (flower)	No.180,R75.

E

365	*é*	鹅	goose	No.726,R196.
366	*é*	俄	Russian	No.726,R9.
367	*é*	额	forehead	No.390,R181.
368	*é*	讹	mistaken	No.287,R149.
369	*ě & è*	恶(惡)	evil	No.181,R61 (61).
370	*è*	饿	hunger	No.726,R184.
371	*ēn*	恩	kindness	No.182,R61.
372	*ér*	而	and	No.184,R126.
373	*ér*	儿(兒)	child	No.183,R10 (10).
374	*ěr*	耳	ear	No.185,R128.
375	*ěr*	尔(爾)	you	No.502,R42 (89).
376	*ěr*	饵	cakes	No.185,R184.
377	*èr*	二	two	No.186,R7.

F

378	*fā*	发(發)	send out	No.187,R29 (105).
378	*fà*	发(髮)	hair	No.187,R29 (190).
379	*fá*	伐	fell	No.884,R9.

380	fá	阀	valve	No.884,R169.
381	fǎ	法	law	No.188,R85.
382	fān	番	time	No.189,R102.
383	fān	翻	overturn	No.189,R124.
384	fán	繁	numerous	No.191,R120.
385	fán	凡	anyone	No.190,R16.
386	fǎn	反	return	No.192,R29.
387	fǎn	返	return	No.192,R162.
388	fàn	范(範)	pattern	No.193,R140 (118).
389	fàn	犯	violate	No.193,R94.
390	fàn	饭	food	No.192,R184.
391	fāng	芳	fragrant	No.194,R140.
392	fāng	方	square	No.194,R70.
393	fáng	房	room	No.194,R63.
394	fáng	防	defend	No.194,R170.
395	fáng	鲂	bream	No.194,R195.
396	fǎng	仿	copy	No.194,R9.
397	fǎng	访	visit	No.194,R149.
398	fǎng	纺	spin	No.194,R120.
399	fàng	放	let go	No.194,R66.
400	fēi	非	wrong	No.196,R175.
401	fēi	飞(飛)	fly	No.195,R5 (183).
402	féi	肥	fat	No.12,R130.
403	fěi	匪	bandit	No.196,R22.
404	fèi	肺	lungs	No.197,R130.
405	fèi	废(廢)	abandon	No.187,R53 (53).
406	fèi	费	fee	No.198,R154.
407	fēn	酚	phenol	No.199,R164.
408	fēn	分	divide	No.199,R18.
	fèn		component	No.199,R18.
409	fěn	粉	powder	No.199,R119.
410	fèn	奋(奮)	lift	No.200,R37 (37).
411	fèn	份	share	No.199,R9.
412	fèn	粪(糞)	excrement	No.201,R119 (119).
413	fēng	丰(豐)	abundant	No.202,R2 (151).
414	fēng	封	seal	No.204,R41.
415	fēng	峰	summit	No.205,R46.

416	fēng	风(風)	wind	No.203,R182 (182).
417	fēng	疯(瘋)	mad	No.203,R104 (104).
418	Féng	冯(馮)	a surname	No.457,R15 (15).
419	féng	缝	sew	No.205,R120.
419	féng		seam	No.205,R120.
420	fèng	奉	give	No.206,R37.
421	fèng	凤(鳳)	phoenix	No.203,R16 (196).
422	fó	佛	Buddha	No.207,R9.
423	fǒu	否	deny	No.208,R30.
424	fū	夫	husband	No.209,R37.
425	fū	孵	hatch	No.212,R39.
422	fú	佛	seem	No.207,R9.
426	fú	扶	support	No.209,R64.
427	fú	幅	size	No.213,R50.
428	fú	氟	fluorine	No.207,R84.
429	fú	伏	bend over	No.210,R9.
430	fú	服	clothes	No.211,R130.
	fù		a dose	No.211,R130.
431	fú	浮	float	No.212,R85.
432	fú	福	good fortune	No.213,R113
433	fú	弗	not	No.207,R57.
434	fǔ	抚(撫)	comfort	No.729,R64 (64).
435	fǔ	辅	assist	No.55,R159.
436	fǔ	府	office	No.215,R53.
437	fǔ	腐	rotten	No.215,R130 also 53.
438	fù	父	father	No.214,R88.
439	fù	赴	attend	No.55,R156.
440	fù	副	deputy	No.213,R18.
441	fù	覆	cover	No.218,R146.
442	fù	赋	bestow	No.732,R154.
443	fù	复(復)	duplicate	No.218,R35 (60).
444	fù	傅	instruct	No.54,R9.
445	fù	付	hand over	No.215,R9.
446	fù	腹	belly	No.218,R130.
447	fù	负	carry	No.216,R154.
448	fù	富	rich	No.213,R40.
449	fù	附	add	No.215,R170.
450	fù	妇(婦)	woman	No.217,R38 (38).

G

451	gāi	该	ought	No.219,R149.
452	gǎi	改	change	No.220,R66.
453	gài	概	approximate	No.222,R75.
454	gài	钙	calcium	No.894,R167.
455	gài	盖(蓋)	cover	No.221,R123 (140).
456	gān	干(乾)	do; dry	No.223,R51 (5).
	gàn	干(幹)	treetrunk	No.223,R51 (51).
457	gān	甘	sweet	No.224,R99.
458	gān	杆	pole	No.223,R75.
	gǎn	杆(桿)	shaft	No.223,R75 (75).
459	gān	肝	liver	No.223,R130.
460	gǎn	赶(趕)	catch up	No.223,R156 (156).
461	gǎn	感	feel	No.226,R61.
462	gǎn	秆(稈)	stalk	No.223,R115 (115).
463	gǎn	敢	bold	No.225,R66.
464	gāng	刚(剛)	firm	No.227,R18 (18).
465	gāng	钢(鋼)	steel	No.227,R167 (167).
	gàng		sharpen	No.227,R167 (167).
466	gāng	缸	vat	No.238,R121.
467	gāng	纲(綱)	principle	No.227,R120 (120).
468	gǎng	岗(崗)	hill	No.227,R46 (46).
469	gǎng	港	port	No.241,R85.
470	gāo	高	tall	No.228,R189.
471	gǎo	搞	do	No.228,R64.
472	gǎo	稿	stalk	No.228,R115.
473	gào	告	tell	No.229,R30.
474	gē	哥	brother	No.230,R30.
475	gē	歌	sing	No.230,R76.
476	gē	戈	weapon	No.884,R62.
477	gē	割	cut	No.266,R18.
478	gé	格	squares	No.234,R75.
479	gé	革	leather	No.231,R177.
480	gé	隔	separate	No.232,R170.
481	gè	各	each	No.234,R30.
482	gè	铬	chromium	No.234,R167.
483	gè	个(個)	a measure	No.233,R2 (9).

484	*gěi*	给	give	No.235,R120.
485	*gēn*	根	root	No.277,R75.
486	*gēn*	跟	heel	No.277,R157.
487	*gēng*	耕	plough	No.237,R127.
488	*gēng*	更	change	No.236,R73.
	gèng		more	No.236,R73.
489	*gōng*	工	labour	No.238,R48.
490	*gōng*	攻	attack	No.238,R66.
491	*gōng*	功	merit	No.238,R19.
492	*gōng*	供	supply	No.241,R9.
	gòng		confess	No.241,R9.
493	*gōng*	公	public	No.240,R12.
494	*gōng*	宫(宮)	palace	No.114,R40 (40).
495	*gōng*	弓	bow	No.239,R57.
496	*gǒng*	汞	mercury	No.238,R85.
497	*gòng*	贡	tribute	No.238,R154.
498	*gòng*	共	common	No.241,R12.
499	*gōu*	钩(鉤)	hook	No.242,R167 (167).
500	*gōu*	勾	cancel	No.242,R20.
501	*gōu*	沟(溝)	ditch	No.242,R85 (85).
502	*gǒu*	狗	dog	No.371,R94.
503	*gòu*	构(構)	compose	No.242,R75 (75).
504	*gòu*	购(購)	buy	No.242,R154 (154).
505	*gòu*	够(夠)	enough	No.371,R36 (36).
506	*gū*	姑	aunt	No.243,R38.
507	*gǔ*	骨	bone	No.244,R188.
508	*gǔ*	鼓	drum	No.245,R207.
509	*gǔ*	古	ancient	No.243,R30.
510	*gǔ*	谷	valley	No.858,R150.
511	*gǔ*	股	thigh	No.597,R130.
512	*gù*	故	incident	No.243,R66.
513	*gù*	顾(顧)	look at	No.246,R181 (181).
514	*gù*	固	firm	No.243,R31.
515	*gù*	雇(僱)	hire	No.246,R63 (9).
516	*guā*	刮(颳)	blow	No.596,R135 (182).
517	*guā*	瓜	melon	No.247,R97.
518	*guà*	挂(掛)	hang	No.248,R64 (64).
519	*guǎi*	拐	turn	No.50,R64.

520	*guài*	怪	strange	No.249,R61.
521	*guān*	关(關)	close	No.250,R12 (169).
522	*guān*	官	official	No.252,R40.
523	*guān*	冠	crown	No.860,R14.
	guàn		precede	No.860,R14.
524	*guān*	观(觀)	look at	No.251,R29 (147).
525	*guǎn*	管	tube	No.252,R118.
526	*guǎn*	馆	hotel	No.252,R184.
527	*guàn*	罐	pot	No.251,R121.
528	*guàn*	惯	be used to	No.253,R61.
529	*guàn*	灌	irrigate	No.251,R85.
530	*guàn*	贯	pass through	No.253,R154.
531	*guāng*	光	light	No.254,R10.
532	*guǎng*	广(廣)	wide	No.255,R53 (53).
533	*guī*	规	rule	No.256,R147.
534	*guī*	圭	jade	No.248,R32.
535	*guī*	硅	silicon	No.248,R112.
536	*guī*	归(歸)	return	No.217,R58 (77).
537	*guǐ*	轨	track	No.362,R159.
538	*guǐ*	鬼	spirit; ghost	No.257,R194.
539	*guì*	桂	laurel	No.248,R75.
540	*guì*	贵	dear	No.258,R154.
541	*gǔn*	滚(滾)	roll	No.259,R85 (85).
542	*guō*	锅(鍋)	pot	No.260,R167 (167).
543	*guō*	郭	a surname	No.758,R163.
544	*guò*	过(過)	cross	No.263,R162 (162).
	guō		excessive	No.263,R162 (162).
545	*guó*	国(國)	country	No.261,R31 (31).
546	*guǒ*	果	fruit	No.262,R75.

H

547	*hā*	哈	breathe out	No.274,R30.
548	*hái*	孩	child	No.219,R39.
549	*hái*	还(還)	still	No.264,R162 (162).
550	*hǎi*	海	sea	No.265,R85.
551	*hài*	害	evil	No.266,R40.
552	*Hán*	韩(韓)	Korea	No.714,R178 (178).
553	*hán*	含	contain	No.267,R30.

554	*hán*	寒	cold	No.268,R40.
555	*hán*	函	letter	No.267,R17.
556	*hǎn*	喊	shout	No.226,R30.
557	*hàn*	旱	drought	No.223,R72.
558	*hàn*	焊	weld	No.223,R86.
559	*hàn*	汗	sweat	No.223,R85.
560	*Hàn*	汉(漢)	Chinese	No.269,R85 (85).
561	*háng*	航	boat	No.383,R137.
562	*háng*	行	profession	No.774,R144.
563	*háo*	豪	hero	No.270,R152.
564	*háo*	毫	writing brush	No.270,R82.
565	*hào*	号(號)	name; number	No.272,R30 (141).
	háo		howl	No.272,R30 (141).
566	*hǎo*	好	good	No.271,R38.
	hào		like	No.271,R38.
567	*hào*	耗	cost	No.463,R127.
568	*hē*	呵	breathe out	No.388,R30.
569	*hē*	喝	drink	No.273,R30.
	hè		shout	No.273,R30.
570	*hé*	荷	lotus	No.388,R140.
	hè		carry	No.388,R140.
571	*hé*	核	nucleus	No.219,R75.
572	*hé*	和	and	No.275,R30.
	hè		compose	No.275,R30.
573	*hé*	何	what?	No.388,R9.
574	*hé*	合	close	No.274,R30.
575	*hé*	盒	box	No.274,R108.
576	*hé*	河	river	No.388,R85.
577	*hè*	赫	grand	No.100,R155.
578	*hè*	褐	brown	No.273,R145.
579	*hè*	贺	congratulate	No.319,R154.
580	*hēi*	黑	black	No.276,R203.
581	*hěn*	很	very	No.277,R60.
582	*hěn*	狠	ruthless	No.277,R94.
583	*hèn*	恨	hate	No.277,R61.
584	*hēng*	哼	snort	No.758,R30.
585	*héng*	横	horizontal	No.293,R75.
	hèng		harsh	No.293,R75.
586	*héng*	衡	weigh	No.341,R144.

587	héng	恒	permanent	No.787,R61.
588	hōng	烘	bake	No.241,R86.
589	hóng	洪	vast	No.241,R85.
590	hóng	红	red	No.238,R120.
591	hóu	侯	nobleman	No.280,R9.
592	hòu	厚	thick	No.279,R27.
593	hòu	候	wait	No.280,R9.
594	hòu	后(後)	behind	No.278,R30 (60).
595	hū	呼	breathe out	No.281,R30.
596	hū	乎	at	No.281,R4.
597	hū	忽	suddenly	No.735,R61.
598	hú	糊	paste	No.282,R119.
599	hú	壶(壺)	pot	No.796,R33 (33).
600	hú	胡	non-Han	No.282,R130.
601	hú	湖	lake	No.282,R85.
602	hú	弧	arc	No.247,R57.
603	hǔ	虎	tiger	No.283,R141.
604	hù	护(護)	protect	No.284,R64 (149).
605	hù	互	mutual	No.285,R7.
606	Hù	沪(滬)	Shanghai	No.284,R85 (85).
607	hù	户	door	No.284,R63.
608	huā	花	flower	No.287,R140.
609	huā	化	spend	No.287,R21 & 9.
	huà		change	No.287,R21 & 9.
610	huá	华(華)	splendid	No.287,R24 (140).
611	huá	滑	smooth	No.244,R85.
612	huá	划(劃)	cut	No.286,R62 & 18 (18).
	huà		plan	No.286,R62 & 18 (18).
613	huà	画(畫)	draw	No.289,R102 (102).
614	huà	话	word	No.288,R149.
615	huà	桦(樺)	birch tree	No.287,R75 (75).
616	huái	怀(懷)	bosom	No.264,R61 (61).
617	huái	淮	Huai River	No.642,R85.
618	huài	坏(壞)	bad	No.264,R32 (32).
619	huān	欢(歡)	joyous	No.251,R29 (76).
620	huán	环(環)	ring	No.264,R96 (96).
621	huán	还(還)	return	No.264,R162 (162).
622	huǎn	缓	slow	No.514,R120.

623	*huàn*	换	exchange	No.290,R64.
624	*huàn*	患	trouble	No.114,R61.
625	*huāng*	荒	wasteland	No.291,R140.
626	*huāng*	慌	flurried	No.291,R61.
627	*huáng*	黄	yellow	No.293,R201.
628	*huáng*	簧	reed	No.293,R118.
629	*huáng*	皇	emperor	No.292,R106.
630	*huī*	灰	ash	No.294,R86.
631	*huī*	挥(揮)	wave	No.378,R64 (64).
632	*huī*	辉	brightness	No.254,R159.
633	*huí*	回	return	No.295,R31.
634	*huǐ*	毁(毀)	destroy	No.296,R79 (79).
635	*huì*	惠	kindness	No.182,R61.
636	*huì*	会(會)	can	No.298,R9 (73).
637	*huì*	汇(匯)	converge	No.297,R85 (22).
638	*huì*	绘(繪)	paint	No.298,R120 (120).
639	*hūn*	昏	dusk	No.299,R72.
640	*hūn*	婚	marry	No.299,R38.
641	*hùn*	混	mix	No.300,R85.
642	*huó*	活	live	No.288,R85.
643	*huǒ*	伙	meals	No.301,R9.
644	*huǒ*	火	fire	No.301,R86.
645	*huò*	获(獲)	obtain	No.304,R140 (94).
646	*huò*	或	perhaps	No.302,R62.
647	*huò*	货	goods	No.303,R154.
648	*huò*	祸(禍)	disaster	No. 260,R113 (113).

J

649	*jī*	击(擊)	attack	No.306,R17 (64).
650	*jī*	基	base	No.309,R32.
651	*jī*	机(機)	machine	No.305,R75 (75).
652	*jī*	积(積)	amass	No.308,R115 (115).
653	*jī*	迹(跡)	trace	No.823,R162 (157).
654	*jī*	激	arouse	No.310,R85.
655	*jī*	鸡(雞)	chicken	No.307,R29 (172).
656	*jī*	绩	achievement	No.875,R120.
657	*jī*	几(幾)	small table	No.305,R16 (52).
	jǐ		how many?	No.305,R16 (52).

658	jī	奇	odd (number)	No.532,R37.
659	jí	吉	lucky	No.343,R30.
660	jí	极(極)	extreme	No.311,R75 (75).
661	jí	辑	edit	No.185,R159.
662	jí	籍	register	No.346,R118.
663	jí	集	assemble	No.315,R172.
664	jí	及	reach	No.311,R29.
665	jí	急	anxious	No.313,R61.
666	jí	疾	disease	No.314,R104.
667	jí	即	even if	No.312,R26.
668	jí	级	rank	No.311,R120.
669	jí	亟	urgently	No.311,R7.
670	jǐ	挤	squeeze	No.530,R64.
671	jǐ	己	oneself	No.316,R49.
672	jì	纪	discipline	No.316,R120.
673	jì	技	skill	No.897,R64.
674	jì	季	season	No.927,R39.
675	jì	祭	hold worship	No.73,R113.
676	jì	剂	pill	No.530,R18.
677	jì	济	cross over	No.530,R85.
678	jì	寄	send	No.532,R40.
679	jì	计	count	No.613,R149.
680	jì	记	remember	No.316,R149.
681	jì	既	since	No.317,R71.
682	jì	际(際)	border	No.73,R170 (170).
683	jì	继(繼)	continue	No.318,R120 (120).
684	jiā	嘉	praise	No.319,R30.
685	jiā	夹(夾)	squeeze	No.320,R37 (37).
	jiá		lined	No.320,R37 (37).
686	jiā	佳	fine	No.248,R9.
687	jiā	家	family	No.321,R40.
688	jiā	加	add	No.319,R19.
689	jiǎ	甲	first	No.322,R102.
690	jiǎ	钾	potassium	No.322,R167.
691	jiǎ	假	false	No.323,R9.
	jià		holiday	No.323,R9.
692	jià	价(價)	price	No.345,R9 (9).
693	jià	架	frame	No.319,R75.

694	*jià*	驾	drive	No.319,R187.
695	*jià*	嫁	marry	No.321,R38.
696	*jiān*	监(監)	supervise	No.327,R108 (108).
697	*jiān*	坚(堅)	firm	No.325,R32 (32).
698	*jiān*	尖	sharp	No.324,R42.
699	*jiān*	间	among	No.329,R169.
	jiàn		space between	No.329,R169.
700	*jiān*	兼	double	No.326,R12.
701	*jiān*	肩	shoulder	No.284,R130.
702	*jiān*	渐	soak	No.348,R85.
	jiàn		gradually	No.348,R85.
703	*jiān*	茧(繭)	cocoon	No.103,R140 (120).
704	*jiǎn*	检(檢)	inspect	No.426,R75 (75).
705	*jiǎn*	柬	card	No.83,R75.
706	*jiǎn*	碱	soda	No.226,R112.
707	*jiǎn*	硷(鹼)	alkali	No.426,R112 (197).
708	*jiǎn*	简	simple	No.329,R118.
709	*jiǎn*	剪	scissors	No.539,R18.
710	*jiǎn*	减	subtract	No.226,R15.
711	*jiàn*	鉴(鑒)	reflect	No.327,R167 (167).
712	*jiàn*	见	see	No.328,R147.
713	*jiàn*	键	key	No.330,R167.
714	*jiàn*	件	measure word	No.508,R9.
715	*jiàn*	健	healthy	No.330,R9.
716	*jiàn*	舰(艦)	warship	No.327,R137 (137).
717	*jiàn*	剑(劍)	sword	No.426,R18 (18).
718	*jiàn*	建	build	No.330,R54.
719	*jiāng*	僵	stiff	No.332,R9.
720	*jiāng*	姜(薑)	ginger	No.332,R123 (140).
721	*jiāng*	将(將)	do	No.331,R90 (90).
	jiàng		general	No.331,R90 (90).
722	*jiāng*	浆(漿)	starch	No.331,R85 (85).
723	*jiāng*	江	large river	No.238,R85.
724	*jiāng*	疆	border	No.332,R57.
725	*jiǎng*	奖(獎)	reward	No.331,R37 (37).
726	*jiǎng*	讲(講)	speak	No.333,R149 (149).
727	*jiàng*	降	fall	No.205,R170.
728	*jiāo*	礁	reef	No.335,R112.

729	*jiāo*	焦	burnt	No.335,R86.
730	*jiāo*	胶(膠)	glue	No.334,R130 (130).
731	*jiāo*	交	hand over	No.334,R8.
732	*jiāo*	浇(澆)	sprinkle	No.567,R85 (85).
733	*jiào*	教	teach	No.338,R66.
734	*jiǎo*	脚(腳)	foot	No.560,R130 (130).
735	*jiǎo*	角	horn	No.336,R148.
736	*jiǎo*	缴	pay	No.310,R120.
737	*jiǎo*	绞	twist	No.334,R120.
738	*jiào*	较	compare	No.334,R159.
739	*jiào*	叫	shout	No.337,R30.
740	*jiào*	觉(覺)	sleep	No.376,R147 (147).
741	*jiē*	揭	tear off	No.273,R64.
742	*jiē*	接	receive	No.340,R64.
743	*jiē*	皆	all	No.339,R106.
744	*jiē*	街	street	No.341,R144.
745	*jiē*	阶(階)	steps	No.339,R170 (170).
746	*jié*	节(節)	joint	No.342,R140 (118).
747	*jié*	结	tie	No.343,R120.
	jiē		bear fruit	No.343,R120.
748	*jié*	截	cut	No.61,R62.
749	*jié*	孑	lonely	No.927,R39.
750	*jiě*	解	separate	No.344,R148.
	jiè		escort	No.344,R148.
751	*jiě*	姐	sister	No.933,R38.
752	*jiè*	界	boundary	No.345,R102.
753	*jiè*	借(藉)	borrow	No.346,R9 (140).
754	*jiè*	介	be situated between	No.345,R9.
755	*jiè*	届(屆)	fall due	No.843,R44 (44).
756	*jīn*	巾	cloth	No.57,R50.
757	*jīn*	筋	muscle	No.342,R118.
758	*jīn*	斤	half kilo	No.348,R69.
759	*jīn*	金	metals	No.349,R167.
760	*jīn*	今	today	No.347,R9.
761	*jīn*	津	ferry	No.350,R85.
762	*jīn*	禁	bear	No.356,R113.
	jìn		prohibit	No.356,R113.
763	*jǐn*	紧(緊)	tight	No.353,R120 (120).

764	jǐn	锦	brocade	No.474,R167.
765	jǐn	仅(僅)	only	No.351,R9 (9).
766	jìn	尽(盡)	utmost	No.352,R44 (108).
	jìn		exhausted	No.352,R44 (108).
767	jìn	进(進)	enter	No.354,R162 (162).
768	jìn	晋	advance	No.527,R72.
769	jìn	近	near	No.355,R162.
770	jìn	浸	soak	No.549,R85.
771	jìn	劲(勁)	energy	No.358,R19 (19).
772	jīng	茎(莖)	stalk	No.358,R140 (140).
773	jīng	晶	crystal	No.524,R72.
774	jīng	京	capital	No.357,R8.
775	jīng	惊(驚)	alarm	No.357,R61 (187).
776	jīng	精	refined	No.551,R119.
777	jīng	经(經)	go through	No.358,R120 (120).
778	jǐng	井	well	No.359,R7.
779	jǐng	警	alert	No.361,R149.
780	jǐng	景	view	No.357,R72.
781	jǐng	颈(頸)	neck	No.358,R181 (181).
782	jìng	静(靜)	quiet	No.892,R174 (174).
783	jìng	境	border	No.360,R32.
784	jìng	敬	respect	No.361,R66.
785	jìng	镜	mirror	No.360,R167.
786	jìng	径(徑)	path	No.358,R60 (60).
787	jìng	竟	complete	No.360,R117.
788	jìng	竞(競)	compete	No.360,R117 (117).
789	jìng	净(淨)	clean	No.892,R15 (85).
790	jiū	究	study	No.362,R116.
791	jiǔ	久	long time	No.363,R4.
792	jiǔ	九	nine	No.362,R5.
793	jiǔ	酒	wine	No.364,R164 (85).
794	jiù	救	save	No.556,R66.
795	jiù	旧(舊)	old	No.365,R72 (134).
796	jiù	就	come near	No.366,R43.
797	jū	居	reside	No.367,R44.
798	jù	据(據)	occupy	No.367,R64 (64).
799	jú	桔(橘)	orange	No.343,R75 (75).
800	jú	菊	chrysanthemum	No.371,R140.

801	*jú*	局	situation	No.368,R44.
802	*jú*	橘	orange	No.343,R75.
803	*jǔ*	矩	rules	No.370,R111.
804	*jǔ*	举(舉)	lift	No.369,R3 (134).
805	*jù*	聚	assemble	No.559,R128.
806	*jù*	拒	refuse	No.370,R64.
807	*jù*	巨	huge	No.370,R48.
808	*jù*	具	tool	No.372,R12.
809	*jù*	距	distance	No.370,R157.
810	*jù*	锯	saw	No.367,R167.
811	*jù*	俱	all	No.372,R9.
812	*jù*	句	sentence	No.371,R30.
813	*jù*	剧(劇)	play	No.367,R18.
814	*juān*	捐	abandon	No.373,R64.
815	*juǎn*	卷	roll up	No.374,R26.
	juàn		book	No.374,R26.
816	*jué*	觉(覺)	feel	No.376,R147 (147).
817	*jué*	决(決)	decide	No.375,R15 (85).
818	*jué*	绝	absolutely	No.377,R120.
819	*jué*	角	role	No.336,R148.
820	*jūn*	均	equal	No.867,R32.
821	*jūn*	菌	fungus	No.404,R140.
	jùn		mushroom	No.404,R140.
822	*jūn*	军(軍)	army	No.378,R14 (159).
823	*jūn*	君	gentleman	No.564,R30.
824	*jùn*	郡	prefecture	No.564,R163.

K

825	*kǎ*	卡	block	No.379,R25.
826	*kāi*	开(開)	open	No.380,R55 (169).
827	*kān*	刊	print	No.223,R18.
828	*kān*	看	look after	No.381,R109.
	kàn		see	No.381,R109.
829	*kǎn*	砍	cut	No.541,R112.
830	*kāng*	康	health	No.382,R53.
831	*káng*	扛	carry	No.238,R64.
832	*kàng*	抗	resist	No.383,R64.
833	*kàng*	炕	kang	No.383,R86.

834	*kǎo*	考	test	No.384,R125.
835	*kǎo*	烤	roast	No.384,R86.
836	*kào*	靠	lean on	No.385,R175.
837	*kē*	棵	measure word	No.262,R75.
838	*kē*	颗	measure word	No.262,R181.
839	*kē*	科	science	No.386,R115.
840	*ké*	壳(殼)	shell	No.387,R33 (79).
841	*kě*	可	can	No.388,R30.
842	*kè*	克	can; overcome	No.389,R10.
843	*kè*	刻	carve	No.219,R18.
844	*kè*	客	guest	No.390,R40.
845	*kè*	课(課)	course	No.391,R149 (149).
846	*kěn*	肯	willing	No.392,R130.
847	*kēng*	坑	hole	No.383,R32.
848	*kōng*	空	empty	No.393,R116.
	kòng		leave blank	No.393,R116.
849	*kǒng*	恐	fear	No.395,R61.
850	*kǒng*	孔	hole	No.394,R39.
851	*kòng*	控	accuse	No.393,R64.
852	*kǒu*	口	mouth	No.396,R30.
853	*kòu*	扣	button up	No.396,R64.
854	*kū*	枯	withered	No.243,R75.
855	*kū*	哭	weep	No.397,R30.
856	*kǔ*	苦	bitter	No.398,R140.
857	*kù*	库(庫)	warehouse	No.399,R53 (53).
858	*kuà*	跨	step	No.400,R157.
859	*kuài*	块(塊)	piece	No.401,R32 (32).
860	*kuài*	快	fast	No.401,R61.
861	*kuān*	宽(寬)	wide	No.402,R40 (40).
862	*kuǎn*	款	sincere	No.403,R76.
863	*kuāng*	筐	basket	No.706,R118.
864	*kuāng & kuàng*	框	frame	No.706,R75.
865	*kuáng*	狂	mad	No.706,R94.
866	*kuàng*	矿(礦)	ore	No.255,R112 (112).
867	*kuàng*	况(況)	condition	No.778,R15 (85).
868	*kuī*	亏(虧)	lose	No.728,R7 (141).
869	*kūn*	昆	elder brother	No.300,R72.
870	*kùn*	困	difficulty	No.404,R31.

| 871 | *kuò* | 扩(擴) | expand | No.255,R64 (64). |
| 872 | *kuò* | 阔 | wide | No.288,R169. |

L

873	*lā*	拉	pull	No.405,R64.
874	*la*	啦	really!	No.405,R30.
875	*là*	蜡(蠟)	wax	No.346,R142 (142).
876	*lái*	来(來)	come	No.406,R75 (9).
877	*lài*	赖	rely on	No.407,R154.
878	*lán*	蓝(藍)	blue	No.327,R140 (140).
879	*lán*	栏(欄)	fence	No.408,R75 (75).
880	*lán*	篮(籃)	basket	No.327,R118 (118).
881	*lán*	兰(蘭)	orchid	No.408,R12 (140).
882	*làn*	烂(爛)	sodden	No.408,R86 (86).
883	*láng*	狼	wolf	No.428,R9.
884	*láng*	郎	young man	No.428,R163.
885	*làng*	浪	wave	No.428,R85.
886	*lāo*	捞(撈)	get	No.409,R64 (64).
887	*láo*	劳(勞)	labour	No.409,R140 (19).
888	*láo*	牢	prison	No.508,R93.
889	*lǎo*	老	old	No.410,R125.
890	*lè*	勒	rein in	No.231,R19.
891	*lè*	乐(樂)	happy	No.411,R4 (75).
892	*le*	了	perfective	No.412,R6.
893	*léi*	雷	thunder	No.413,R173.
894	*lěi* *léi* *lèi*	累	pile up clusters. tired.	No.414,R120.
895	*lèi*	类(類)	kind	No.415,R119 (181).
896	*lèi*	泪(淚)	tears	No.488,R85 (85).
897	*léng*	棱(稜)	edge	No.416,R75 (115).
898	*lěng*	冷	cold	No.439,R15.
899	*lī & li*	哩	a particle	No.420,R30.
900	*lí*	犁	plough	No.423,R93.
901	*lí*	黎	multitude	No.429,R202.
902	*lí*	离(離)	leave	No.417,R114 (172).
903	*lì*	丽(麗)	beautiful	No.737,R1 (198).
904	*lǐ*	理	reason	No.420,R96.

905	lǐ	李	plum	No.419,R75.
906	lǐ	里(裡,裏)	inside	No.420,R166 (145,145).
907	lǐ	礼(禮)	courtesy	No.418,R113 (113).
908	lì	吏	official	No.618,R30.
909	lì	励(勵)	encourage	No.421,R19 (19).
910	lì	历(歷)	experience	No.421,R27 (77).
911	lì	利	sharp	No.423,R18.
912	lì	例	example	No.434,R9.
913	lì	立	stand	No.422,R117.
914	lì	粒	grain	No.422,R119.
915	lì	隶(隸)	under	No.350,R171 (171).
916	lì	力	power	No.421,R19.
917	liǎ	俩(倆)	two	No.431,R9 (9).
918	lián	联(聯)	unite	No.425,R128 (128).
919	lián	莲	lotus	No.424,R140.
920	lián	连(連)	link	No.424,R162 (162).
921	lián	廉	honest	No.326,R53.
922	liǎn	脸(臉)	face	No.426,R130 (130).
923	liàn	链	chain	No.424,R167.
924	liàn	炼(煉)	refine	No.427,R86 (86).
925	liàn	练(練)	train	No.427,R120 (120).
926	liáng	粮(糧)	grain	No.428,R119 (119).
927	liáng liàng	凉	cool make cool.	No.357,R15.
928	liáng	梁	ridge	No.429,R75.
929	liáng	良	good	No.428,R138.
930	liáng liàng	量	measure capacity.	No.430,R166.
931	liǎng	两(兩)	two	No.431,R1 (1).
932	liàng	辆(輛)	a measure	No.431,R159 (159).
933	liàng	亮	bright	No.432,R8.
934	liáo	僚	official	No.433,R9.
935	liáo	辽(遼)	distant	No.433,R162 (162).
936	liǎo liào	了(瞭)	understand watch	No.433. R6 (109).
937	liào	料	material	No.168,R68.
938	liè	裂	split	No.434,R145.
939	liè	列	arrange	No.434,R18.

940	*liè*	烈	violent	No.434,R86.
941	*lín*	林	forest	No.435,R75.
942	*lín*	磷	phosphorus	No.439,R112.
943	*lín*	临(臨)	face	No.436,R2 (131).
944	*lín*	邻(鄰)	neighbour	No.439,R163 (163).
945	*lín* *lìn*	淋	drench filter.	No.435,R85.
946	*líng*	玲	tinkle	No.439,R96.
947	*líng*	零	zero	No.439,R173.
948	*líng*	龄	age	No.439,R211.
949	*líng*	铃	bell	No.439,R167.
950	*líng*	灵(靈)	clever	No.437,R58 (173).
951	*líng*	陵	hill	No.416,R170.
952	*lìng*	令	cause	No.439,R9.
953	*lǐng*	岭(嶺)	mountains	No.439,R46 (46).
954	*lǐng*	领	neck	No.439,R181.
955	*lìng*	另	other	No.438,R30.
956	*liū* *liù*	溜	slide swift current.	No.441,R85.
957	*liú*	硫	sulphur	No.440,R112.
958	*liú*	留	remain	No.441,R102.
959	*Liú*	刘(劉)	Liu(name)	No.723,R18 & 67 (18).
960	*liú*	流	flow	No.440,R85.
961	*liǔ*	柳	willow	No.312,R75.
962	*liù*	六	six	No.442,R12.
963	*lóng*	龙(龍)	dragon	No.443,R212 (212).
964	*lóng* *lǒng*	笼(籠)	cage envelop.	No.443,R118 (118).
965	*lóu*	楼(樓)	building	No.444,R75 (75).
966	*lòu*	漏	leak	No.445,R85.
967	*lòu*	露	reveal	No.445,R173.
968	*lú*	炉(爐)	stove	No.446,R86 (86).
969	*lǔ*	鲁	stupid	No.852,R195.
970	*lù*	露	dew	No.449,R173.
971	*lù*	路	road	No.449,R157.
972	*lù*	录(錄)	record	No.448,R58 (167).
973	*lù*	陆(陸)	mainland	No.447,R170 (170).
974	*Lü* (third tone)	吕(呂)	Lu(name)	No.114,R30 (30).

975	*lü* (third tone)	铝(鋁)	aluminium	No.114,R167 (167).
976	*lü* (third tone)	旅	travel	No.450,R70.
977	*lü* (fourth tone)	虑(慮)	consider	No.767,R141 (61).
978	*lü* (fourth tone)	氯	chlorine	No.448,R84.
979	*lü* (fourth tone)	律	law	No.451,R60.
980	*lü* (fourth tone)	率	rate	No.640,R95.
981	*lü* (fourth tone)	滤(濾)	filter	No.767,R85 (85).
982	*lü* (fourth tone)	绿	green	No.448,R120.
983	*luǎn*	卵	egg	No.212,R26.
984	*luàn*	乱(亂)	chaos	No.452,R5 (5).
985	*lüè*	略	brief	No.234,R102.
986	*lún*	轮(輪)	wheel	No.453,R159 (159).
987	*lún*	伦(倫)	logic	No.453,R9 (9).
988	*lùn*	论(論)	discuss	No.453,R149 (149).
989	*luó*	螺	snail	No.414,R142.
990	*luó*	罗(羅)	net	No.454,R122 (122).
991	*luó*	落	fall	No.455,R140.
992	*Luò*	洛	Luo(name)	No.234,R85.

M

993	*mā*	妈	mummy	No.457,R38.
994	*má*	麻	hemp	No.456,R200.
995	*ma*	吗	(a final particle) marking a question	No.457,R30.
996	*mǎ*	码	sign	No.457,R112.
997	*mǎ*	马(馬)	horse	No.457,R187 (187).
998	*mà*	骂(罵)	curse	No.457,R187 (122).
999	*ma*	嘛	(a final particle) giving the sense of 'after all'	No.456,R30.
1,000	*mái*	埋	bury	No.420,R32.
1,001	*mǎi*	买(買)	buy	No.458,R5 (154).
1,002	*mài*	麦(麥)	wheat	No.459,R199 (199).
1,003	*mài*	卖(賣)	sell	No.458,R24 (154).
1,004	*mài*	迈(邁)	stride	No.705,R162 (162).
1,005	*mài*	脉(脈)	vein	No.840,R130 (130).
1,006	*mǎn*	满	full	No.460,R85.
1,007	*màn*	曼	graceful	No.461,R73.
1,008	*màn*	慢	slow	No.461,R61.

1,009 *máng*	忙	busy	No.462,R61.
1,010 *máo*	毛	hair	No.463,R82.
1,011 *mào*	冒	emit	No.464,R13.
1,012 *mào*	帽	hat	No.464,R50.
1,013 *mào*	贸	trade	No.303,R154.
1,014 *me*	么(麼)	what	No.456,R4 (200).
1,015 *méi*	枚	(a measure word)	No.487,R75.
1,016 *méi*	梅	plum	No.466,R75.
1,017 *méi*	酶	ferment	No.466,R164.
1,018 *méi*	霉	mildew	No.466,R173.
1,019 *méi*	煤	coal	No.485,R86.
1,020 *méi*	没	not	No.465,R85.
1,021 *méi*	眉	eyebrow	No.488,R109.
1,022 *měi*	镁	magnesium	No.467,R167.
1,023 *měi*	**每**	every	No.466,R80.
1,024 *měi*	美	beautiful	No.467,R123.
1,025 *mèi*	妹	sister	No.718,R38.
1,026 *mēn*	闷	stuffy	No.468,R61.
mèn		bored	
1,027 *mén*	门(門)	door	No.468,R169 (169).
1,028 *men*	们	indicator of plural	No.468,R9.
1,029 *méng*	蒙	cover	No.469,R140.
měng		cheat	
Měng		Mongol	
1,030 *méng*	盟	alliance	No.481,R108.
1,031 *měng*	锰	manganese	No.470,R167.
1,032 *měng*	猛	violent	No.470,R94.
1,033 *mèng*	梦(夢)	dream	No.471,R36 (36).
1,034 *mèng*	孟	first month of a season	No.470,R39.
1,035 *mí*	迷	lost	No.472,R162.
1,036 *mǐ*	米	rice	No.472,R119.
1,037 *mì*	秘	secret	No.473,R115.
1,038 *mì*	密	dense	No.473,R40.
1,039 *mì*	幂	power (in maths)	No.489,R14.
1,040 *mián*	棉	cotton	No.474,R75.
1,041 *miǎn*	免	avoid	No.475,R10.
1,042 *miàn*	面	face	No.476,R176.
1,043 *miáo*	苗	young plant	No.477,R140.

1,044	*miǎo*	秒	a second	No.595,R115.
1,045	*miào*	庙(廟)	temple	No.843,R53 (53).
1,046	*miào*	妙	wonderful	No.595,R38.
1,047	*miè*	灭(滅)	extinguish	No.478,R86 (85).
1,048	*mín*	民	people	No.479,R83.
1,049	*míng*	明	bright	No.481,R72.
1,050	*míng*	鸣	cry of birds	No.506,R30.
1,051	*míng*	名	name	No.480,R30.
1,052	*mìng*	命	life	No.482,R30.
1,053	*mō*	摸	stroke	No.484,R64.
1,054	*mó*	模	model	No.484,R75.
1,055	*mó*	膜	membrane	No.484,R130.
1,056	*mó* *mò*	磨	rub mill	No.456,R112.
1,057	*mǒ* *mò*	抹	smear on plaster	No.483,R64.
1,058	*mò*	末	tip	No.483,R75.
1,059	*mò*	莫	not	No.484,R140.
1,060	*mò*	墨	ink	No.276,R32.
1,061	*móu*	谋	stratagem	No.485,R149.
1,062	*mǒu*	某	some	No.485,R75.
1,063	*mú*	模	mould	No.484,R75.
1,064	*mǔ*	亩(畝)	a mu (unit of area)	No.682,R8 (102).
1,065	*mǔ*	姆	nurse	No.486,R38.
1,066	*mǔ*	母	mother	No.486,R80.
1,067	*mù*	墓	grave	No.489,R32.
1,068	*mù*	幕	screen	No.489,R50.
1,069	*mù*	木	tree; wood	No.487,R75.
1,070	*mù*	目	eye	No.488,R109.
1,071	*mù*	穆	solemn	No.15,R115.

N

1,072	*nà*	那	that	No.491,R163.
1,073	*ná*	拿	take	No.490,R64.
1,074	*nǎ*	哪	which	No.491,R30.
1,075	*nà*	钠	sodium	No.499,R167.
1,076	*nà*	纳	receive	No.499,R120.
1,077	*nǎi*	乃	be	No.492,R4.

1,078 *nài*	耐	be patient	No.493,R126.
1,079 *nán*	南	south	No.495,R24.
1,080 *nán*	男	male	No.494,R102.
1,081 *nán* *nàn*	难(難)	difficult disaster.	No.496,R172 & 29 (172).
1,082 *náng*	囊	pocket	No.566,R30.
1,083 *nǎo*	脑(腦)	brain	No.497,R130 (130).
1,084 *nào*	闹(鬧)	noisy	No.498,R169 (191).
1,085 *ne*	呢	(a final particle) marking a question	No.501,R30.
1,086 *nèi*	内	within	No.499,R11.
1,087 *nèn*	嫩	tender	No.656,R38.
1,088 *néng*	能	ability	No.500,R130.
1,089 *ng*	嗯	exclamation. what?!	No.182,R30.
1,090 *ní*	呢	wool cloth	No.501,R30.
1,091 *ní* *nì*	泥	mud cover with plaster.	No.501,R85.
1,092 *ní*	尼	Buddhist nun	No.501,R44.
1,093 *nǐ*	拟(擬)	draft	No.821,R64 (64).
1,094 *nǐ*	你	you	No.502,R9.
1,095 *nì*	逆	contrary	No.503,R162.
1,096 *nián*	年	year	No.504,R51.
1,097 *nián*	粘(黏)	sticky	No.879,R119 (202).
1,098 *niǎn*	捻	twist	No.505,R64.
1,099 *niàn*	念	read	No.505,R61.
1,100 *niáng*	娘	young woman	No.428,R38.
1,101 *niǎo*	鸟(鳥)	bird	No.506,R196 (196).
1,102 *niào*	尿	urine	No.643,R44.
1,103 *niē*	捏(揑)	pinch	No.696,R64 (64).
1,104 *niè*	镍	nickel	No.487,R167.
1,105 *nín*	您	you	No.502,R61.
1,106 *níng*	凝	congeal	No.818,R15.
1,107 *níng* *nìng*	宁(寧)	peaceful would rather.	No.507,R40 (40).
1,108 *níng* *nǐng*	拧(擰)	twist twist.	No.507,R64 (64).
1,109 *niú*	牛	ox	No.508,R93.
1,110 *niǔ*	扭	twist	No.509,R64.
1,111 *niǔ*	纽	handle	No.509,R120.

1,112	*nóng*	浓(濃)	dense	No.510,R85.
1,113	*nóng*	农(農)	agriculture	No.510,R14 (161).
1,114	*nòng*	弄	play with	No.511,R55.
1,115	*nǔ*	努	make an effort	No.512,R19.
1,116	*nù*	怒	anger	No.512,R61.
1,117	*nü* (third tone)	女	woman	No.513,R38.
1,118	*nuǎn*	暖	warm	No.514,R72.
1,119	*nuò*	诺	promise	No.581,R149.

O

1,120	*ō*	噢	oh!	No.10,R30.
1,121	*ó & ò*	哦	what! & oh!	No.726,R30.
1,122	*ōu*	欧(歐)	Europe	No.557,R76 (76).
1,123	*ǒu*	偶	image	No.859,R9.

P

1,124	*pá*	耙	rake	No.12,R127.
1,125	*pá*	爬	crawl	No.12,R87.
1,126	*pà*	怕	fear	No.15,R61.
1,127	*pāi*	拍	beat	No.15,R64.
1,128	*pái*	排	arrange	No.515,R64.
1,129	*pái*	牌	signpost	No.29,R91.
1,130	*pài*	派	send	No.516,R85.
1,131	*pán*	盘(盤)	dish	No.20,R108 & 137 (108).
1,132	*pàn*	判	distinguish	No.22,R18.
1,133	*páng*	旁	side	No.517,R70.
1,134	*pāo*	抛	throw	No.518,R64.
1,135	*pāo* *pào*	泡	spongy bubble.	No.24,R85.
1,136	*páo* *pào*	炮	roast gun.	No.24,R86.
1,137	*pǎo*	跑	run	No.24,R157.
1,138	*péi*	培	foster	No.34,R32.
1,139	*péi*	陪	accompany	No.34,R170.
1,140	*pèi*	配	join	No.519,R164.
1,141	*pēn*	喷	gush	No.258,R30.
1,142	*pén*	盆	basin	No.199,R108.

1,143 *péng*	棚	canopy	No.520,R75.
1,144 *pěng*	捧	carry	No.206,R64.
1,145 *pèng*	碰	bump into	No.52,R112.
1,146 *pī*	坯	base	No.56,R32.
1,147 *pī*	批	slap	No.38,R64.
1,148 *pī*	披	put on	No.521,R64.
1,149 *pī*	劈	chop	No.42,R18.
1,150 *pí*	皮	skin	No.521,R107.
1,151 *pǐ*	匹(疋)	equal to	No.651,R23 (103).
1,152 *pì*	辟	open up	No.42,R160.
1,153 *piān*	篇	sheet	No.44,R118.
1,154 *piān*	偏	partial	No.44,R9.
1,155 *piān* *piàn*	片	film slice.	No.522,R91.
1,156 *piāo*	飘	flutter	No.523,R182.
1,157 *piāo*	漂	float	No.523,R85.

piǎo bleach & *piào* handsome.

1,158 *piào*	票	ticket	No.523,R113.
1,159 *pīn*	拼(拚)	put together	No.52,R64 (64).
1,160 *pín*	频	frequently	No.58,R181.
1,161 *pín*	贫	poor	No.199,R154.
1,162 *pǐn*	品	article	No.524,R30.
1,163 *píng*	萍	duckweed	No.525,R140.
1,164 *píng*	平	flat	No.525,R51.
1,165 *píng*	凭(憑)	rely on	No.526,R16 (61).
1,166 *píng*	瓶	bottle	No.52,R98.
1,167 *píng*	评	criticise	No.525,R149.
1,168 *píng*	屏	screen	No.52,R44.
1,169 *pō*	坡	slope	No.521,R32.
1,170 *pō*	颇	rather	No.521,R181.
1,171 *pò*	破	broken	No.521,R112.
1,172 *pò*	迫	compel	No.15,R162.
1,173 *pū*	扑(撲)	pounce	No.55,R64 (64).
1,174 *pū* *pù*	铺	spread shop.	No.55,R167.
1,175 *pú*	仆(僕)	servant	No.55,R9 (9).
1,176 *pǔ*	普	general	No.527,R72.
1,177 *pǔ*	谱	register	No.527,R149.

Q

1,178	qī	期	period of time	No.531,R74.
1,179	qī	欺	deceive	No.531,R76.
1,180	qī	妻	wife	No.529,R38.
1,181	qī	七	seven	No.528,R1.
1,182	qī	漆	paint	No.879,R85.
1,183	qí	其	his	No.531,R12.
1,184	qí	棋	chess	No.531,R75.
1,185	qí	奇	strange	No.532,R37.
1,186	qí	歧	fork	No.897,R77.
1,187	qí	齐(齊)	neat	No.530,R67 (210).
1,188	qí	旗	flag	No.531,R70.
1,189	qí	祈	pray	No.348,R113.
1,190	qí	骑	ride	No.532,R187.
1,191	qǐ	起	begin	No.534,R156.
1,192	qǐ	岂(豈)	question particle	No.169,R46 (151).
1,193	qǐ	乞	beg	No.533,R5.
1,194	qǐ	启(啟)	open	No.284,R63 (30).
1,195	qì	砌	build	No.546,R112.
1,196	qì	器	utensil	No.537,R30.
1,197	qì	气(氣)	gas	No.535,R84 (84).
1,198	qì	弃(棄)	abandon	No.536,R8 (75).
1,199	qì	汽	steam	No.535,R85.
1,200	qiān	牵(牽)	lead along	No.508,R37 (93).
1,201	qiān	铅	lead	No.801,R167.
1,202	qiān	千	thousand	No.538,R24.
1,203	qiān	迁(遷)	move	No.538,R162.
1,204	qiān	签(簽)(籤)	sign	No.426,R118.
1,205	qiān	谦	modest	No.326,R149.
1,206	qián	乾	male	No.223,R5.
1,207	qián	钱(錢)	money	No.540,R167 (167).
1,208	qián	前	front	No.539,R18.
1,209	qián	潜(潛)	latent	No.680,R85 (85).
1,210	qiǎn	浅(淺)	shallow	No.540,R85 (85).
1,211	qiàn	欠	owe	No.541,R76.
1,212	qiàn	纤(纖)	tow line	No.538,R120 (120).
1,213	qiāng	枪(槍)	rifle	No.64,R75 (75).
1,214	qiāng	腔	cavity	No.393,R130.

1,215 *qiǎng*	抢(搶)	rob	No.64,R64 (64).
1,216 *qiáng*	墙(牆)	wall	No.543,R32 (90).
1,217 *qiáng*	强(強)	strong	No.542,R57 (57).
qiǎng		make an effort.	
1,218 *qiāo*	敲	knock	No.228,R66.
1,219 *qiáo*	桥(橋)	bridge	No.544,R75 (75).
1,220 *qiáo*	瞧	look	No.335,R109.
1,221 *qiáo*	乔(喬)	tall	No.544,R4 (30).
1,222 *qiǎo*	巧	skilful	No.545,R48.
1,223 *qiē*	切	cut	No.546,R18.
qiè		correspond to.	
1,224 *qiě*	且	just	No.547,R1.
1,225 *qīn*	侵	invade	No.549,R9.
1,226 *qīn*	亲(親)	parent	No.548,R117 (147).
1,227 *Qín*	秦	a proper name	No.206,R115.
1,228 *qín*	琴	a musical instrument	No.347,R96.
1,229 *qín*	勤	diligent	No.550,R19.
1,230 *qín*	禽	birds	No.417,R114.
1,231 *qīng*	青	green	No.551,R174.
1,232 *qīng*	轻(輕)	light	No.358,R159 (159).
1,233 *qīng*	氢(氫)	hydrogen	No.535,R84 (84).
1,234 *qīng*	倾	incline	No.552,R9.
1,235 *qīng*	卿	minister	No.312,R26.
1,236 *qīng*	清	clear	No.551,R85.
1,237 *qíng*	晴	fine	No.551,R72.
1,238 *qíng*	氰	cyanogen	No.551,R84.
1,239 *qíng*	情	feeling	No.551,R61.
1,240 *qǐng*	顷	unit of area	No.552,R181.
1,241 *qǐng*	请	request	No.551,R149.
1,242 *qìng*	庆(慶)	celebrate	No.553,R53 (61).
1,243 *qióng*	穷(窮)	poor	No.554,R116 (116).
1,244 *qiū*	秋	autumn	No.555,R115.
1,245 *qiú*	球	sphere	No.556,R96.
1,246 *qiú*	求	beg	No.556,R85.
1,247 *qū*	趋(趨)	hasten	No.558,R156 (156).
1,248 *qū*	区(區)	district	No.557,R23 (23).
1,249 *qū*	曲	crooked	No.155,R73.
qǔ		melody.	
1,250 *qū*	屈	injustice	No.106,R44.

1,251 *qū*	驱(驅)	drive	No.557,R187 (187).
1,252 *qú*	渠	canal	No.370,R85.
1,253 *qǔ*	取	get	No.559,R29.
1,254 *qù*	去	go	No.560,R28.
1,255 *quān*	圈	circle	No.374,R31.
1,256 *quán*	权(權)	right	No.251,R75 (75).
1,257 *quán*	泉	spring	No.643,R85.
1,258 *quán*	全	complete	No.561,R11.
1,259 *quǎn*	犬	dog	No.210,R94.
1,260 *quàn*	劝(勸)	urge	No.251,R19 (19).
1,261 *quē*	缺	lack	No.562,R121.
1,262 *què*	却(卻)	however	No.560,R26 (26).
1,263 *què*	确(確)	true	No.563,R112 (112).
1,264 *qún*	群(羣)	crowd	No.564,R123 (123).

R

1,265 *rán*	然	correct	No.565,R86.
1,266 *rán*	燃	burn	No.565,R86.
1,267 *rǎn*	染	dye	No.180,R75.
1,268 *rāng & rǎng*	嚷	shout	No.566,R30.
1,269 *ràng*	让(讓)	yield	No.566,R149 (149).
1,270 *rào*	绕(繞)	wind	No.567,R120 (120).
1,271 *rè*	热(熱)	heat	No.568,R86 (86).
1,272 *rén*	仁	benevolence	No.570,R9.
1,273 *rén*	人	man	No.569,R9.
1,274 *rèn*	任	appoint	No.572,R9.
1,275 *rěn*	忍	bear	No.571,R61.
1,276 *rèn*	认(認)	know	No.569,R149 (149).
1,277 *rèn*	刃	edge of a knife	No.571,R18.
1,278 *rēng*	扔	throw	No.573,R64.
1,279 *réng*	仍	remain	No.573,R9.
1,280 *rì*	日	day	No.574,R72.
1,281 *róng*	荣(榮)	flourish	No.575,R75 (75).
1,282 *róng*	融	melt	No.232,R142.
1,283 *róng*	熔	melt	No.577,R86.
1,284 *róng*	溶	dissolve	No.577,R85.
1,285 *róng*	容	contain	No.577,R40.

1,286 *róng*	绒	fine hair	No.576,R120.
1,287 *róu*	揉	rub	No.419,R64.
1,288 *róu*	柔	soft	No.419,R75.
1,289 *ròu*	肉	flesh	No.578,R130.
1,290 *rú*	儒	Confucianism	No.785,R9.
1,291 *rú*	如	according to	No.579,R38.
1,292 *rǔ*	乳	breast	No.212,R5.
1,293 *rǔ*	汝	you	No.513,R85.
1,294 *rù*	入	enter	No.580,R11.
1,295 *ruǎn*	软	soft	No.541,R159.
1,296 *rùn*	润	moist	No.706,R85.
1,297 *ruò*	若	like	No.581,R140.
1,298 *ruò*	弱	weak	No.582,R57.

S

1,299 *sā* *sǎ*	撒	let go scatter.	No.585,R64.
1,300 *sǎ*	洒(灑)	sprinkle	No.737,R85 (85).
1,301 *Sà*	萨(薩)	a name	No.75,R140 (140).
1,302 *sāi* *sài*	塞	squeeze in strategic point.	No.583,R32.
1,303 *sài*	赛	competition	No.583,R154.
1,304 *sān*	三	three	No.584,R1.
1,305 *sǎn*	伞(傘)	umbrella	No.640,R9 (9).
1,306 *sǎn* *sàn*	散	come loose disperse.	No.585,R66.
1,307 *sāng*	桑	mulberry	No.846,R75.
1,308 *sǎo*	扫(掃)	sweep	No.217,R64 (64).
1,309 *sǎo*	嫂	sister-in-law	No.586,R38.
1,310 *sè*	色	colour	No.587,R139.
1,311 *sēn*	森	dark	No.487,R75.
1,312 *sēng*	僧	Buddhist monk	No.68,R9.
1,313 *shā*	砂	grit	No.595,R112.
1,314 *shā*	杀(殺)	kill	No.588,R75 (79).
1,315 *shā*	沙	sand	No.595,R85.
1,316 *shā*	纱	yarn	No.595,R120.
1,317 *shà*	啥	what	No.596,R30.
1,318 *shāi*	筛(篩)	sieve	No.610,R118 (118).

1,319	*shài*	晒(曬)	shine upon	No.737,R72 (72).
1,320	*shān*	杉	China fir	No.487,R75.
1,321	*shān*	山	mountain	No.589,R46.
1,322	*shān & shàn*	扇	fan	No.284,R63.
1,323	*shǎn*	闪	flash	No.468,R169.
1,324	*shàn*	善	good	No.590,R30.
1,325	*shāng*	伤(傷)	wound	No.591,R9 (9).
1,326	*shāng*	商	consult	No.592,R30.
1,327	*shǎng*	赏	reward	No.78,R154.
1,328	*shàng*	上	upper	No.593,R1.
1,329	*shàng*	尚	still	No.594,R42.
1,330	*shāo*	梢	tip	No.762,R75.
1,331	*shāo*	稍	a little	No.762,R115.
1,332	*shāo*	烧(燒)	burn	No.567,R86 (86).
1,333	*shǎo*	少	few	No.595,R42.
1,334	*shé*	舌	tongue	No.596,R135.
1,335	*shě* *shè*	舍	abandon shed.	No.596,R135.
1,336	*shè*	摄(攝)	photograph	No.185,R64 (64).
1,337	*shè*	射	shoot	No.600,R41.
1,338	*shè*	涉	ford	No.58,R85.
1,339	*shè*	社	society	No.598,R113.
1,340	*shè*	设	establish	No.597,R149.
1,341	*shēn*	申	explain	No.599,R102.
1,342	*shēn*	伸	extend	No.599,R9.
1,343	*shēn*	身	body	No.600,R158.
1,344	*shēn*	深	deep	No.601,R85.
1,345	*shēn*	绅	gentry	No.599,R120.
1,346	*shén*	神	spirit	No.599,R113.
1,347	*shén*	什(甚)	what?	No.602,R9 (99).
1,348	*Shěn*	沈	Shenyang	No.87,R85.
1,349	*shěn*	审(審)	examine	No.599,R40 (40).
1,350	*shěn*	婶(嬸)	aunt	No.599,R38 (38).
1,351	*shèn*	甚	very	No.602,R99.
1,352	*shēng*	声(聲)	sound	No.605,R33 (128).
1,353	*shēng*	生	life	No.604,R100.
1,354	*shēng*	升	rise	No.603,R24.
1,355	*shèng*	胜(勝)	victory	No.604,R130 (130).

1,356	*shēng*	笙	reed pipe	No.604,R118.
1,357	*shéng*	绳(繩)	rope	No.606,R120 (120).
1,358	*shěng*	省	save	No.607,R109.
1,359	*shèng*	盛	flourishing	No.92,R108.
1,360	*shèng*	剩	surplus	No.95,R18.
1,361	*shèng*	圣(聖)	saint	No.249,R32 (128).
1,362	*shī*	师(師)	master	No.610,R50 (50).
1,363	*shī*	失	lose	No.609,R37.
1,364	*shī*	施	carry out	No.611,R70.
1,365	*shī*	湿(濕)	wet	No.612,R85 (85).
1,366	*shī*	诗	poetry	No.615,R149.
1,367	*shī*	尸	corpse	No.608,R44.
1,368	*shí*	十	ten	No.613,R24.
1,369	*shí*	石	stone	No.614,R112.
1,370	*shí*	拾	pick up	No.274,R64.
1,371	*shí*	时(時)	time	No.615,R72 (72).
1,372	*shí*	饣(食)	food	No.617,R184 (184).
1,373	*shí*	蚀	corrode	No.103,R142.
1,374	*shí*	实(實)	true	No.616,R40 (40).
1,375	*shí*	识(識)	know	No.902,R149 (149).
1,376	*shǐ*	史	history	No.236,R30.
1,377	*shǐ*	使	send	No.618,R9.
1,378	*shǐ*	驶	drive	No.618,R187.
1,379	*shǐ*	始	beginning	No.668,R38.
1,380	*shì*	式	type	No.622,R56.
1,381	*shì*	示	show	No.620,R113.
1,382	*shì*	士	scholar	No.696,R33.
1,383	*shì*	世	lifetime	No.621,R1.
1,384	*shì*	事	affair	No.623,R6.
1,385	*shì*	势(勢)	power	No.899,R19 (19).
1,386	*shì*	是	be	No.624,R72.
1,387	*shì*	适(適)	proper	No.596,R162 (162).
1,388	*shì*	释(釋)	explain	No.825,R165 (165).
1,389	*shì*	饰	adorn	No.610,R184.
1,390	*shì*	氏	surname	No.903,R83.
1,391	*shì*	市	market	No.619,R50.
1,392	*shì*	室	room	No.905,R40.
1,393	*shì*	视	look at	No.328,R147.

1,394	*shì*	试	test	No.622,R149.
1,395	*shōu*	收	receive	No.625,R66.
1,396	*shóu*	熟	ripe	No.633,R86.
1,397	*shǒu*	手	hand	No.626,R64.
1,398	*shǒu*	首	head	No.628,R185.
1,399	*shǒu*	守	guard	No.627,R40.
1,400	*shòu*	寿(壽)	longevity	No.629,R41 (33).
1,401	*shòu*	授	award	No.630,R64.
1,402	*shòu*	售	sell	No.642,R30.
1,403	*shòu*	受	receive	No.630,R29.
1,404	*shòu*	瘦	thin	No.586,R104.
1,405	*shū*	殊	different	No.915,R78.
1,406	*shū*	输	transport	No.691,R159.
1,407	*shū*	叔	uncle	No.632,R29.
1,408	*shū*	疏	sparse	No.440,R103.
1,409	*shū*	书(書)	book	No.631,R2 (73).
1,410	*shū*	殳	ancient weapon	No.597,R79.
1,396	*shú*	熟	ripe	No.633,R86.
1,411	*shǔ*	薯	potato	No.916,R140.
1,412	*shǔ*	署	government office	No.916,R122.
1,413	*Shǔ*	蜀	Sichuan	No.111,R142.
1,414	*shǔ*	鼠	mouse	No.636,R208.
1,415	*shǔ*	属(屬)	category	No.634,R44 (44).
1,416	*shǔ* *shù*	数(數)	count a number.	No.635,R66 (66).
1,417	*shù*	术(術)	art	No.637,R75 (144).
1,418	*shù*	述(述)	relate	No.637,R162 (162).
1,419	*shù*	树(樹)	tree	No.638,R75 (75).
1,420	*shù*	束	tie	No.656,R75.
1,421	*shù*	竖(豎)	vertical	No.353,R117 (151).
1,422	*shuā*	刷	brush	No.639,R18.
1,423	*shuǎi*	甩	swing	No.841,R101.
980	*shuài*	率	lead	No.640,R95.
1,424	*shuān*	拴	fasten	No.561,R64.
1,425	*shuāng*	霜	frost	No.756,R173.
1,426	*shuāng*	双(雙)	both	No.641,R29 (172).
1,427	*shuí*	谁	who?	No.642,R149.
1,428	*shuǐ*	水	water	No.643,R85.

1,429 *shuì*	睡	sleep	No.118,R109.
1,430 *shuì*	税	tax	No.645,R115.
1,431 *shùn*	瞬	wink	No.439,R109.
1,432 *shùn*	顺	along	No.644,R181.
1,433 *shuō*	说	speak	No.645,R149.
1,434 *sī*	斯	this	No.649,R69.
1,435 *sī*	撕	tear	No.649,R64.
1,436 *sī*	思	think	No.648,R61.
1,437 *sī*	私	private	No.647,R115.
1,438 *sī*	司	take charge	No.121,R30.
1,439 *sī*	丝(絲)	silk	No.646,R1 (120).
1,440 *sǐ*	死	die	No.650,R78.
1,441 *sì*	寺	temple	No.97,R41.
1,442 *sì*	四	four	No.651,R31.
1,443 *sì*	似	similar	No.821,R9.
1,444 *sì*	饲	rear	No.121,R184.
1,445 *sōng*	松(鬆)	relax	No.240,R75 (190).
1,446 *sòng*	颂	praise	No.240,R181.
1,447 *sòng*	送	deliver	No.652,R162.
1,448 *Sòng*	宋	Song dynasty	No.929,R40.
1,449 *sōu*	艘	measure (for ships)	No.586,R137.
1,450 *sū*	苏(蘇)	revive	No.21,R140 (140).
1,451 *sú*	俗	vulgar	No.858,R9.
1,452 *sù*	素	white	No.655,R120.
1,453 *sù*	速	speed	No.656,R162.
1,454 *sù*	塑	model	No.657,R32.
1,455 *sù*	诉(訴)	tell	No.653,R149 (149).
1,456 *sù*	肃(肅)	solemn	No.654,R129 (129).
1,457 *suān*	酸	sour	No.658,R164.
1,458 *suàn*	算	calculate	No.659,R118.
1,459 *suī*	虽(雖)	although	No.660,R30&142 (172).
1,460 *suí*	隋	Sui dynasty	No.661,R170.
1,461 *suí*	随(隨)	follow	No.661,R170 (170).
1,462 *suì*	遂	satisfy	No.652,R162.
1,463 *suì*	碎	smash	No.938,R112.
1,464 *suì*	岁(歲)	age	No.662,R46 (77).
1,465 *suì*	穗	fringe	No.182,R115.
1,466 *sūn*	孙(孫)	grandson	No.763,R39 (39).

1,467	*sǔn*	损	damage	No.861,R64.
1,468	*suō*	梭	shuttle	No.658,R75.
1,469	*suō*	缩	shrink	No.663,R120.
1,470	*suǒ*	索	rope	No.655,R120.
1,471	*suǒ*	锁	lock	No.762,R167.
1,472	*suǒ*	所	place	No.664,R63.

T

1,473	*tā*	他	he	No.666, R9.
1,474	*tā*	它(牠)	it	No.665,R40 (93).
1,475	*tā*	她	she	No.666,R38.
1,476	*tà*	踏	step on	No.667,R157.
1,477	*tǎ*	塔	tower	No.128,R32.
1,478	*tāi*	胎	foetus	No.668,R130.
1,479	*tái*	台(臺)	platform	No.668,R30 (133).
1,480	*tái*	抬	lift	No.668,R64.
1,481	*tài*	泰	peaceful	No.206,R85.
1,482	*tài*	太	too	No.669,R37.
1,483	*tài*	态(態)	attitude	No.669,R61 (61).
1,484	*tān*	摊(攤)	spread out	No.496,R64 (64).
1,485	*tān*	贪	corrupt	No.267,R154.
1,486	*tān*	滩(灘)	beach	No.496,R85 (85).
275	*tán*	弹(彈)	shoot	No.135,R57 (57).
1,487	*tán*	谈(談)	chat	No.670,R149.
1,488	*tán*	昙(曇)	cloud-covered	No.866,R72 (72).
1,489	*tàn*	碳	carbon	No.294,R112.
1,490	*tàn*	探	explore	No.601,R64.
1,491	*tàn*	叹(嘆)	sigh	No.496,R30 (30).
1,492	*tàn*	炭	charcoal	No.294,R86.
1,493	*tāng*	汤(湯)	soup	No.77,R85 (85).
1,494	*tàng*	趟	measure word for times	No.594,R156.
1,495	*táng*	塘	dyke	No.671,R32.
1,496	*táng*	堂	hall	No.672,R32.
1,497	*Táng*	唐	Tang dynasty	No.671,R30.
1,498	*táng*	糖	sugar	No.671,R119.
1,499	*tǎng*	倘	if	No.594,R9.
1,500	*tǎng*	躺	lie down	No.594,R158.

1,501 *tàng*	烫(燙)	scald	No.77,R86 (86).
1,502 *tāo*	掏	draw out	No.673,R64.
1,503 *tāo*	涛(濤)	billows	No.629,R85 (85).
1,504 *táo*	桃	peach	No.674,R75.
1,505 *táo*	逃	escape	No.674,R162.
1,506 *tǎo*	讨	suppress	No.127,R149.
1,507 *tào*	套	sheath	No.675,R37.
1,508 *tè*	特	special	No.676,R93.
1,509 *téng*	腾	gallop	No.206,R187 & 130.
1,510 *tī*	踢	kick	No.826,R157.
1,511 *tí*	提	lift	No.677,R64.
1,512 *tí*	题	topic	No.677,R181.
1,513 *tǐ*	体(體)	body	No.679,R9 (188).
1,514 *tì*	替	substitute for	No.680,R73.
1,515 *tiān*	天	heaven	No.681,R37.
1,516 *tiān*	添	add	No.681,R85.
1,517 *tián*	填	fill	No.890,R32.
1,518 *tián*	田	field	No.682,R102.
1,519 *tián*	甜	sweet	No.224,R99.
1,520 *tiāo* *tiǎo*	挑	choose push; poke	No.674,R64.
318 *tiáo*	调	mix	No.160,R149.
1,521 *tiáo*	条(條)	twig	No.683,R75 (75 & 9).
1,522 *tiào*	跳	jump	No.674,R157.
1,523 *tiē*	贴	paste	No.879,R154.
1,524 *tiě*	铁(鐵)	iron	No.684,R167 (167).
1,525 *tīng*	厅(廳)	hall	No.162,R27 (53).
1,526 *tīng*	听(聽)	listen	No.685,R30 (128).
1,527 *tīng*	烃(烴)	hydrocarbon	No.358,R86 (86).
1,528 *tíng*	廷	feudal court	No.687,R54.
1,529 *tíng*	停	stop	No.686,R9.
1,530 *tíng*	亭	kiosk	No.686,R8.
1,531 *tíng*	庭	courtyard	No.687,R53.
1,532 *tǐng*	挺	straight	No.687,R64.
1,533 *tōng*	通	through	No.688,R162.
1,534 *tóng*	同	same	No.689,R30.
1,535 *tóng*	铜	copper	No.689,R167.
1,536 *tóng*	童	child	No.690,R117.

1,537 tǒng	桶	bucket	No.688,R75.
1,538 tǒng	筒	tube	No.689,R118.
1,539 tǒng	统	system	No.102,R120.
1,540 tòng	痛	pain	No.688,R104.
1,541 tòng	恸(慟)	deep sorrow	No.166,R61 (61).
1,542 tōu	偷	steal	No.691,R9.
1,543 tóu	投	throw	No.597,R64.
1,544 tóu	头(頭)	head	No.692,R37 & 3 (181).
1,545 tòu	透	penetrate	No.693,R162.
1,546 tū	凸	protruding	No.8,R17.
1,547 tū	突	dash forward	No.694,R116.
1,548 tú	图(圖)	map	No.695,R31 (31).
1,549 tú	徒	on foot	No.931,R60.
1,550 tú	途	route	No.851,R162.
1,551 tú	涂	smear on	No.851,R85.
1,552 tǔ	土	earth	No.696,R32.
1,553 tǔ tù	吐	spit vomit.	No.696,R30.
1,554 tù	兔	rabbit	No.475,R10.
1,555 tuán	团(團)	round	No.921,R31 (31).
1,556 tuī	推	push	No.697,R64.
1,557 tuǐ	腿	leg	No.698,R130.
1,558 tuì	退	retreat	No.698,R162.
1,559 tún	屯	collect	No.127,R45.
1,560 tuō	拖	pull	No.611,R64.
1,561 tuō	托	entrust	No.699,R64.
1,562 tuō	脱	shed	No.645,R130.

W

1,563 wā	挖	dig	No.700,R64.
1,564 wā	哇	noise of crying	No.248,R30.
1,565 wá	娃	baby	No.248,R38.
1,566 wǎ & wà	瓦	tile	No.701,R98.
1,567 wāi	歪	crooked	No.56,R77.
1,568 wài	外	foreign	No.702,R36.
1,569 wān	弯(彎)	curved	No.45,R57 (57).
1,570 wān	湾(灣)	bay	No.45,R85 (85).
1,571 wán	玩	have fun; joke	No.703,R96.

1,572	*wán*	完	whole	No.703,R40.
1,573	*wǎn*	碗	bowl	No.704,R112.
1,574	*wǎn*	晚	late	No.475,R72.
1,575	*wàn*	万(萬)	ten thousand	No.705,R1 (140).
1,576	*wāng*	汪	accumulate	No.706,R85.
1,577	*wáng*	王	king	No.706,R96.
1,578	*wáng*	亡	flee	No.708,R8.
1,579	*wàng*	忘	forget	No.708,R61.
1,580	*wǎng*	网(網)	net	No.707,R122 (120).
1,581	*wǎng & wàng*	往	towards	No.918,R60.
1,582	*wàng*	旺	prosperous	No.706,R72.
1,583	*wàng*	望	gaze	No.709,R74.
1,584	*wēi*	威	might	No.711,R38.
1,585	*wēi*	微	tiny	No.712,R60.
1,586	*wēi*	危	danger	No.710,R26.
1,587	*wéi*	围(圍)	enclose	No.714,R31 (31).
1,588	*wéi*	唯	only	No.642,R30.
1,589	*wéi*	惟	only	No.642,R61.
1,590	*wéi* / *wèi*	为(為)	act / for.	No.713,R3 (87).
1,591	*wéi*	维	tie up	No.642,R120.
1,592	*wěi*	委	entrust	No.716,R38.
1,593	*wěi*	伟(偉)	great	No.714,R9 (9).
1,594	*wěi*	伪(偽)	false	No.713,R9 (9).
1,595	*wěi*	尾	tail	No.715,R44.
1,596	*wěi*	纬(緯)	latitude	No.714,R120 (120).
1,597	*wèi*	未	not	No.718,R75.
1,598	*wèi*	味	taste	No.718,R30.
1,599	*wèi*	胃	stomach	No.720,R130.
1,600	*wèi*	喂	hello	No.721,R30.
1,601	*Wèi*	魏	a proper name	No.716,R194.
1,602	*wèi*	位	place	No.719,R9.
1,603	*wèi*	谓	call	No.720,R149.
1,604	*wèi*	卫(衛)	guard	No.717,R26 (144).
1,605	*wēn*	温	warm	No.722,R85.
1,606	*wén*	文	writing	No.723,R67.
1,607	*wén*	闻	hear	No.724,R128 & 169.
1,608	*wén*	纹	wrinkles	No.723,R120.

1,609	*wěn*	稳(穩)	steady	No.313,R115 (115).
1,610	*wèn*	问	ask	No.725,R30.
1,611	*wō*	涡(渦)	whirlpool	No.260,R85 (85).
1,612	*wō*	窝(窩)	nest	No.260, R116 (116).
1,613	*wǒ*	我	I	No.726,R62.
1,614	*wò*	卧(臥)	lie	No.727,R131 (131).
1,615	*wò*	握	grasp	No.905,R64.
1,616	*wū*	乌(烏)	crow	No.506,R4 (86).
1,617	*wū*	污(汙)	dirt	No.728,R85 (85).
1,618	*wū*	屋	house	No.905,R44.
1,619	*wú*	无(無)	not	No.729,R71 (86).
1,620	*wú*	吾	I or we	No.730,R30.
1,621	*Wú*	吴(吳)	a surname	No.736,R30 (30).
1,622	*wǔ*	武	military	No.732,R77.
1,623	*wǔ*	五	five	No.730,R7.
1,624	*wǔ*	午	noon	No.731,R24.
1,625	*wǔ*	舞	dance	No.733,R136.
1,626	*wǔ*	伍	five	No.730,R9.
1,627	*wù*	雾(霧)	fog	No.734,R173 (173).
1,628	*wù*	物	matter	No.735,R93.
1,629	*wù*	勿	not	No.735,R20.
1,630	*wù*	务(務)	affair	No.734,R19 (19).
1,631	*wù*	悟	realise	No.856,R61.
1,632	*wù*	误(誤)	mistake	No.736,R149 (149).

X

1,633	*xī*	栖	perch	No.737,R75.
1,634	*xī*	析	analyse	No.739,R75.
1,635	*xī*	西	west	No.737,R146.
1,636	*xī*	吸	breathe in	No.311,R30.
1,637	*xī*	锡	tin	No.826,R167.
1,638	*xī*	稀	rare	No.738,R115.
1,639	*xī*	息	breath	No.740,R61.
1,640	*xī*	希	hope	No.738,R50.
1,641	*xī*	悉	know	No.745,R61.
1,642	*xī*	烯	alkene	No.738,R86.
1,643	*xī*	溪	small stream	No.745,R85.

1,644	*xí*	席	mat	No.171,R50.
1,645	*xí*	习(習)	practise	No.741,R5 (124).
1,646	*xǐ*	喜	like	No.743,R30.
1,647	*xǐ*	洗	wash	No.742,R85.
1,648	*xì*	系(係)(繫)	system	No.745,R120 (9) (120).
1,649	*xì*	戏(戲)	play	No.744,R29 & 62 (62).
1,650	*xì*	细(細)	thin	No.744,R120 (120).
1,651	*xiā*	虾(蝦)	shrimp	No.747,R142 (142).
1,652	*xiá*	霞	rosy clouds	No.323,R173.
1,653	*xiá*	狭(狹)	narrow	No.320,R94 (94).
1,654	*xià*	下	below	No.747,R1.
1,655	*xià*	夏	summer	No.748,R35.
1,656	*xià*	吓(嚇)	frighten	No.747,R30 (30).
1,657	*xiān*	先	first	No.749,R10.
1,658	*xiān*	仙	immortal	No.589,R9.
1,659	*xiān* *xiǎn*	鲜	fresh rare.	No.805,R195.
1,212	*xiān*	纤(纖)	fine	No.538,R120 (120).
1,660	*xián*	咸(鹹)	salty	No.226,R30 (197).
1,661	*xián*	贤(賢)	virtuous	No.325,R154 (154).
1,662	*xián*	闲	idle	No.468,R169.
1,663	*xián*	弦	bowstring	No.788,R57.
1,664	*xián*	嫌	suspicion	No.326,R38.
1,665	*xiǎn*	显(顯)	obvious	No.750,R72 (181).
1,666	*xiǎn*	险(險)	danger	No.426,R170 (170).
1,667	*xiàn*	现	present	No.752,R96.
1,668	*xiàn*	献(獻)	offer	No.754,R94 (94).
1,669	*xiàn*	县(縣)	county	No.751,R28 (120).
1,670	*xiàn*	腺	gland	No.643,R130.
1,671	*xiàn*	宪(憲)	constitution	No.749,R40 (61).
1,672	*xiàn*	陷	trap	No.753,R170.
1,673	*xiàn*	限	limit	No.277,R170.
1,674	*xiàn*	线(線)	thread	No.540,R120 (120).
1,675	*xiāng* *xiàng*	相	each other appearance.	No.756,R109 & 75.
1,676	*xiāng*	镶	inlay	No.566,R167.
1,677	*xiāng*	香	fragrant	No.757,R186.
1,678	*xiāng*	箱	chest	No.756,R118.

1,679	Xiāng	湘	Hunan	No.756,R85.
1,680	xiāng	乡(鄉)	countryside	No.755,R5 (163).
1,681	xiáng	祥	auspicious	No.805,R113.
1,682	xiáng	详	detailed	No.805,R149.
1,683	xiǎng	想	think	No.759,R61.
1,684	xiǎng	响(響)	sound	No.760,R30 (180).
1,685	xiǎng	享	enjoy	No.758,R8.
1,686	xiàng	项	an item	No.238,R181.
1,687	xiàng	巷	alley	No.241,R49.
1,688	xiàng	像	likeness	No.761,R9.
1,689	xiàng	向	direction	No.760,R30.
1,690	xiàng	象	elephant	No.761,R152.
1,691	xiāo	萧(蕭)	desolate	No.654,R140 (140).
1,692	xiāo	削	peel	No.762,R18.
1,693	xiāo	销	melt	No.762,R167.
1,694	xiāo	消	disappear	No.762,R85.
1,695	xiǎo	晓(曉)	dawn	No.567,R72 (72).
1,696	xiǎo	小	small	No.763,R42.
1,697	xiào	孝	filial piety; mourning	No.887,R39.
1,698	xiào	校	school	No.334,R75.
1,699	xiào	笑	smile	No.764,R118.
1,700	xiào	效	effect	No.334,R66.
1,701	xiē	楔	wedge	No.429,R75.
1,702	xiē	些	these	No.122,R7.
1,703	xiē	歇	rest	No.273,R76.
1,704	xié	鞋	shoes	No.248,R177.
1,705	xié	协(協)	common	No.21,R24 (24).
1,706	xié	斜	oblique	No.851,R68.
1,707	xiě	写(寫)	write	No.765,R14 (40).
1,708	xiè	械	tool	No.576,R75.
1,709	xiè	卸	unload	No.562,R26.
1,710	xiè	蟹	crab	No.344,R142.
1,711	xiè	谢	thank	No.766,R149.
1,712	xiè	屑	scraps	No.762,R44.
1,713	xīn / xìn	芯	wick / core.	No.767,R140.
1,714	xīn	锌	zinc	No.768,R167.
1,715	xīn	辛	hot; pungent	No.768,R160.

1,716	*xīn*	新	new	No.769,R69.
1,717	*xīn*	心	heart	No.767,R61.
1,718	*xìn*	信	trust	No.770,R9.
1,719	*xīng*	星	star	No.772,R72.
1,720	*xīng* xìng	兴(興)	prosper mood.	No.771,R12 (134).
1,721	*xíng*	刑	punishment	No.773,R18.
1,722	*xíng*	型	mould	No.773,R32.
1,723	*xíng*	形	form	No.775,R59.
562	*xíng*	行	go	No.774,R144.
1,724	*xīng*	星	star	No.772,R72.
1,725	*xìng*	幸	good fortune	No.768,R51.
1,726	*xìng*	杏	apricot	No.26,R75.
1,727	*xìng*	性	nature	No.776,R61.
1,728	*xìng*	姓	surname	No.604,R38.
1,729	*xiōng*	兄	elder brother	No.778,R10.
1,730	*xiōng*	凶	fierce	No.777,R17.
1,731	*xiōng*	胸	chest	No.777,R130.
1,732	*xióng*	雄	male	No.779,R172.
1,733	*xiū*	休	rest	No.780,R9.
1,734	*xiū*	修	repair	No.781,R9.
1,735	*xiǔ*	朽	rotten	No.545,R75.
1,736	*xiù*	秀	elegant	No.782,R115.
1,737	*xiù*	绣(繡)	embroider	No.782,R120 (120).
1,738	*xū*	需	need	No.785,R173.
1,739	*xū*	虚	void	No.784,R141.
1,740	*xū*	须(鬚)	must; have to; beard	No.783,R181 & 59 (190).
1,741	*xú*	徐	slowly	No.851,R60.
1,742	*xǔ*	许	praise	No.731,R149.
1,743	*xù*	蓄	store up	No.786,R140.
1,744	*xù*	序	order	No.850,R53.
1,745	*xù*	畜	raise	No.786,R102.
1,746	*xù*	续(續)	continue	No.458,R120 (120).
1,747	*xuān*	宣	declare	No.787,R40.
1,748	*xuán*	悬(懸)	hang	No.751,R61 (61).
1,749	*xuán*	旋	turn	No.611,R70.
1,750	*xuán*	玄	black	No.788,R95.
1,751	*xuǎn*	选(選)	select	No.789,R162 (162).

1,752 *xué*	学(學)	study	No.790,R39 (39).
1,753 *xué*	穴	cave	No.11,R116.
1,754 *xuě*	雪	snow	No.413,R173.
1,755 *xuè*	血	blood	No.791,R143.
1,756 *xún*	旬	period of ten days/years	No.371,R72.
1,757 *xún*	寻(尋)	look for	No.792,R41 & 58 (41).
1,758 *xún*	巡	patrol	No.644,R47.
1,759 *xùn*	汛	flood	No.793,R85.
1,760 *xùn*	训	lecture	No.644,R149.
1,761 *xùn*	讯(訊)	interrogate	No.793,R149 (149).

Y

1,762 *yā*	压(壓)	press down	No.794,R27 (32).
1,763 *yā*	鸭	duck	No.322,R196.
1,764 *yā*	呀	Oh!	No.795,R30.
1,765 *yǎ*	雅	elegant	No.795,R172.
1,766 *yá*	芽	bud	No.795,R140.
1,767 *yá*	牙	tooth	No.795,R92.
1,768 *yá*	崖	cliff	No.248,R46.
1,769 *yà*	亚(亞)	inferior	No.796,R1 (7).
1,770 *yà*	轧	run over	No.877,R159.
1,771 *yān*	焉	how?	No.141,R86.
1,772 *yān* *yàn*	咽	pharynx swallow.	No.797,R30.
1,773 *yān*	烟(煙)	smoke	No.797,R86 (86).
1,774 *yàn*	燕	swallow (bird)	No.797,R86.
1,775 *yán*	盐(鹽)	salt	No.802,R108 (197).
1,776 *yán*	严(嚴)	strict	No.800,R1 (30).
1,777 *yán*	研	study	No.614,R112.
1,778 *yán*	岩(巖)	cliff	No.614,R46 (46).
1,779 *yán*	延	prolong	No.798,R54.
1,780 *yán*	讠(言)	speech	No.799,R149 (149).
1,781 *yán*	颜	colour	No.75,R181.
1,782 *yán*	炎	burning hot	No.670,R86.
1,783 *yán* *yàn*	沿	along water's edge.	No.801,R85.
1,784 *yǎn*	眼	eye	No.803,R109.
1,785 *yǎn*	演	act	No.804,R85.

1,786 *yàn*	验(驗)	examine	No.426,R187 (187).
1,787 *yāng*	秧	seedling	No.836,R115.
1,788 *yáng*	杨(楊)	poplar	No.77,R75 (75).
1,789 *yáng*	扬(揚)	raise	No.77,R64 (64).
1,790 *yáng*	羊	sheep	No.805,R123.
1,791 *yáng*	洋	vast	No.805,R85.
1,792 *yáng*	阳(陽)	sun	No.77,R170 (170).
1,793 *yǎng*	氧	oxygen	No.535,R84.
1,794 *yǎng*	仰	look up to	No.837,R9.
1,795 *yǎng*	养(養)	provide for	No.806,R12 (184).
1,796 *yàng*	样(樣)	appearance	No.805,R75 (75).
1,797 *yāo*	腰	waist	No.808,R130.
1,798 *yào* *yāo*	要	wish demand.	No.808,R146.
1,799 *yáo*	摇	shake	No.807,R64.
1,800 *yáo*	窑(窯)	kiln	No.562,R116 (116).
1,801 *Yáo*	姚	a surname	No.674,R38.
1,802 *yǎo*	咬	bite	No.334,R30.
1,803 *yào*	药(藥)	medicine	No.863,R140 (140).
1,804 *yé*	爷(爺)	father	No.214,R88 (88).
1,805 *yě*	野	wild	No.810,R166.
1,806 *yě*	也	also	No.809,R5.
1,807 *yè*	页	page	No.813,R181.
1,808 *yè*	业(業)	business	No.811,R1 (75).
1,809 *yè*	叶(葉)	leaf	No.812,R30 (140).
1,810 *yè*	夜	night	No.814,R36.
1,811 *yè*	液	liquid	No.814,R85.
1,812 *yī*	一	one	No.815,R1.
1,813 *yī*	医(醫)	doctor	No.817,R23 (164).
1,814 *yī*	依	depend on	No.816,R9.
1,815 *yī*	伊	he or she	No.564,R9.
1,816 *yī*	衣	clothing	No.816,R145.
1,817 *yí*	夷	smooth	No.153,R37.
1,818 *yí*	遗	leave behind	No.258,R162.
1,819 *yí*	移	move	No.178,R115.
1,820 *yí*	仪(儀)	ceremony	No.822,R9 (9).
1,821 *yí*	疑	doubt	No.818,R103.
1,822 *yí*	宜	suitable	No.547,R40.

1,823	*yǐ*	倚	rely on	No.532,R9.
1,824	*yǐ*	已	stop; already	No.820,R49.
1,825	*yǐ*	乙	second	No.819,R5.
1,826	*yǐ*	矣	final particle denoting completion	No.2,R111.
1,827	*yǐ*	以	use	No.821,R9.
1,828	*yì*	艺(藝)	skill	No.819,R140 (140).
1,829	*yì*	抑	restrain	No.837,R64.
1,830	*yì*	易	easy	No.826,R72.
1,831	*yì*	亿(億)	a hundred million	No.819,R9 (9).
1,832	*yì*	役	labour	No.597,R60.
1,833	*yì*	逸	ease	No.475,R162.
1,834	*yì*	亦	also	No.823,R8.
1,835	*yì*	意	meaning	No.828,R61.
1,836	*yì*	忆(憶)	recall	No.819,R61 (61).
1,837	*yì*	义(義)	justice	No.822,R3 (123).
1,838	*yì*	益	benefit	No.827,R108.
1,839	*yì*	议(議)	opinion	No.822,R149 (149).
1,840	*yì*	译(譯)	translate	No.825,R149 (149).
1,841	*yì*	异(異)	strange	No.824,R49 (102).
1,842	*yì*	翼	wing	No.854,R124.
1,843	*yīn*	因	because of	No.829,R31.
1,844	*yīn*	殷	abundant	No.597,R79.
1,845	*yīn*	音	sound	No.831,R180.
1,846	*yīn*	阴(陰)	shade	No.830,R170 (170).
1,847	*yín*	银	silver	No.277,R167.
1,848	*yǐn* *yìn*	饮	drink to water animals.	No.541,R184.
1,849	*yǐn*	引	attract	No.832,R57.
1,850	*yǐn*	隐(隱)	concealed	No.833,R170 (170).
1,851	*yìn*	印	seal	No.834,R26.
1,852	*yīng*	英	hero	No.836,R140.
1,853	*yīng & yìng*	应(應)	answer	No.835,R53 (53 & 61).
1,854	*yíng*	营(營)	camp	No.838,R140 (86).
1,855	*yíng*	迎	go to meet	No.837,R162.
1,856	*yǐng*	影	shadow	No.839,R59.
1,857	*yìng*	硬	hard	No.236,R112.
1,858	*yìng*	映	reflect	No.836,R72.

1,859	*yō & yo*	哟	oh! & ho!	No.863,R30.
1,860	*yōng*	拥(擁)	embrace	No.841,R64 (64).
1,861	*yǒng*	涌	well up	No.688,R85.
1,862	*yǒng*	永	forever	No.840,R85.
1,863	*yǒng*	勇	brave	No.688,R19.
1,864	*yòng*	用	use	No.841,R101.
1,865	*yōu*	优(優)	excellent	No.842,R9 (9).
1,866	*yóu*	尤	outstanding	No.842,R43.
1,867	*yóu*	由	cause	No.843,R102.
1,868	*yóu*	铀	uranium	No.843,R167.
1,869	*yóu*	犹(猶)	just as	No.842,R94 (94).
1,870	*yóu*	油	oil	No.843,R85.
1,871	*yóu*	游	swim	No.844,R85.
1,872	*yǒu*	酉	tenth	No.364,R164.
1,873	*yǒu*	有	have	No.845,R74.
1,874	*yǒu*	友	friend	No.847,R29.
1,875	*yòu*	右	right	No.847,R30.
1,876	*yòu*	釉	glaze	No.843,R165.
1,877	*yòu*	又	again	No.846,R29.
1,878	*yòu*	幼	young	No.848,R52.
1,879	*yú*	于(於)	in	No.849,R7 (70).
1,880	*yú*	愚	foolish	No.859,R61.
1,881	*yú*	余(餘)	surplus	No.851,R9 (184).
1,882	*yú*	鱼(魚)	fish	No.852,R195 (195).
1,883	*yú*	渔(漁)	fishing	No.852,R85.
1,884	*yú* *yù*	予	I give.	No.850,R6.
1,885	*yǔ & yú* *yù*	与(與)	give take part in.	No.853,R1 (134).
1,886	*yǔ*	雨	rain	No.855,R173.
1,887	*yǔ*	语(語)	language	No.856,R149.
1,888	*yǔ*	羽	feather	No.854,R124.
1,889	*yù*	玉	jade	No.706,R96.
1,890	*yù*	域	territory	No.302,R32.
1,891	*yù*	遇	meet	No.859,R162.
1,892	*yù*	愈	heal	No.691,R61.
1,893	*yù*	欲	desire	No.858,R76.
1,894	*yù*	狱	prison	No.210,R94.

1,895 *yù*	育	rear	No.857,R130.
1,896 *yù*	寓	reside	No.859,R40.
1,897 *yù*	裕	abundant	No.858,R145.
1,898 *yù*	预	in advance	No.850,R181.
1,899 *yù*	豫	pleased	No.850,R152.
1,900 *yù*	聿	pencil	No.350,R129.
1,901 *yuān*	冤	wrong	No.475,R14.
1,902 *yuán*	元	first	No.860,R10.
1,903 *yuán*	原	original	No.862,R27.
1,904 *yuán*	援	hold	No.514,R64.
1,905 *yuán*	园(園)	garden	No.860,R31 (31).
1,906 *yuán*	员	member	No.861,R30.
1,907 *yuán*	圆	round	No.861,R31.
1,908 *yuán*	源	source	No.862,R85.
1,909 *yuán*	缘	reason	No.448,R120.
1,910 *yuǎn*	远(遠)	distant	No.860,R162 (162).
1,911 *yuàn*	愿(願)	willing	No.862,R61 (181).
1,912 *yuàn*	怨	resentment	No.512,R61.
1,913 *yuàn*	院	courtyard	No.860,R170.
1,914 *yuē*	曰	say	No.574,R73.
1,915 *yuē*	约(約)	arrange	No.863,R120 (120).
891 *yuè*	乐(樂)	music	No.411,R4 (75).
1,916 *yuè*	越	exceed	No.865,R156.
1,917 *yuè*	跃(躍)	leap	No.854,R157 (157).
1,918 *yuè*	月	moon	No.864,R74 & 130.
1,919 *yuè*	阅	read	No.645,R169.
1,920 *yún*	云(雲)	cloud	No.866,R7 (173).
1,921 *yún*	匀	even	No.867,R20.
1,922 *yùn*	运(運)	movement	No.866,R162 (162).
1,923 *yùn*	韵(韻)	musical sound	No.867,R180 (180).

Z

1,924 *zá*	杂(雜)	sundry	No.868,R75 (172).
1,925 *zāi*	栽	plant	No.61,R75.
1,926 *zāi*	灾(災)	calamity	No.301,R40 (86).
1,927 *zǎi* *zài*	载	year transport.	No.61,R159.

1,928	zài	再	again	No.869,R13.
1,929	zài	在	at	No.870,R32.
1,930	zán	咱	we	No.928,R30.
1,931	zàn	暂	temporary	No.348,R72.
1,932	zàn	赞	praise	No.871,R154.
1,933	zāng	脏(髒)	dirty	No.65,R130 (188).
	zàng	脏(臟)	internal organs	No.65,R130 (130).
132	zàng	藏	storing place	No.65,R140.
1,934	zāo	遭	suffer	No.872,R162.
1,935	zǎo	早	early morning	No.873,R72.
1,936	zào	造	create	No.229,R162.
1,937	zé	责	duty	No.875,R154.
1,938	zé	择(擇)	select	No.825,R64 (64).
1,939	zé	则	standard	No.874,R18.
1,940	zé	泽(澤)	pool	No.825,R85.
1,941	zè	仄	narrow	No.569,R9.
1,942	zéi	贼	thief	No.576,R154.
1,943	zěn	怎	how?	No.876,R61.
1,944	zēng	增	add	No.68,R32.
1,945	zhā zhá	扎	prick pitch (tent).	No.877,R64.
1,946	zhā	渣	dregs	No.72,R85.
1,770	zhá	轧	roll (steel)	No.877,R159.
1,947	zhá	闸	floodgate	No.322,R169.
1,948	zhá zhà	炸	fry explode.	No.876,R86.
1,949	zhāi	摘	pluck	No.151,R64.
1,950	zhāi	斋(齋)	abstain	No.184,R67 (40).
1,951	zhǎi	窄	narrow	No.876,R116.
1,952	zhài	债	debt	No.875,R9.
1,953	zhài	寨	stockade	No.583,R40.
1,954	zhàn zhān	占(佔)	occupy practise divination.	No.879,R25 (9).
1,955	zhān	沾	moisten	No.879,R85.
1,956	zhǎn	展	open up	No.878,R44.
1,957	zhǎn	斩	cut	No.348,R69.
1,958	zhàn	站	stand	No.879,R117.
1,959	zhàn	战(戰)	war	No.879,R62 (62).

1,960 *zhāng*	章	chapter	No.880,R117.
1,961 *zhāng*	张	display	No.76,R57.
159 *zhǎng*	长(長)	senior	No.76,R4 (168).
1,962 *zhǎng*	掌	palm	No.881,R64.
1,963 *zhǎng* *zhàng*	涨	rise swell.	No.76,R85.
1,964 *zhàng*	丈	husband; measure of length (3$^1/_3$ metres)	No.882,R1.
1,965 *zhàng*	帐	curtain	No.76,R50.
1,966 *zhàng*	仗	weaponry	No.882,R9.
1,967 *zhàng*	胀	expand	No.76,R130.
1,968 *zhāo*	招	beckon	No.883,R64.
1,978 *zhāo* *zháo*	着(著)	a move touch.	No.889,R123 (140).
1,969 *zhǎo*	找	look for	No.884,R64.
1,970 *Zhào*	赵(趙)	a surname	No.762,R156 (156).
1,971 *zhào*	照	shine	No.885,R86.
1,972 *zhào*	罩	cover	No.161,R122.
1,973 *zhào*	召	summon	No.883,R30.
1,974 *zhē*	折	roll over	No.886,R64.
zhé	折(摺)	break	No.886,R64 (64).
1,975 *zhě*	者	person performing an action	No.887,R125.
1,976 *zhè*	这(這)	this	No.888,R162 (162).
1,977 *Zhè*	浙	Zhejiang Province	No.886,R85.
1,978 *zhe*	着(著)	indicates continuing action	No.889,R123 (140).
1,979 *zhēn*	珍	treasure	No.90,R96.
1,980 *zhēn*	真	true	No.890,R109.
1,981 *zhēn*	贞	loyal	No.879,R154.
1,982 *zhēn*	针	needle	No.613,R167.
1,983 *zhèn*	震	shock	No.891,R173.
1,984 *zhèn*	振	shake	No.891,R64.
1,985 *zhèn*	镇	press down	No.890,R167.
1,986 *zhèn*	阵	battle front	No.83,R170.
1,987 *zhēng*	蒸	steam food	No.94,R140.
1,988 *zhēng*	睁	open the eyes	No.892,R109.
1,989 *zhēng*	征(徵)	go on a journey	No.894,R60 (60).
1,990 *zhēng*	争(爭)	struggle	No.892,R18 (87).

1,991	*zhèng*	正	straight	No.894,R77.
	zhēng		first month of lunar year.	
1,992	*zhēng* & *zhèng*	症(癥)	illness	No.894,R104 (104).
1,993	*zhěng*	整	whole	No.893,R66.
1,994	*zhèng*	政	politics	No.895,R66.
1,995	*Zhèng*	郑(鄭)	a surname	No.250,R163 (163).
1,996	*zhèng*	证(證)	proof	No.894,R149 (149).
1,997	*zhī*	芝	occurs only in compounds	No.896,R140.
1,998	*zhī*	枝	branch	No.897,R75.
1,999	*zhī*	支	prop up	No.897,R65.
2,074	*zhī*	吱	creak	No.897,R30.
2,000	*zhī*	知	know	No.898,R111.
2,001	*zhī*	脂	fat	No.904,R130.
2,002	*zhī*	汁	juice	No.613,R85.
2,003	*zhī*	之	sign of the genitive	No.896,R4.
2,004	*zhī*	织(織)	weave	No.902,R120 (120).
2,005	*zhǐ*	指	point to	No.904,R64.
	zhī		nail.	
	zhí		finger or toe.	
2,006	*zhǐ*	只(祇)	only	No.902,R30 (113).
	zhī	只(隻)	single	No.902,R30 (172).
2,007	*zhī* & *zhì*	掷(擲)	throw	No.250,R64 (64).
2,008	*zhí*	职(職)	duty	No.902,R128 (128).
2,009	*zhí*	直	straight	No.900,R109.
2,010	*zhí*	植	plant	No.900,R75.
2,011	*zhí*	执(執)	grasp	No.899,R64 (32).
2,012	*zhí*	值	value	No.900,R9.
2,013	*zhǐ*	止	stop	No.901,R77.
2,014	*zhǐ*	纸(紙)	paper	No.903,R120 (120).
2,015	*zhǐ*	酯	ester	No.904,R164.
2,016	*zhì*	志(誌)	will	No.906,R61 (149).
2,017	*zhì*	至	until	No.905,R133.
2,018	*zhì*	致	send	No.905,R133.
2,019	*zhì*	置	put	No.900,R122.
2,020	*zhì*	制(製)	manufacture	No.909,R18 (145).
2,021	*zhì*	智	wisdom	No.898,R72.
2,022	*zhì*	质(質)	nature	No.908,R154 (154).
2,023	*zhì*	治	rule	No.907,R85.

2,024	zhōng	中	centre	No.910,R2.
	zhòng		hit.	
2,025	zhōng	忠	loyal	No.910,R61.
2,026	zhōng	钟(鐘)	bell	No.910,R167 (167).
2,027	zhōng	终	end	No.165,R120.
2,028	zhǒng	种(種)	species	No.910,R115 (115).
	zhòng		grow.	
2,028	zhòng	重	heavy	No.912,R166.
2,029	zhòng	仲	second	No.910,R9.
2,030	zhòng	众(眾)	crowd	No.911,R9 (109).
2,031	zhōu	舟	boat	No.113,R137.
2,032	zhōu	周(週)	all around	No.914,R30 (162).
2,033	zhōu	州	prefecture	No.913,R47.
2,034	zhōu	洲	continent	No.913,R85.
2,035	zhóu	轴	axle	No.843,R159.
2,036	zhòu	皱(皺)	wrinkle	No.558,R107 (107).
2,037	zhū	珠	pearl	No.915,R96.
2,038	zhū	株	trunk of a tree	No.915,R75.
2,039	zhū	朱(硃)	vermilion	No.915,R75 (112).
2,040	zhū	猪(豬)	pig	No.916,R94 (152).
2,041	zhū	诸(諸)	all	No.916,R149 (149).
2,042	zhú	逐	pursue	No.652,R162.
2,043	zhú	竹	bamboo	No.917,R118.
2,044	zhù	筑(築)	build	No.395,R118 (118).
2,045	zhǔ	煮	boil	No.916,R86.
2,046	zhǔ	拄	lean on	No.918,R64.
2,047	zhǔ	主	host	No.918,R3.
2,048	zhù	著	outstanding	No.916,R140.
2,049	zhù	柱	post	No.918,R75.
2,050	zhù	助	help	No.919,R19.
2,051	zhù	贮(貯)	store	No.507,R154 (154).
2,052	zhù	铸(鑄)	casting	No.629,R167 (167).
2,053	zhù	住	live	No.918,R9.
2,054	zhù	注(註)	pour	No.918,R85 (149).
2,055	zhù	祝	express good wishes	No.778,R113.
2,056	zhù	驻	halt	No.918,R187.
2,057	zhuā	抓	seize	No.920,R64.
2,058	zhuān	专(專)	special	No.921,R7 (41).

2,059	*zhuān*	砖(磚)	brick	No.921,R112 (112).
2,060	*zhuǎn* *zhuàn*	转(轉)	turn revolve.	No.921,R159 (159).
219	*zhuàn*	传(傳)	commentaries on classics	No.921,R9 (9).
2,061	*zhuāng*	桩(椿)	stake	No.922,R75 (75).
2,062	*zhuāng*	庄(莊)	village	No.696,R53 (140).
2,063	*zhuāng*	装(裝)	dress up	No.922,R145 (145).
2,064	*zhuàng*	撞	bump into	No.923,R64.
2,065	*zhuàng*	壮(壯)	strong	No.922,R90 (33).
2,066	*zhuàng*	状(狀)	form	No.922,R90 (94).
2,067	*zhuī*	隹	short-tailed birds	No.335,R172.
2,068	*zhuī*	锥	awl	No.642,R167.
2,069	*zhuī*	追	pursue	No.924,R162.
2,070	*zhǔn*	准(準)	allow	No.925,R15 (24).
2,071	*zhuō*	捉	grasp	No.934,R64.
2,072	*zhuō*	卓	eminent	No.161,R24.
2,073	*zhuō*	桌	table	No.161,R75.
1,978	*zhuó*	着(著)	wear	No.889,R123 (140).
2,074	*zī*	吱	squeak	No.897,R30.
2,075	*zī*	兹(茲)	this	No.926,R12 (140).
2,076	*zī*	资	expenses	No.123,R154.
2,077	*zǐ*	紫	purple	No.122,R120.
2,078	*zǐ*	仔	young animal	No.927,R9.
2,079	*zǐ*	籽	seed	No.927,R119.
2,080	*zǐ* *zi*	子	son indicates one of a set.	No.927,R39.
2,081	*zì*	自	oneself	No.928,R132.
2,082	*zì*	字	word	No.927,R39.
2,083	*zōng*	宗	ancestor	No.929,R40.
2,084	*zōng*	综	sum up	No.929,R120.
2,085	*zǒng*	总(總)	assemble	No.930,R61 (120).
2,086	*zòng*	纵(縱)	vertical	No.125,R120 (120).
2,087	*zǒu*	走	walk	No.931,R156.
2,088	*zòu*	奏	play music	No.932,R37.
2,089	*zū*	租	rent	No.933,R115.
2,090	*zú*	足	foot	No.934,R157.
2,091	*zú*	卒	soldier	No.938,R24.
2,092	*zú*	族	race	No.611,R70.

2,093 *zǔ*	祖	grandfather	No.933,R113.
2,094 *zǔ*	阻	hinder	No.933,R170.
2,095 *zǔ*	组	organise	No.933,R120.
2,096 *zuān & zuàn*	钻(鑽)	drill	No.871,R167 (167).
2,097 *zuǐ*	嘴	mouth	No.935,R30.
2,098 *zuì*	醉	drunk	No.938,R164.
2,099 *zuì*	最	the most	No.936,R73.
2,100 *zuì*	罪	crime	No.937,R122.
2,101 *zūn*	尊	senior	No.939,R41.
2,102 *zūn*	遵	obey	No.939,R162.
2,103 *zuò, zuō & zuó*	作	do	No.942,R9.
2,104 *zuó*	昨	yesterday	No.942,R72.
2,105 *zuǒ*	左	left	No.940,R48.
2,106 *zuò*	做(作)	make	No.943,R9 (9).
2,107 *zuò*	坐	sit	No.941,R32.
2,108 *zuò*	座	seat	No.941,R53.

Radical index for the Dictionary

All the 2,108 characters mentioned in the Dictionary appear below, assigned to the appropriate radical. The number below a character is the number of the entry in the Dictionary where it appears. Key characters are shown in bold. Traditional characters are shown in brackets.

To assist in locating characters in the more frequently used radicals the number of strokes added to the radical is indicated by the number placed above the line[1].

Radical + Strokes   2   3   4

1:   一　七　丁　三　丈　上　下　万　不　丑　与　丛　丝　世　丙　东　且　业
     815　528　162　584　882　593　747　705　56　509　853　125　646　621　53　164　547　811

       5　 6　 8
   (册)　亚　丢　丽　两　严　(兩)　(並)
    67　796　560　737　431　800　431　 52

2:   个　中　丰　书　电　串　临
   233　910　202　631　157　114　436

3:   义　丹　为　主　头　举
   822　190　713　918　692　369

4:   乃　么　久　长　乌　之　乐　乎　乔　乘
   492　456　363　76　506　896　411　281　544　95

[1] Note on the allocation of simplified characters to one of the 214 traditional radicals:

Most simplified characters have the same radical as the corresponding traditional character, or have a radical which corresponds to one of the 214 traditional radicals, and therefore present no problem in allocation.

For those few simplified characters which are not so readily allocated I have considered the practice followed in two modern dictionaries:

1. *A Chinese-English Dictionary* ed.Wu Jingrong, Beijing 1987; and
2. *Xiàndài Hànyǔ Cídiǎn*, Beijing 1988.

Both these dictionaries deal with these cases by allocating them to new radicals created for this purpose and I have not attempted to follow this practice but have preferred to assign them to the most appropriate of the 214 traditional radicals. In a small number of cases, where there may be some doubt, I have followed the practice in the second of the dictionaries above and listed a character under two radicals. This occurs for instance with 难 *nán*, listed both under radical 29, 又 , and under radical 172, 隹.

The radical under which a character is to be found is given in its entry in the pinyin index, thus for *nán* the entry reads: R 172 & 29.

5:　乙 九 飞 习 乞 也 乡 买 乱 乳 (乾) (亂)
819 362 195 741 533 809 755 458 452 212 223 452

6:　了 予 事
412 850 623

7:　二 专 于 亏 云 互 井 五 些 (亞) 亟
186 921 849 728 866 285 359 730 122 796 311

8:　亡 交 亦 亩 弃 享 京 亮 亭
708 334 823 682 536 758 357 432 686

9:
　　　　　　　　2　　　　　　　　　　　　　3
人 亿 化 仓 仅 今 仍 介 仁 从 什 仆 仄 们 仪 仗 令 以
569 819 287 64 351 347 573 345 570 125 602 55 569 468 822 882 439 821

　　　3　　　　　　4
他 仔 付 仙 代 价 伦 传 仲 伞 伤 伪 伟 优 众 会 伍 份
666 927 215 589 132 345 453 921 910 640 591 713 714 842 911 298 730 199

　　4　　　　　　　　5
仰 任 伊 伐 仿 休 伙 件 伏 余 作 住 你 似 (佔) 何 佛
837 572 564 884 194 780 301 508 210 851 942 918 502 821 879 388 207

　　　5　6　　　　　　7
但 体 低 伸 伯 位 侧 (來) 供 例 使 佳 依 俩 侵 保 俄
136 679 150 599 15 719 874 406 241 434 618 248 816 431 549 26 726

　　　　　8　　　　8
便 侯 (係) 信 俗 促 借 倾 (條) 债 (倫) (倆) 俱 倒 倍 (倉)
46 280 745 770 934 346 552 683 875 453 431 372 142 34 64

　　　　　　　9　　　　　　　9　　　　10
(個) 倚 俺 倘 修 值 候 停 偷 健 偏 做 假 偶 (偉) (傘) 傅
233 532 157 594 781 900 280 686 691 330 44 943 323 859 714 640 54

　　11　15　　12　　　　　　13　　13
(備) 储 (僅) (傳) 催 (傷) 僚 僧 (偽) (僕) 像 (儘) (億) 僵 (儀)
32 916 351 921 642 591 433 68 713 55 761 246 819 332 822

　14　15
(價) 儒 (優)
345 785 842

10:　儿 元 充 兄 光 先 克 兔 兔 (兒) 党
183 860 102 778 254 749 389 475 475 183 139

11:　入 内 全
580 499 561

12:　八 兰 六 公 关 共 并 兴 兵 其 具 典 兹 养 兼
11 408 442 240 250 241 52 771 51 531 372 155 926 806 326

13:　册 再 冒
67 869 464

14:　军 农 写 冠 冤 幂
378 510 765 860 475 489

15:　冯 冬 冲 冰 决 冻 况 冷 净 凉 (凍) 准 减 凑 (馮) 凝
457 165 101 643 375 164 778 439 892 357 164 925 226 932 457 818

16:   几 凡 凤 凭
305 190 203 526

17:   击 凶 凸 凹 出 函
306 777 8 8 106 267

                    4   5

18:   刀 刃 分 切 刊 刘 刚 创 则 争 刑 划 列 刨 判 别 利 初
140 571 199 546 223 723 227 64 874 892 773 286 434 24 22 50 423 107

   6   6   7   8   9   10
剂 刻 制 刷 刺 到 剑 前 削 剧 (刚) 剥 剪 副 剩 (創) 割
530 219 909 639 124 142 426 539 762 367 227 448 539 213 95 64 266

   12   13   13
(劃) (劍) (劇) 劈 (劉)
286 426 367 42 723

           2   3   4   5   6   7   9

19:   力 办 劝 务 加 功 动 劲 励 助 努 势 (劲) 勇 (务) (动) 勒
421 21 251 734 319 238 166 358 421 919 512 899 358 688 734 166 231

   10   11   15   18
(勝) (勞) (勢) 勤 (勵) (勸)
604 409 899 550 421 251

20:   勿 匀 勾 包
735 867 242 24

21:   化 北
287 31

22:   匪 (匯)
196 297

23:   区 匹 医 (區)
557 651 817 557

24:   十 千 升 午 半 协 华 卖 卒 (協) 卓 卑 单 南 博 (準)
613 538 603 731 22 21 287 458 938 21 161 29 135 495 54 925

25:   卜 处 占 卡
55 109 879 379

26:   卫 却 印 危 即 卵 卷 卸 (卻) 卿
717 560 834 710 312 212 374 562 560 312

27:   厂 历 厅 压 厚 原
80 421 162 794 279 862

28:   去 县 参 (參)
560 751 63 63

                      3   6   8

29:   又 叉 反 友 及 双 对 发 戏 观 欢 鸡 变 叔 受 取 难
846 846 192 847 311 641 177 187 744 251 251 307 45 632 630 559 496

叠 (叢)
846 125

51:　干　平　年　幸　(幹)
　　　223　525　504　768　223

52:　幼　(幾)
　　　848　305

　　　　　　　　　　　　4　　　　　　　5　　　　　　　　　6　　7　　　　　8
53:　广　庆　庄　库　应　序　床　废　府　店　底　庙　度　座　庭　(庫)　康
　　　255　553　696　399　835　850　116　187　215　158　150　843　171　941　687　399　382
　　　10　　11　　12　　　　　　　13　　22
　　　廉　腐　(廠)　(廟)　(廢)　(廣)　(應)　(廳)
　　　326　215　80　843　187　255　835　162

54:　廷　延　建
　　　687　798　330

55:　开　弄　弊
　　　380　511　40

56:　式
　　　622

57:　弓　引　弗　张　弟　弦　弧　弯　弱　弹　强　(強)　(彈)　疆　(彎)
　　　239　832　207　76　153　788　247　45　582　135　542　542　135　332　45

58:　归　灵　录　寻
　　　217　437　448　792

59:　形　须　彪　彩　影
　　　775　783　283　62　839

　　　　　　　　　5　　　　　　　　6　　　　　　　　7　　　　　　8　　　　　9　　10
60:　役　径　往　征　彼　(後)　待　律　很　徐　(徑)　徒　(從)　得　(復)　微
　　　597　358　918　894　521　278　615　451　277　851　358　931　125　145　218　712
　　　12
　　　德　(徵)
　　　146　894

　　　　　　　　　　　　　　　　　　　　4　　　　　　　　5
61:　心　忆　必　闷　忙　忘　忍　志　态　怀　忠　念　忽　快　总　怎　怨　怪
　　　767　819　41　468　462　708　571　906　669　264　910　505　735　401　930　876　512　249
　　　5　　　　　　　6　　　　　　　　　　7　　　　　　　8
　　　怒　急　性　思　怕　恶　恸　恒　恩　恐　息　恨　悬　患　您　悟　悉　惊
　　　512　313　776　648　15　181　166　787　182　395　740　277　751　114　502　856　745　357
　　　　　　8　　　　　　9　　　　　　　　　　　　　　　10　　　　　　11
　　　(恶)　惠　惟　情　愈　感　(愛)　想　愚　愁　惯　意　愿　(態)　慌　(慟)
　　　181　182　642　551　691　226　4　759　859　555　253　828　862　669　291　166
　　　　　　12　　　　　13　　　　　16
　　　(慶)　慢　(慮)　(憲)　(憑)　(憶)　懂　(應)　(懸)　(懷)
　　　553　461　767　749　526　819　104　835　751　264

62:　戈　划　戏　成　我　或　战　截　(戰)　(戲)　戴
　　　884　286　744　92　726　302　879　61　879　744　134

63:　户　启　所　房　扁　扇　雇
　　　284　284　664　194　44　284　246

64:
3
手 才 扎 打 扔 扑 扩 扫 扬 **托** 执 扣 扛 护 拟 抢 扭 承
626 60 877 130 573 55 255 217 77 699 899 396 238 284 821 64 509 94

4
报 抗 抛 抑 扳 扶 抚 把 **找** 技 抖 **折** 扯 投 批 **抓** 拧 拥
27 383 518 837 192 209 729 12 884 897 168 886 901 597 38 920 507 841

5
择 挂 拖 抱 拜 拌 **招** 拐 抬 拒 (拼) 拆 担 抹 抵 **拔** 抽 拍
825 918 611 24 18 22 883 50 668 370 52 653 136 483 150 13 843 15

6
披 拉 拨 挡 挥 挤 拼 挑 拴 拿 拾 挂 按 **持** 指 挖 捞 损
521 405 187 138 378 530 52 674 561 490 274 248 5 97 904 700 409 861

捐 捏 (捏) **挺** 捕 **挨** 捉 **振** 掺 据 掷 **掏** 掉 (掛) 授 捧 接
373 696 696 687 55 2 934 891 63 367 250 673 161 248 630 206 340

8
掌 (婦) 捻 探 控 (採) 推 排 挽 **换** 握 揭 提 (揚) 揉 援 插
881 217 505 601 393 62 697 515 63 290 905 273 677 77 419 514 70

10 **11** **12**
(揮) 搞 **摆** 摄 摊 (搶) **摇** 搬 搭 摘 (摺) 摸 (撈) 撑 (撐) **撤** 撒
378 228 14 185 496 64 807 20 128 151 886 484 409 881 881 84 585

12 **13** **14**
撕 (撫) 播 (撥) 撞 (撲) **操** (擊) (擋) (擇) (擔) (據) (擁) (擰) 擦
649 729 189 187 923 55 66 306 138 825 136 367 841 507 73

15 **18** **19**
(擬) (擴) (擺) (擲) (攝) (攤)
821 255 14 250 185 496

65: 支
897

66: 收 攻 改 败 放 故 政 效 **教** 救 **敢** 散 数 敬 敲 (敵)
625 238 220 17 194 243 895 334 338 556 225 585 635 361 228 151

(數) 整
635 893

67: 文 刘 齐 斋 斑
723 723 530 184 19

68: 斗 料 斜
168 168 851

69: 斤 斥 斩 **斯** 断 新 (斷)
348 348 348 649 175 769 175

70: 方 (於) 施 旅 旁 旋 族 旗
194 849 611 450 517 611 611 531

71: 无 既
729 317

72: 日 旧 旬 早 时 旱 昙 易 昌 明 昆 昏 旺 显 昨 春 映 星
574 365 371 873 615 223 866 826 81 481 300 299 706 750 942 119 836 772

是 晓 晋 (時) 晒 晚 晨 暂 普 景 晶 智 晴 暖 暗 暴 (曉)
624 567 527 615 737 475 891 348 527 357 524 898 551 514 7 28 567

(曇) (曬)
866 737

73: 曰 电 曲 更 (書) 曼 曹 曾 最 替 (會)
574 157 155 236 631 461 872 68 936 680 298

74: 月 有 望 期 朝
864 845 709 531 82

75: 木 术 朱 末 本 未 机 权 杀 杂 朽 朵 极 来 条 杨 杏 呆
487 637 915 483 36 718 305 251 588 868 545 180 311 406 683 77 26 26

束 杜 李 村 杆 杉 材 构 枪 松 杯 板 枝 枚 析 (東) 林 棵
656 696 419 127 223 487 60 242 64 240 56 192 897 487 739 164 435 262

栏 荣 树 相 柄 标 柱 架 枯 查 柴 染 某 柔 柬 柳 档 桦
408 575 638 756 53 48 918 319 243 72 122 180 485 419 83 312 138 287

桥 样 桩 核 校 桃 框 桑 桔 格 桂 案 栽 桌 株 根 栖 检
544 805 922 219 334 674 706 846 343 234 248 6 61 161 915 277 737 426

梭 械 (條) (桿) 梅 梁 桶 梢 棱 (極) (棄) 棒 棋 棉 棚 棵 森
658 576 683 223 466 429 688 762 416 311 536 206 531 474 520 262 487

植 楼 楔 (楊) 楚 (業) (槍) (構) (榮) (樓) (樂) 概 (樣) 槽 (標)
900 444 429 77 110 811 64 242 575 444 411 222 805 872 48

(椿) 模 (橋) (樹) (機) (橘) (樺) 横 (檢) (檔) (欄) (權)
922 484 544 638 305 343 287 293 426 138 408 251

76: 欠 欧 次 欲 欺 款 歇 歌 (歐) (歡)
541 557 123 858 531 403 273 230 557 251

77: 止 正 此 步 歪 武 歧 (歲) (歷) (歸)
901 894 122 57 56 732 897 662 421 217

78: 死 残 殊 (殘)
650 540 915 540

79: 殳 段 殷 (殺) (殼) 殿 毁 (毀)
597 174 597 588 387 241 296 296

80: 母 每 毒
486 466 170

81: 比 毕
38 38

82: 毛 毫
463 270

83: 氏 民
903 479

84: 气 氢 氟 氨 (氫) 氮 (氣) 氰 氧 氯
535 535 207 5 535 670 535 551 535 448

                 3   4

85: 水 永 汉 汇 求 汁 汤 池 污 (汗) 汛 汝 汞 江 汗 沟 泸 沉
643 840 269 297 556 613 77 809 728 728 793 513 238 238 223 242 284 87

         4   5

沈 (决) 沙 没 汽 汪 浅 泽 注 (况) 泡 法 沾 治 河 沿 泰 泥
87 375 595 465 535 706 540 825 918 778 24 188 879 907 388 801 206 501

         5   6

油 泉 泊 波 泪 测 济 浆 浇 浓 派 洗 洪 洛 洞 洲 洋 津
843 643 15 521 488 874 530 331 567 510 516 742 241 234 689 913 805 350

         7   8

活 洒 酒 润 涛 流 涡 涂 浸 浮 浙 涉 海 涌 消 浪 渐 渔
288 737 364 706 629 440 260 851 549 212 886 58 265 688 762 428 348 852

         8   9

液 添 (淺) (淚) 混 淋 深 淡 (淨) 准 清 湿 湾 港 (渦) (湊)
814 681 540 488 300 435 601 670 892 642 551 612 45 241 260 932

         9   10

渡 游 (湯) 渣 渠 温 湘 湖 滚 滤 摊 (溝) 源 溪 溶 (滅) 溜
171 844 77 72 370 722 756 282 259 767 496 242 862 745 577 478 441

         11   11   12

滑 (滾) 滴 演 漏 涨 漆 (漿) 漂 满 (漢) (滬) (澆) 潜 (潛) 潮
244 259 151 804 445 6 879 331 523 460 269 284 567 680 680 82

         13   14   15   18   19   22

激 (澤) (濃) (濤) (濕) (濾) 灌 (灘) (灑) (灣)
310 825 510 629 612 767 251 496 737 45

         4   5   6

86: 火 灭 灯 灰 (災) 炉 炕 炒 炎 烂 炼 烃 炳 炸 炮 点 炭 热
301 478 148 294 301 446 383 595 670 408 427 358 53 876 24 156 294 568

         6   7   8   9

烧 烫 (烏) 烘 烈 烟 烤 焊 (煙) 烯 焉 (無) 然 焦 (煙) 照
567 77 506 241 434 797 384 223 358 738 141 729 565 335 797 885

         10 11   12   13 15 16   17

(煉) 煤 煮 熔 (熱) 熟 熬 燕 (燒) (燙) 燃 (燈) (營) 爆 (爐) (爛)
427 485 916 577 568 633 9 797 567 77 565 148 838 28 446 408

87: 爱 爬 (爭) (為)
4 12 892 713

88: 父 爷 爸 爹 (爺)
214 214 12 178 214

89: (爾)
502

90: 将 (將) 壮 状 (牆)
331 331 922 922 543

91: 片 版 牌
522 192 29

92: 牙
795

93: 牛 (牠) 牢 物 特 (牽) 犁
508 665 508 735 676 508 423

                4   5   6   7   8   9

94: 犬 犯 犹 (狀) 狂 狗 独 狭 狱 狼 (狹) 狼 猛 猜 献 (猶)
210 193 842 922 706 371 103 320 210 277 320 428 470 551 754 842

  13   14   16

(獨) (獲) (獻)
103 304 754

95: 玄 率
788 640

96: 王 玉 环 现 玩 玲 珍 珠 班 球 理 琴 (環)
706 706 264 752 703 439 90 915 19 556 420 347 264

97: 瓜
247

98: 瓶 瓷
701 52 123

99: 甘 甚 甜
224 602 224

100: 生 (產)
604 75

101: 用 甩
841 841

             2   3   4   5   6   7

102: 田 甲 申 由 男 备 画 界 留 (畝) 畜 (異) (畢) 略 (畫) 番
682 322 599 843 494 32 289 345 441 682 786 824 38 234 289 189

  8   17

(當) (疊)
138 846

103: (疋) 疏 疑
651 440 818

104: 疯 病 症 疾 痛 (瘋) 瘦 (癲)
203 53 894 314 688 203 586 894

105: 登 (發)
148 187

106: 白 百 的 皆 皇
15 16 147 339 292

107: 皮 皱 (皺)
521 558 558

108: 盐 盆 监 益 盘 盒 盗 盛 盟 (盡) (監) (盤)
802 199 327 827 20 274 123 92 481 352 327 20

109: 目 盯 直 看 眉 省 相 真 (眾) 眼 督 睡 睁 (瞭) 瞧 瞬
488 162 900 381 488 607 756 890 911 803 632 118 892 433 335 439

111: 矣 知 矩 短 矮
2 898 370 173 3

         3   4   5   6   7   8
112: 石 矿 码 泵 砖 砌 砂 砍 研 破 硅 (硃) 硷 确 硫 硬 碘
614 255 457 643 921 546 595 541 614 521 248 915 426 563 440 236 155

      8   9   11   12   15
     碎 碗 碳 碱 碰 磁 (確) (磚) 磨 礁 磷 (礦)
     938 704 294 226 52 926 563 921 456 335 439 255

113: 示 礼 社 祈 祖 祝 (祇) 神 祭 祥 票 祸 禁 (禍) 福 (禮)
620 418 598 348 933 778 902 599 73 805 523 260 356 260 213 418

114: 离 禽
417 551

           3   4   5   6   7
115: 秀 私 秆 种 秒 科 秋 称 积 租 秦 秧 秘 移 税 程 稀
782 647 223 910 595 386 555 91 308 933 206 836 473 178 645 93 738

           8   9   10   11   12   14
     (稈) 稍 (稜) 稳 (稱) (種) 稻 稿 穆 (積) 穗 (穩)
     223 762 416 313 91 910 144 228 15 308 182 313

116: 穴 穷 究 空 穿 突 窄 窑 窗 窝 (窩) (窯) (窮)
11 554 362 393 114 694 876 562 115 260 260 562 554

117: 立 产 亲 竖 竞 站 竟 章 童 端 (競)
422 75 548 353 360 879 360 880 690 172 360

           4   5   6   7
118: 竹 笔 笑 笼 第 笙 筛 筐 答 筒 等 筑 策 (筆) 筋 筹 简
917 39 764 443 153 604 610 706 128 689 149 395 124 39 342 629 329

           8   9   10   12   13   14
     签 管 算 (節) 篇 箱 (範) 篮 (篩) (築) 篡 簧 (簽) (籌) (籃) 籍
     426 252 659 342 44 756 193 327 610 395 489 293 426 629 327 346

          16   17
     (籠) (籤)
     443 426

119: 米 类 籽 粉 粗 粘 粒 粪 粮 精 糊 糖 (糞) (糧)
472 415 927 199 933 879 422 201 428 551 282 671 201 428

          3   4
120: 系 纤 约 (約) 红 纪 纲 紧 纬 纵 纽 素 纳 索 级 纱 纯 纹
745 538 863 863 238 316 227 353 714 125 509 655 499 655 311 595 120 723

                  5   6
     纺 纸 (紙) 经 练 线 织 组 终 绅 紫 细 (細) 累 绘 绕 绞
     194 903 903 358 427 540 902 933 165 599 122 746 746 414 298 567 334

7　　　　　　8

统 结 给 绒 (絲) 绝 继 绣 (經) 绩 绳 续 综 (綱) 绿 (網) (緊)
102 343 235 576 646 377 318 782 358 875 606 458 929 227 448 707 353

9　　　　　　　10　　　11　　　　　　12

维 缘 编 (練) (線) 缓 (緯) 缠 (縣) 缩 (縱) (總) 繁 缝 (繞) (織)
642 448 44 427 540 514 714 74 751 663 125 930 191 205 567 902

13　　　　　　14 15　　　17

(繡) 缴 (繪) (繫) (繭) (繩) (繼) (纏) (續) (纖)
782 310 298 745 103 606 318 74 458 538

121: 缸 缺 罐
238 562 251

122: 网 罗 罢 罩 置 罪 署 (罷) (罵) (羅)
707 454 14 161 900 937 916 14 457 454

123: 羊 姜 美 盖 着 群 (羣) (義)
805 332 467 221 889 564 564 822

124: 羽 翅 (習) 翠 翼 翻
854 854 741 938 854 189

125: 老 考 者
410 384 887

126: 而 耐
184 493

127: 耗 耕 耙
463 237 12

128: 耳 闻 联 (聖) 聚 (聯) (聲) (聽)
185 724 425 249 559 425 605 685

129: 聿 肃 (肅)
350 654 654

3　　4　　　　　　　　　5

130: 月 肉 肝 服 胀 育 肥 肺 肩 股 肯 脉 胜 胞 背 胡 胎 胆
864 578 223 211 76 857 12 197 284 597 392 840 604 24 30 282 668 136

6　　　　　　　　7　　　　8　　　　9

胃 胺 胶 脑 脏 (脈) 胸 脆 能 脂 脸 脱 脚 (勝) 腐 腔 腾
720 5 334 497 65 840 777 710 500 904 426 560 604 215 393 206

9　　　　　10　11　　13　　　18

(腳) 腹 (腦) (腸) 腺 腰 腿 (膠) 膜 (臉) (膽) 臂 (臟)
560 218 497 77 643 808 698 334 484 426 136 42 65

131: 臣 卧 (臥) (臨)
86 727 727 436

132: 自 臭
928 105

133: 至 致 (臺)
905 905 668

134: (與) (興) (舉) (舊)
853 771 369 365

135: 舌 刮 舍 敌
     596 596 596 151

136: 舞
     733

137: 舟 舰 航 **般** 盘 船 艘 (艦)
     113 327 383 20 20 113 586 327

138: 良
     428

139: 色
     587

| | 4 | 5 | 6 |
140: 艺 节 劳 苏 芝 花 芯 芳 芽 苯 茎 若 苦 英 范 **苗** 茧 药
     819 342 409 21 896 287 767 194 795 36 358 581 398 836 193 477 103 863

      6   7   8
     荒 (茲) 草 茬 茶 获 莲 荷 (莊) 莫 (茎) 萨 萧 营 (華) 菊 菌
     291 926 873 870 71 304 424 388 696 484 358 75 654 838 287 371 404

     9   9   10   12 13
     萍 菜 蒂 葱 (葉) 落 (萬) (著) 著 董 蓝 蒙 蒸 蓄 (蓋) (蕭) 薄
     525 62 154 735 812 455 705 889 916 104 327 469 94 786 221 654 54

      14   15   16   17
     (薑) (薩) (藍) 薯 (藉) 藏 (藝) (藥) (蘇) (蘭)
     332 75 327 916 346 65 819 863 21 408

141: 虎 虑 (處) 虚 (號) (虧)
     283 767 109 784 272 728

142: 虫 蚀 虽 虾 蚕 蛋 蜀 蜡 (蝦) 融 螺 (蟲) 蟹 (蠟) (蠶)
     103 103 660 747 681 137 111 346 747 232 414 103 344 346 681

143: 血
     791

144: 行 (術) 街 (衝) (衛) 衡
     774 637 341 101 717 341

       5   6   7   8 9 16
145: 衣 补 衬 表 袋 被 装 裂 裁 (裝) (補) 裕 (裡) (裏) (製) 褐 襯
     816 55 89 49 132 33 922 434 61 922 55 858 420 420 909 273 89

146: 西 要 覆
     737 808 218

147: 见 觉 规 视 (親) (覺) (觀)
     328 376 256 328 548 376 251

148: 角 触 解 (觸)
     336 111 344 111

       2   3   4
149: 讠 (言) 认 订 计 让 议 讯 (訊) 讨 训 记 讲 论 讹 许 访 设
     799 799 569 162 613 566 822 793 793 127 644 316 333 453 287 731 194 597

     5   6   7
     识 译 证 (註) 词 评 诉 (訴) 该 诗 试 详 话 误 说 语 (語)
     902 825 894 918 121 525 653 653 219 615 622 805 288 736 645 856 856

8 9
(誤) (誌) (認) 诚 读 (論) 调 课 (課) 谈 (談) 谁 请 谋 诸 (諸)
736 906 569 92 458 453 160 391 391 670 670 642 551 485 916 916

10 11 12 13 13 14 15 16 17
谓 诺 谦 (講) 谢 (謝) (識) (證) 警 谱 (譯) (議) (護) (讀) (變) (讓)
720 581 326 333 766 766 902 894 361 527 825 822 284 458 45 566

150: 谷
858

151: 豆 (豈) (豎) (豐)
169 169 353 202

152: 象 豪 (豬) 豫
761 270 916 850

4 5
154: 贝 (貝) 贞 负 贡 财 购 贤 贮 责 质 货 贪 贫 贯 贷 贸
17 17 879 216 238 60 242 325 507 875 908 303 267 199 253 132 303

5 6 8 9
贺 贵 贴 (貯) 费 (買) 贼 资 (賣) 赞 赏 (質) 赐 赋 (賢) 赖
319 258 879 507 198 458 576 123 458 871 78 908 826 732 325 407

10
(購) 赛
242 583

155: 赤 赫
100 100

156: 走 赵 赴 起 赶 趋 趁 超 越 (趕) (趙) 趟 (趨)
931 762 55 534 223 558 90 883 865 223 762 594 558

157: 足 跃 跑 跌 距 (跡) 跳 路 跨 跟 踢 踏 蹲 (躍)
934 854 24 609 370 823 674 449 400 277 826 667 939 854

158: 身 躲 躺
600 180 594

2 4 5 6 7 8
159: 车 (車) 轧 轨 (軍) 轮 转 软 轻 轴 较 载 辆 (輕) 辅 (輪) 辉
83 83 877 362 378 453 921 541 358 843 334 61 431 358 55 453 254

9 11
(輛) 辈 输 辑 (轉)
431 196 691 185 921

160: 辛 辟 辞 (辭) 瓣 辨 辩
768 42 596 596 21 47 47

161: (農)
510

2 3 4 5
162: 辽 边 达 迈 迁 过 进 连 远 运 还 迎 返 这 近 迟 述 迭
433 43 129 705 538 263 354 424 860 866 264 837 192 888 355 98 637 609

5 6 7
(述) 迫 适 选 追 迹 逃 送 逆 迷 退 递 途 造 速 通 透
637 15 596 789 924 823 674 652 503 472 698 153 851 229 656 688 693

175: 非 靠
196 385

176: 面
476

177: 革 鞋
231 177

178: 韩 (韓)
714 714

180: 音 韵 (韻) (響)
831 867 867 760

                          4   5   7

181: 页 (頁) 顶 顷 须 顺 项 预 颂 顾 顿 颈 领 颇 (頸) 频 (頭)
813 813 162 552 783 644 238 850 240 246 120 358 439 521 358 58 692

     8   9   10   12   14

      颗 额 颜 题 (願) (類) (顧) (顯)
262 390 75 678 862 415 246 750

182: 风 (風) (颶) 飘
203 203 596 523

183: (飛)
195

184: 饣 (食) 饭 饮 饲 饱 饰 饼 饵 (養) (餘) 饿 馆
617 617 192 541 121 24 610 52 185 806 851 726 252

185: 首
628

186: 香
757

187: 马 (馬) 驱 驻 驾 驶 骂 验 骑 腾 (驅) (驗) (驚)
457 457 557 918 319 618 457 426 532 206 557 426 357

188: 骨 (髒) (體)
244 65 679

189: 高
228

190: (髮) (鬆) (鬚)
187 240 783

191: (鬥) (鬧)
168 498

194: 鬼 魏
257 716

195: 鱼 (魚) 鲂 鲁 鲜
852 852 194 852 805

196: 鸟 (鳥) 鳳 鸣 鸭 鹅
506 506 203 506 322 726

197: (鹹) (鹼) (鹽)
226 426 802

198: (麗)
737

199: 麦 (麥)
459 459

200: 麻 (麼)
456 456

201: 黄
293

202: 黎 (黏)
429 879

203: 黑 (點) (黨)
276 156 139

207: 鼓
245

208: 鼠
636

209: 鼻
37

210: (齊) (齋)
530 184

211: 齿 (齒) 龄
99   99   439

212: 龙 (龍)
443 443